With Commodore Perry to Japan

New Perspectives on Maritime History and Nautical Archaeology
James C. Bradford and Gene A. Smith, editors

Rivers, seas, oceans, and lakes have provided food and transportation for man since the beginning of time. As avenues of communication they link the peoples of the world, continuing to the present to transport more commodities and trade goods than all other methods of conveyance combined. The New Perspectives on Maritime History and Nautical Archaeology series is devoted to exploring the significance of the earth's waterways while providing lively and important books that cover the spectrum of maritime history and nautical archaeology broadly defined. The series includes works that focus on the role of canals, rivers, lakes, and oceans in history; on the economic, military, and political use of those waters; on the exploration of waters and their secrets by seafarers, archeologists, oceanographers, and other scientists; and upon the people, communities, and industries that support maritime endeavors. Limited by neither geography nor time, volumes in the series contribute to the overall understanding of maritime history and can be read with profit by both general readers and specialists alike.

With Commodore Perry to Japan

The Journal of William Speiden Jr., 1852–1855

Edited by John A. Wolter,
David A. Ranzan,
and John J. McDonough

Naval Institute Press • Annapolis, Maryland

Naval Institute Press
291 Wood Road
Annapolis, MD 21402

Library of Congress Cataloging-in-Publication Data
Speiden, William, 1797–1861
  With Commodore Perry to Japan : the journal of William Speiden Jr., 1852–1855 / edited by John A. Wolter, David A. Ranzan, and John J. McDonough.
    pages cm — (New perspectives on maritime history and nautical archaeology)
  Includes bibliographical references.
  ISBN 978-1-61251-238-9 (pbk. : alk. paper) — ISBN 978-1-61251-337-9 (ebook) 1. Speiden, William, approximately 1836–approximately 1910—Diaries. 2. United States Naval Expedition to Japan (1852–1854) 3. Perry, Matthew Calbraith, 1794–1858. 4. Sailors—United States—Diaries. 5. Mississippi (Side-wheel steamer) 6. United States. Navy—Sea life. 7. United States. Navy—Biography. 8. Coasts—China—Description and travel. 9. Japan—Foreign relations—United States. 10. United States—Foreign relations—Japan. I. Wolter, John Amadeus, date, editor. II. Ranzan, David A., editor. III. McDonough, John J., editor. IV. Title.
  DS881.8.S68 2013
  952'.025—dc23

                                                                              2013027467

21 20 19 18 17 16 15 14 13   9 8 7 6 5 4 3 2 1
First printing

To John Joseph McDonough Jr. (1926–2009),
friend, scholar, historian

Contents

—ᴧᴧ—

Maps

—⁓—

Preface

William S. Speiden Jr., purser's clerk on the U.S. frigate *Mississippi,* kept a regular diary of the events transpiring all around him, written with the unpracticed hand of a mere boy during the momentous U.S. naval expedition to open Japan to the trade of the Western world in 1852–1854. Although some entries were extracted verbatim from the deck log of the *Mississippi,* the journal recounts the stirring scenes that were vividly impressed upon Speiden's mind while sailing to the Pacific Ocean via the Cape of Good Hope. In addition, the journal is filled with images ranging from hand-drawn, pen-and-ink scenes of everyday life sketched by Speiden and other members of the crew to exquisitely colored and detailed pith paintings by Chinese artists. Except for a few instances, naval historians have mostly ignored the journal. The editors hope this fascinating account of the expedition through the eyes of the purser's clerk of the *Mississippi* will further illuminate Commodore Perry's expedition to Japan.

The editors' intent has been to transcribe the text as accurately and literally as possible in the hope of preserving the style of the nineteenth-century writing. In the interests of consistency and clarity, however, the editors have made a few changes in punctuation and spelling. Speiden used capitalizations very freely and was not consistent in their use. In order to make the sentences more intelligible, his usage has been altered. However, the editors were generous in allowing his capitalizations, especially if the context is forgiving. Speiden was especially indiscriminant in his use of commas, using them for any and all purposes. The editors have omitted many altogether and converted others to other forms of punctuation: periods especially, but semicolons also. Where there was no punctuation at all and the sense of the sentence called for it, the editors created and enclosed it within brackets. It was not necessary to use brackets for dates or locations (e.g., May 12, 1853, or Norfolk, Virginia). The datelines at the start of each entry have been standardized as follows: place (when given), name of the day, month, and numerical day. The editors have dropped the "th," as in 9th, or "d," as in 2d. The place at which an entry was written is cited only when it differed from the previous entry. Any errors in dates are kept as they were, followed by the corrections in brackets. Interlineations were brought down to the line of the text at the place indicated, as well as addition in the margins. Marginal insertions were enclosed within braces.

Speiden almost always enclosed ship names in quotation marks. The editors did not retain these, and all ship names were italicized. In addition, the editors removed quotation marks enclosing geographical locations. When an incomplete or incorrect word could be expanded or corrected by a bracketed insertion, the editors did so. However, if it was too awkward to do this, then the full correct word was placed in brackets, following the incorrect word. If there was no confusion, or if the word added flavor, it was unaltered. General orders and other correspondence inserted throughout the journal were transcribed and placed as appendices with notes indicating their placement in the journal.

Acknowledgments

When a book is so many years in preparation, it involves a very large number of people, and although to list them all is not possible, their help is a pleasure to acknowledge. To those we do not list we offer our apologies. First we must thank Roger A. Bruns and Michael T. Meier at the National Historical Public Records Commission who saw merit in our efforts and gave our project their endorsed-documentary-edition status. We also thank the five anonymous readers who criticized our proposal and gave us their thoughtful and encouraging comments.

A special thanks to Ralph E. Ehrenberg and John Herbert, former and current chiefs of the Library of Congress Geography and Map Division, who provided their expertise and encouragement during the early years of the project. Ralph Ehrenberg returned as division chief and is once again providing us with much-needed advice and assistance. Present and former staff members Edward Redmond, Michael Buscher, and James Flatness are also owed our thanks. In the Library's Manuscript Division, James Hutson, chief; Gerard W. Gawalt, manuscript historian; and the late Mary Wolfskill were also very helpful during the early stages of our research.

At the University of Arizona, Professors David Plaine and John Paul Jones III, successive Geography and Regional Development Department heads, kindly arranged visitor privileges, and subsequently visiting scholar status, for Dr. Wolter. Christine Kollen of the Reference Department, and special studies librarians in the Chinese and Japanese Collections, provided assistance in the University of Arizona libraries. Dr. Wolter's colleague from their service on the U.S. National Committee for the International Geographical Union, Professor Janice Monk, was also most helpful.

The librarians of Salisbury University's Blackwell Library have been gracious and helpful with its interlibrary loans, Internet access to special collections, and the speedy emergency response when Dr. Wolter fell and broke his hip near the Government Documents Section of the Library. Special thanks to former dean of libraries and instructional resources, Dr. Alice H. Bahr; former associate dean, Judith Fischer; Head of Circulations Sharon Payne; and Access Services Technician Debbie Malone. The geographers of the Salisbury University Geography and Geosciences Department have been unfailingly generous with their time. Professor Michael Scott kindly arranged for and oversaw the map compilations by geography intern Alexander Paul Nohe, who deserves special mention. Our appreciation also extends to Associate Dean Michael Folkoff, Chairman Brent Skeeter, and Professor Daniel Harris for their kindness and generosity.

A special thanks goes to Bill and Sandra Speiden of Orange, Virginia. Bill is a descendant of this famous U.S. Navy family. They were our gracious hosts some years ago and gave us access to their collection of materials relating to the Speiden family, including a 1950s typescript of a portion of the journal.

We are humbled that the Naval Institute Press will be publishing the edition. We are indebted to series editor and fellow colleague from the North American Society for Oceanic History, James C. Bradford, and the Press' senior acquisitions editor, Adam Kane; production editor, Emily Bakely; marketing manager, Claire Noble; and copy editor, Marla Johanning.

Finally, we shall not forget our significant others—Dorothy, Joan, and Kelly—for without their support and understanding, the manuscript never would have come to fruition. Dorothy invaluably helped with the transcription and typing of the first draft of the manuscript; Joan worked on the first batch of annotations, and Kelly helped copyedit the final version of the manuscript.

This project has seen an abundance of unforeseen problems. John J. McDonough, our friend and colleague and the originator of the project, passed away after a long and debilitating series of illnesses. At the same time, John Wolter required two major surgeries, which also limited his involvement. Thus, the project was put on hold. However, four years ago, Dr. Wolter discussed the problem with Professor G. Ray Thompson, director of the Edward H. Nabb Research Center for Delmarva History and Culture at Salisbury University. Professor Thompson suggested that David Ranzan, the Salisbury University archivist, might be persuaded to help in co-editing the manuscript. David graciously accepted this new task, and with his enthusiasm and expertise, we were able to complete the editing and prepare the journal for publication.

The journal of William S. Speiden Jr. is one of some 254 individual collections in the Naval Historical Foundation Manuscript Collection housed in the Library of Congress Manuscript Division. The collection, on deposit since 1949, was formally acquired by the Library in 1998. The fragile physical condition of the two-volume journal required repair by the Library's Conservation and Restoration Division. Conservator Terry Boone disbound the volumes and cleaned and repaired the various items, including pith paintings and sketches. The two volumes were rebound with new leather and boards and with facsimiles of the original fragile pith paintings. Digital images of all the artwork were included before the entire journal was microfilmed. The result is a beautifully restored work that can be examined in the Manuscript Division reading room by the interested researcher.

Selected Chronology

—✦—

Volume One (1852–1854)

1852

March 9	Appointment as purser's clerk to U.S. frigate *Mississippi*, Philadelphia Navy Yard
March 21	At Navy Yard getting ship ready for sea
May 11	First mention of intended voyage to Island of Japan, "with which country we hope to come to a treaty."
May 17	Arrive Boston
May 24	Standing up Chesapeake Bay to Baltimore
May 31	To New York and Brooklyn
July 3	M. C. Perry comes on board and hoists "his broad pennant as Commander in Chief of the East India Squadron."
July 31	Sails for Fishing Banks (disputes with English)
August 6	Arrive St. John, New Brunswick
August 15–19	At Halifax
August 26	Sails for New York City
September 1	At Brooklyn
October 26	Off Annapolis
November 8	President Millard Fillmore and Secretary of the Navy John P. Kennedy visit ship

November 19	Norfolk
November 24	At sea, headed "across the waters of the broad Atlantic"
December 12	Arrive Madeira

1853

January 10–11	At St. Helena. Visits house and grave of Napoleon.
January 24	At Cape Town
January 28–February 2	At Cape Town. Ashore.
February 18–25	At Port Louis, Mauritius. Ashore.
March 11	Arrive Point de Galle, Ceylon
March 25–27	Singapore. Ashore.
April 7	Macao. Hong Kong.
April 19	M. C. Perry leaves for Canton
April 21	Speiden goes to Canton
April 28–May 4	Heads for Shanghai. At Shanghai.
May 26	At "Napa" (Naha-Okinawa)
July 2	At sea. Names accompanying ships.
July 8	Arrives Bay of Jedo
July 8–17	Bay of Jedo
July 25	Back at Naha
August 7	Hong Kong
September 23	Rumors of rebels threatening Canton (Taiping Rebellion)
September 26	Speiden's eighteenth birthday. Hong Kong, Macao, Canton, Whampoa.

1854

January 21	Arrive Naha, Lew Chew
February 3	Account of Perry's visit to Prince Regent of Lew Chew. Speiden goes ashore.
February 13	American anchorage at Bay of Jedo
March 8	Second grand landing of the Americans in Japan
March 27	Banquet on *Powhatan* for Japanese

March 31	Treaty signed
April 10–18	Up and down Bay of Jedo
April 22	At Shimoda (first treaty port)
May 17	At Hakodate (second treaty port)
June 7	Back at Shimoda
June 30	Perry boards an English vessel and learns that England and France are at war with Russia
July 2	At Naha

Volume Two (1854–1855)
1854

July 6–7	Men sent ashore to get authorities to find the murderer of a crew member
July 11	Compact made between United States and Lew Chew
July 17	Depart Lew Chew
July 22	Hong Kong
August 22	Robert McLane, U.S. minister to China, arrives
September 11	Perry and Silas Bent leave the *Mississippi* to return home via Europe, "overland"
September 12	Speiden and *Mississippi* return via Pacific
October 23	At Oahu, Honolulu
October 24	Speiden with group presented to King Kamehameha III
November 9	Leaves Honolulu for San Francisco
November 21	At San Francisco
December 16	At sea. Gives retrospective account of stay in California.

1855

January 3	At Taboga Island, Gulf of Panama
February 1	Valparaiso, Chile
February 16	Last entry. Two dogs died. "Happy dogs to die, Upon the broad blue sea."

Introduction

William S. Speiden Jr. (1835–1920) received an appointment as purser's clerk of the U.S. steam frigate *Mississippi* in March 1852. Born September 26, 1835, he was a resident of Washington, D.C., and only sixteen years old when he left for Philadelphia to join his father, who was already on duty as the *Mississippi*'s purser. The *Mississippi* had been laid down in 1839, launched in 1842, and after service in the Home Squadron she had seen considerable action during the War with Mexico while under the command of Commo. Matthew Calbraith Perry. When young Speiden joined her, she had only recently returned from the Mediterranean with the exiled Hungarian patriot Louis Kossuth. She was "very dirty" according to Speiden, but was soon put "to rights" in preparation for her role as the squadron flagship in Commodore Perry's expedition to Japan.[1] That excursion, one of the more striking in diplomatic annals, had as its principal aim the negotiation of a treaty that would provide for the protection of American seamen, permit the provisioning of American vessels in Japanese waters, and open Japanese ports for trade. The success of the expedition has always been attributed to its leader, Commodore Perry, whose biographer, Samuel Eliot Morison, proclaimed the Japan expedition to be Perry's "supreme achievement." Perry had conceived and carried it through "not as a one-sided push for trade and influence, but as the means to bring a highly civilized, but rigidly secluded people into the comity of nations."[2] As a young purser's clerk, Speiden played only a minor role in these historic undertakings.

1

Nonetheless, he was enthusiastic and alert, and he made the most of his situation and the opportunities it presented.

Nothing is known of Speiden's early education and training, but he wrote clearly and well. His journal, comprising two stout volumes, bears the hand-lettered title "Journal of a Cruise in the U.S. Steam Frigate Mississippi." Speiden kept entries on a regular basis, although not always daily, and he filled more than three hundred closely written pages dating from March 9, 1852, to February 16, 1855. The last entry was recorded at sea a few days out of Valparaiso, Chile, on the homeward leg of the cruise. Nearly fifty illustrations, including a number of original drawings and sketches, add significantly to the interest of Speiden's account. The journal has a polished and finished appearance, suggesting that Speiden prepared it at a later date or during leisure hours, and based it on a rougher version recorded closer to the actual time of the events described. The smoothness of the handwriting, its uniform character, the sameness of the ink, the occasional repetition of words and phrases, and the manner in which the illustrations are placed in the volume all lead to such an opinion.[3]

Before her departure for Japan, the *Mississippi* made calls at several ports on the East Coast and also devoted more than a month to investigating problems involving fishing rights in Canadian waters. On November 24, 1852, however, following a visit from President Millard Fillmore, Speiden announced that the *Mississippi* was headed "across the waters of the broad Atlantic." After a brief stop at Madeira and a visit ashore at St. Helena, where Speiden described and sketched Napoleon's gravesite, the *Mississippi* headed for the Cape of Good Hope, and Speiden rhymed: "The sea smooth, the moon bright, and now into my Hammock to pass away the night."[4] They reached Cape Town on January 24, and after a stay of ten days the voyage continued across the Indian Ocean by way of Mauritius, Ceylon, Malacca, and Singapore, to Macao and Hong Kong. For the better part of a month the *Mississippi* remained on the China coast, during which time Speiden took a side trip by "Fast Boat" up the Pearl River to Canton. Upon their departure from the city, Speiden and his energetic companions "had a jolly time firing crackers and sending off Rockets," leading to the conviction that "the Chinamen must have thought that we were a set of demons just let loose."[5]

The more serious business of the expedition soon resumed as the *Mississippi* "hove up the anchor" and "stood out of the Harbour" for Shanghai, where Perry transferred his flag to the *Susquehanna*. On May 23, after the ships were scraped and painted, the squadron sailed for "Napa Riang" (Naha) in the Lew Chew Islands.[6] Remaining there through the end of June, the crew surveyed the harbor and coastline, explored the interior, and made and received formal and informal visits on board and ashore. By daybreak of July 2, coaled and freshly provisioned, the *Susquehanna*, *Mississippi*, *Plymouth*, and *Saratoga* made the final approach to Japan. The crew observed the Fourth of July at sea with "a salute of 17 guns in honor of the day," and in the evening, "in order to wet poor Jacks parched lips," the main brace was spliced.[7]

The first sighting of Japan came early in the morning of July 8, and the four ships proceeded up the "Bay of Jedo" (Yedo or Tokyo Bay) to a point "Oposite [*sic*] the Town of 'Oragawa'" (Uraga), where they anchored at 5:30 p.m. There was immediate contact with the Japanese.

As soon as [the *Mississippi*] anchored a number of Japanese Boats came alongside several of them attempted to board us, called away the First Division of Boarders and repelled them, they after making a great many signs, and endeavoring without success to put on board of us the usual implications [*sic*] to Foreigners to depart, left us and went toward the shore, w[h]ere they must certainly have all come to the opinion that we were a queer sort of people.[8]

Boats had also clustered around Perry's *Susquehanna*, the crews declaring it to be their custom to do so. Perry, however, signified that "it was not an American custom, and if all the boats were not away in fifteen minutes, he would not be responsible for the consequences."[9] Speiden remarked, "They took the hint and soon vamo[o]sed." This visit, which was intended as a preliminary overture lasting only a few days, involved some maneuvering and posturing on both sides before arrangements could be made for the delivery of a letter from President Fillmore to the Japanese emperor, and for the presentation of Perry's letter of credence. Finally, on July 14, Perry went ashore for the first time, and Speiden was privileged to be included as a member of the commodore's large and regal escort. The Americans were met on the shoreline near Oragawa by the Japanese "to the number of six thousand." It was an impressive scene, because the Japanese were "drawn up in lines along the borders of the Bay, their front files extended over a mile, and with their Banners innumerable and blue and scarlet pennants, present-ed a most beautiful . . . appearance." When the bands from the *Susquehanna* and *Mississippi* struck up "Hail Columbia," Speiden said it "made the blood thrill in my veins." After the proper ceremonials had been observed and the demands of etiquette met, the president's letter and Perry's credentials were presented, and it was agreed that Perry would return in the spring for formal discussions.

Perry's squadron left Japan on July 17, calling at Naha for several days before returning to Hong Kong. Over the next five months the *Mississippi* remained on the China coast, during which time Speiden celebrated his eighteenth birthday, thinking it "not of much consequence." During those same months he often recorded in his journal that "nothing of much interest has occurred," although the Taiping Rebellion was a nearby, ominous pres-ence that kept American residents in China in a permanent state of alarm. Perry remained intent on fulfilling his mission, however, and as soon as pos-sible sailed again for Japan, once more by way of Lew Chew.

Early on the morning of February 13, as the squadron approached Ja-pan, Speiden went on deck and saw "Mount Fusi [Fuji] in the distance all covered with snow."[10] Soon thereafter the American ships entered "Jeddo Bay," and shipboard visits with Japanese officials began anew. The Japa-nese emperor, in response to President Fillmore's letter, had conceded that Japan should not "continue bigotedly attached to the ancient laws." To do so would seem "to misunderstand the spirit of the age," and Japan wished, rather, "to conform to what necessity requires."[11] The earliest discussions on board the ships, however, became mired in contentious debate over the site for the treaty negotiations. The Japanese insisted that they be held at Oragawa, where the earlier landing had been made, whereas Perry held out for Yedo. The parties agreed to a compromise of Yokohama, the nearby outpost for Yedo. When the elaborate preparations at the new site were finally completed on March 8, Speiden was not fortunate enough to be included in the party that went ashore, but he enlisted the good offices of the ship's chaplain, who furnished him with a full account of the proceedings.

Speiden recognized that it was "an important and great day," deserving of all the panoply to which it gave rise. In the morning, the nine American ships took up assigned positions with their broadsides brought to bear on the shore at the point of landing. Twenty-seven boats bearing the five hundred members of the American treaty party—"Marines and armed sailors and officers," as well as "Three Bands of Music"—then headed for the beach where they formed to await Commodore Perry's arrival on his barge, heralded by a seventeen-gun salute from the *Macedonian*. The reception ashore, involving "the usual flourish of drums, arms, etc."; the procession to the hall erected for the discussions; the exchange of gun salutes; the elegance of the receiving rooms; the various ceremonies; and the food and drink are all reported upon by Speiden. The first day of the conference ended at 3:30 p.m., and the Americans returned to their ships. Speiden was optimistic about the eventual outcome: "We think that the Commodore will get all he can reasonably ask for or expect at this time . . . they seem to show every disposition to be accommodating." Three sketches greatly enhance the account of the first day's deliberations: an intricate diagram of the landing, showing the distribution of ships and boats in the bay and the arrangement of buildings and troops ashore; a contemporary likeness of Commodore Perry by a Japanese artist; and a view of the treaty conference room with portraits of the participants drawn by Antón Portman, a Dutch interpreter whom Perry had engaged at Shanghai.[12]

On March 17 Perry went ashore again to continue the negotiations with "some High Prince" recently arrived from Jedo. Another group from the squadron was also ashore, busily assembling some of the gifts to be presented to the Japanese, one of the more remarkable being a miniature railroad consisting of the "Engine, Car & Tender" and a length of track. Speiden had not seen it but had heard it was "a magnificent affair and perfect piece of workmanship."[13] Another noteworthy event was a banquet on board the *Powhatan* tendered by Perry for the Japanese commissioners and American officers, including Speiden. In this relaxed atmosphere of good fellowship, meant to smooth the way for diplomacy, some of the commissioners became "a little tinged from the effects of 'old tom,' alias cherry cordial and champagne," and one who had "taken over his allowance" was seen to throw an arm around the commodore's neck, "rest his head on his epaulette, and laugh and chat at a great rate." Speiden used the occasion to look ahead to the years to come.

> Really the whole thing from beginning to end, was no doubt a remark-able circumstance, and we all hope that the Americans and Japanese will soon be on lasting terms of friendship with each other, and I truly believe that the new era which is now about to take place in the History of the Japanese Empire, will be one in which far more greater changes will occur than we have at this time any reason to anticipate, and that too before many years have passed.[14]

On the following day Perry met with the commissioners to conclude the treaty arrangements, and on March 31 the treaty was signed. Speiden was among the "few select officers" in the landing party "on this great occasion," along with the *Powhatan*'s marine guard and band. The names of the ports to be opened were left blank in the treaty, but it was understood that Perry favored "Shamodi" and "Chak-a-date"—Shimoda and Hakodate—with two or three more to be opened within a year or so. The entry in Speiden's jour-nal for this day proclaims exuberantly in a bold hand, "Commodore Perry for next President of the United States," and asks, "Will not all the world be astonished to hear of our success in making a Treaty with Japan[?]" On April 10, Perry attempted to see the forbidden city of Jedo, but, responsive to the pleas of the alarmed Japanese officials who threatened "Hare Kari," he stopped well short of anchoring there and saluting the Emperor.[15]

In the days that followed, the squadron began to disperse, and on April 18 the *Powhatan*—with Perry on board—and the *Mississippi* sailed to make calls upon the ports of Shimoda and Hakodate. Both places are described at length in sev-eral of Speiden's journal entries in the months of April and May. The squadron made a return visit to Shimoda, occupying most of June, before sailing for Hong Kong by way of the Lew Chew Islands. Perry left the squadron on September 11, having arranged to take passage home on a British mail steamer. Speiden and the *Mississippi* went to sea the following day, and the remainder of his journal, filling thirty-two pages, recounts visits to Honolulu, San Francisco (including a trip to the gold fields near Sacramento), and Valparaiso. In his final entry, February 16, 1855, Speiden tells of the shipboard deaths of two dogs, gifts from the Japanese to Perry, and he memorialized them in this way:

Happy dogs to die
  Upon the broad blue sea,
For there your bones will lie,
  Buried, and forever, be.[16]

No other papers were associated with Speiden's journal when it was received in the Manuscript Division, but because he applied for a pension several times early in the twentieth century, information concerning him is available in the National Archives and Records Administration. For example, a questionnaire filled out for the Department of Interior's Bureau of Pensions on September 20, 1906, when Speiden was seventy-one years old, gives his height as 5 feet 7½ inches and his weight as 140 pounds. His eyes were blue and his complexion fair. On October 17, 1860, he had married Marion McKeever (1836–1924), the daughter of Isaac McKeever, a naval officer who had taken part in critical naval actions against the British during the New Orleans campaign of 1814. Other papers and correspondence in support of Speiden's pension claim reveal that he returned to China in 1856 with an appointment as U.S. Naval Storekeeper at Hong Kong. For health reasons he returned to the United States in 1860, but he resumed his post in 1861, remaining there until 1864. He was employed by the U.S. Customs Service at the port of New York from 1870 to 1910, where he was in charge of the Coastwise Entrance and Clearance desk.[17] His claims for a pension, based on his service as a storekeeper during the Civil War, were rejected on the grounds that his employment was essentially civilian in character and conferred no entitlement to a pension.[18] He passed away at his residence, 124 East Eighty-first Street in New York City, on August 20, 1920, and he was interred at the Green-Wood Cemetery in Brooklyn, New York, three days later.[19]

Speiden's journal was donated to the Naval Historical Foundation in the summer of 1946 by Mrs. C. H. W. Foster of Marblehead, Massachusetts, a daughter of the compiler. The journal does not appear to have been widely used. Capt. Roger Pineau lists it in his edition of *The Japan Expedition, 1852–54: The Personal Journal of Commodore Matthew C. Perry* (Washington, D.C.: Smithsonian Institution Press, 1968), and Pineau published the Portman sketch of the conference room and conferees at Yokohama. Both volumes of Speiden's journal were also included in the Smithsonian Institution's major exhibit on Perry's expedition held in 1968. Peter Booth Wiley and Korogi Ichiro cite Speiden in *Yankees in the Land of the Gods: Commodore Perry and the Opening of Japan* (New York: Viking, 1990), but Samuel Eliot Morison in his 1967 biography of Perry does not. Perry himself, in his three-volume *Narrative of the Expedition of an American Squadron to the China Seas and Japan* (Washington, D.C.: B. Tucker, 1856), is also silent on the subject of Speiden and his journal. It is a matter of much interest, therefore, that the journal of William S. Speiden Jr. now takes its proper place in the fascinating canon of the Perry expedition to Japan.

I

Volume One: 1852

—◦◦◦—

In 1852 an expedition was fitted out by the Government of the United States for Japan & the East; & I, tho' yet in my teens, was fortunate enough to hold a position in it. Very much of interest & novelty were anticipated for it, both in our own country & throughout the world, as well as by those engaged in the expedition. With this feeling, I have kept a Journal of such objects & events as have come under my observation, designing to collect & arrange such flowers & fruits as presented themselves to the passerby, rather than aspiring to gather the full harvest of grain, which is left to older & abler hands. Such being my intention, my Journal will be duly appreciated by my family & friends, & will always be a pleasant remembrancer of interesting events in my early life.

WILLIAM SPEIDEN JR.

Philadelphia, Navy Yard, Tuesday, March 9. Yesterday, having received the Appointment as Pursers Clerk of the United States Steam Frigate *Mississippi*,[1] I proceeded from Washington (my home) to this place, this morning, and reported to William Speiden (Purser of the *Mi.*)[2] for duty on board.

The *Mississippi* is very dirty, having not long since returned from a cruise to the Mediter[r]anean and also went to the Dardanelles, at which place the

9

great Hungarian Exile, Louis Kossuth,[3] was taken on board and brought to this Country, where he is now creating a great excitement.

New York, Sunday, March 21. Last Thursday, the *Miss'ppi* having been by that time set a little to rights, her crew was put on board and yesterday we got steam up, and proceeded to this place, where we arrived today about 3 P.M. At 4 o'clock, the men were all sent on board the Rec[eivin]g ship *North Carolina*,[4] to remain there until this ship is got ready for sea, which will be near two months.

Tuesday, May 11. This morning the *Mi.* was put into commission, and commanded by Captain Wm. J. McCluney.[5] All the men and officers are now on board. Our intended voyage is to the Island of Japan with which country we hope to come to a treaty, but our final start for that place will be in three of four months[,] or we will say about August next. It is the intention now of taking the *Mi.* to Boston for the purpose of towing the Steamer *Princeton*[6] from that place to Baltimore, where she is to receive her boilers and machinery. We are now on the eve of starting.

Thursday [Wednesday], May 12. This morning we started from the Navy Yard (about 12 M.), but came to anchor a few miles down the bay from New York. We took in our powder this evening and will remain here all night.

Thursday, May 13. This morning about 10 A.M. we hove up our anchor and stood out of the Bay of N.Y. It is now raining and the weather is very disagreeable.

At Sea, Saturday, May 15. We came to anchor this morning about 10 miles from Boston. We were unable to proceed directly up to the city on account of the shallowness of the water at that time.

Monday, May 17. This morning about 10 A.M. all hands were called to heave in anchor. Shortly after we had taken it in, the fine Frigate *Cumberland* (the Flag Ship of the Mediter[r]anean Squadron under Commodore

Stringham),[7] under full sail came gliding along like an Eagle, on her outward passage. She passed very close astern of us, so that anyone of any agility whatever could have reached her deck from our vessel. As she was passing, all our men manned the rigging and gave three hearty cheers, which was returned by the men on the *Cumberland*. Im[m]ediately after the cheering our Band topped everything off with the tunes of "Hail Columbia" & the "Star Spangled Banner;" it was really a beautiful sight, and went off in fine style. The beauty of a scene of this kind cannot half be immagined [*sic*] by one who has never seen it. We arrived at the Navy Yard about noon and dropped our anchor. Crowds of persons were on the shore, and welcomed us with many cheers. We expect to leave tomorrow with the *Princeton* in tow for Baltimore.

Boston, Navy Yard, Tuesday, May 18. It was our intention to have left this place this morning, but owing to some delay are compelled to remain another day. Having never visited the place before, I left the ship after dinner to see what could be seen. I jumped into an omnibus and rode out to Jamaica Plains[8] about six miles from the city to visit a friend of mine who resided at that place. I spent two very pleasant hours, and would have remained much longer, had I not made an engagement to spend the evening at the house of Purser Buchanan,[9] who gave a little entertainment in honor of our arrival. I returned to the ship near 11 o'clock, having enjoyed myself very much. The Country Seats around Boston are all owned by wealthy individuals. Everything is done by them to make the place look beautiful and attractive, and they now succeed well, as the Summer has just commenced to make its way through the Trees and Flowers. While on shore I saw the Bunker Hill Monument. It is a grand structure of Architecture; as one looks upon it, his mind is thrown back to the time when all was strife and warfare between our now Glorious and Independent Country and our Fatherland. I intended visiting Mount Auburn Cemetary,[10] but was prevented from so doing for want of time.

Wednesday, May 19. We left Boston this morning about 9 o'clock and dropped our pilot off Point Judith.

Friday, May 21. It has been a lovely day & our fine ship is making her way along the boarders [*sic*] of the broad Atlantic in fine style. This morning, on opening the Spirit Room, we found it overflowed, one of the cocks which are used to admit water into the ship, in case of fire, became loose, & therefore occasioned the overflow. The shell room was also flooded, nearly all the shells were destroyed. During the day, two or three of the wet ones were shot off, but did not succeed in bursting them, also one of those which were not wet, it burst, and we were satisfied that those which got wet, were rendered unfit for service.

Saturday, May 22. This morning a general survey was called upon all the stores in the Spirit Room. All the sugar, with the exception of two barrels were spoiled, occasioned by the overflow of yesterday; these were condemned and thrown overboard. The other stores were sufficiently protected, as not to admit any water.

Sunday, May 23. It has been a beautiful day, the sun shining forth in all glory, we are now standing up Chesapeake Bay, having made Cape Henry[11] about 5 o'clock this evening.

Monday, May 24. We are now at anchor a few miles below Baltimore, having arrived here this morning with the *Princeton*. She will be towed up some time tomorrow. We are unable to proceed with any safety up to B.[,] the draught of the *Mi*. being 20½. ft. and the water is not so deep up the river.

Baltimore, Wednesday, May 26. We rec'd orders this morning to proceed up to this place, and wait for further news. We got here near one o'clock, scraping bottom with our keel all the way we came. We were several times aground, but the immense power of the engine[12] enabled the ship to get here safely.

Washington, Thursday, May 27. Hundreds of the Citizens of B. visited the *Mi*. this morning and at 5 o'clock this evening I left B. to pay a short visit to my family at their place.[13]

[**Baltimore**], **Monday, May 31.** I arrived on board this morning, having spent a very pleasant time at home. Saturday night a Ball was given at B. to our officers, most of whom were present, during my absence. Thousands of persons visited the ship, and at 12 M. this morning we started off for New York.

Brooklyn, Wednesday, June 2. We discharged our Baltimore pilot about 11 o'clock yesterday morning off Cape Henry and took a New York pilot this morning about half past five. As we came up the Bay the Steamer *Northern Light*, from Chagres,[14] with two or three hundred passengers on board, caught up with and went ahead of us. As she passed, our band played several beautiful airs, and salutes were exchanged between the two vessels. We arrived here near 5 o'clock.

Saturday, July 3. We have been lying at anchor here for the last month, in a state of tranquility. This morning Commodore Matthew C. Perry came on board and hoisted his broad Pennant, as Commander in Chief of the East India Squ[a]dron.[15] His Flag was saluted with 13 guns. Near noon the Colors were struck to half mast in honor to the Memory of the Hon. Henry Clay, having just received the sorrowful tidings of his death.[16] He had been in a dying state for a long time. He has often prayed for death and now God has granted it unto him. A few hours after his death it was known throug[h]- out the United States. The following is an extract taken from a speach [*sic*] of his, "I have wished the good opinion of the world, but I defy the most malignant of my enemies to show that I have ever attempted to gain it by any low, or grovelling [*sic*] acts, by any mean or unworthy sacrifice, by a violation of any of the obligations of honor, or by a breach of any of the du- ties which I owed my country."

At Sea, Saturday, July 31. We left our anchorage this morning at 10 o'clock, and dropped round to the Battery to take Commo. Perry on board. We then stood down the Bay. The Mail Steamer *Humbolt* [*sic*] passed us, outward bound. We have received orders to proceed to the Fishing Banks,[17] where difficulties have arisen between our Fishermen and the English, and we are now on our way to Eastport, Me., en route to the Banks.

Monday, August 2. Near 8 o'clock this morning, a Fleet of fishing smacks came in sight (about 80 in number). We stood for[,] and in about two hours came up to them, stopped the engine and lowered a boat, which was sent amongst them, in charge of our Master (Mr. Webb)[18] for the purpose of ascertaining if they had heard anything of the above named difficulties. They knew nothing of them. He presented them with some papers, in return for which they gave him some Mackerel (fresh and salt). As we passed close by one of these smacks, the men on board were so busily employed in catching the fish, that they did not look up from what they were doing to see who we were. They caught them very fast. Some of the vessels had only been out a week or so, but had nearly 150 barrels of fish.

Eastport, Maine, Tuesday, August 3. At 8 o'clock this evening all hands were called to bring ship to anchor, and near 8½ we came too [*sic*] with the port anchor in this port. We discovered Seal Island[19] about noon, and shortly after took Obediah Brown "Pilot"[20] on board. At 4 P.M. made the Grand Manan Island.[21] While standing up the Bay, we passed an U.S. Revenue Cutter coasting along the Island. The following is some "Machine Poetry" we made on arriving here.

> *One eve, one eve in the Month of July*
> *We left New York with our hopes raised high,*
> *To go to the Banks, where playing their pranks,*
> *The Fishermen were for a very long time.*
>
> *So we sailed and we sailed*
> *With a great deal of sport,*
> *'Till we dropped our great Anchor*
> *Off the town of Eastport.*
>
> *The Girls and the Boys*
> *Came down in large flocks,*

And welcomed us heartily
  From off their high Docks.

Oh my! Such cheers they did us give
  I won't forget as long as we live,
'Till Commo. P. who them
  Could no longer withstand
Sent an order from the Cabin
  To get up the Band.

Our *Poetry* should have gone on further, but as we could not get out of our heads what we wished to say, we cut it off short.

Wednesday, August 4. A few Army officers from the Fort and a number of citizens visited the ship this morning. At noon we were saluted by the Fort with 13 Guns, which was returned by our vessel.

Thursday, August 5. It has been a cold, damp, rainy and disagre[e]able day, but notwithstanding that, the ship has been visited by a number of Ladies and Gentlemen from the Town. Last night we were invited on shore to a small party given by the English Consul (Mr. Sherwood).[22] We returned on board about 12 o'clock having enjoyed ourselves very much. I there fell in with a friend whom I met while in Boston last Spring. The officers have been invited to a Ball on shore tonight, several have attended. It is now at 8 P.M. quite clear, but very chilly indeed. Capt. Adams[23] left the ship this evening for St. Johns,[24] [*sic*] where he will join us in a few days.

Friday, August 6. This evening Commo. Perry visited the English ketch *Nettley* at Campo Bello.[25] She saluted him with 13 guns, which this ship returned. He also called on Mr. Owen,[26] an old, retired English Admiral. The ship has been crowded with visitors nearly all day.

St. Johns, New Brunswick, Saturday, August 7. We got steam up near daybreak this morning, and expected to leave Eastport about 5 o'clock, but owing to the dense fog we were not able to leave until eleven o'clock, when we got underway and arrived here near 6 P.M. We are now safely moored in the St. Johns River between St. Johns & Calton.[27] The vessels in this port are nearly all Yankees.

Sunday, August 8. It has been a pleasant day, the sun shining brightly. I have been on shore twice to church during the day. Several English officers came on board this evening.

Monday, August 9. At Eight o'clock this morning we saluted the Town with 15 Guns, which was returned from the Fort at this place. Our Commodore visited the Colonel in command of the Garrison, and was rec'd on the w[h]arf by the LXXII Regiment of Highlanders, who escorted him to his residence, and from there he went to Frederickton[28] to visit the Governor of New Brunswick. The English ketch *Nettley* arrived here this morning from Eastport. The ship has also been visited by a large number of Ladies and Gentlemen.

Tuesday, August 10. Today we took on board a supply of 500 bags of coal, and in the Carpenter's Department, several hundred feet of lumber. Near noon a very large American ship, by the name of *Tenelli*, arrived here. This evening Capt. McCluney was visited by several of the officers belonging to H.B.M. Highland Regiment.

Thursday, August 12. At daybreak this morning, Commo. Perry returned from his visit to Frederickton. A number of English officers escorted him back. They were received on board this evening, when we saluted Lieut. Col. Murray,[29] Acting Governor, with 15 Guns[,] the English Flag flying at our foremast.

At Sea, Friday, August 13. The Artillery at St. Johns returned the salute fired yesterday. This morning near 9 o'clock & at 9½ we fired one gun and hoisted the Cornet[30] at the foremast. The Administrator & suite came on board soon after. They remained an hour or so looking about the ship. We then got underway and stood out of the Harbour & took Capt. Findlay[,] coast pilot[,] to Halifax.

Saturday, August 14. We spoke the schooner *Mary Ann* (this morning) 10 days from Boston, & near 10 o'clock we stopped the engine & fished for about an hour, but did not succeed in catching anything. In the meantime a boat came alongside from the schooner; we purchased a quantity of fish for the crew.

Halifax, Nova Scotia, Sunday, August 15. A more beautiful day we have not had for some time past. At daybreak made land. 6 A.M. made Cross Head Island,[31] and near 7 o'clock a pilot boat bore down for us, from which we took a Halifax Harbour pilot. We passed by many small sailing craft, and at 8 made Sambro Light House and stood into this harbour. At 10½ o'clock came to Anchor about a mile from the shore. We found the English Admiral Ship *Cumberland* in port, commanded by Admiral Sir George Seymour.[32] We saluted the city with 21 guns, which was returned by the Fort on shore. We then dropped the fore-topsail and saluted the A[d]miral with 15 guns, which was returned from his Flag Ship. The Admiral's ship then saluted Commodore Perry with 13 guns. Returned the salute. Admiral Sir G. S. and Commodore M.C.P. exchanged visits.

Monday, August 16. At 11 o'clock this morning Commodore M.C.P. visited the shore and was received with a salute of 11 guns, returned gun for gun from this ship. The Arch Bishop of Nova Scotia together with Arch Bishop Hughes[33] (of New York) and a suite of Bishops visited the ship. We were also visited by the Commander of the Forces at Halifax in compliment to whom a salute of 11 guns was fired, which was returned by the battery on shore. The night before leaving St. Johns a large Ball was given to the Officers of the *Mississippi*; most of us attended and enjoyed ourselves very much indeed. The Band belonging to the LXXII Regiment of Hig[h]landers was in attendance and played beautifully.

Tuesday, August 17. We coaled ship today; nothing of any interest has occurred.

Wednesday, August 18. A great number of the citizens visited the ship today and were very much pleased with everything they saw.

At Sea, Thursday, August 19. This morning we received a Harbour and Coasting pilot on board and at 11½ o'clock all hands were called to heave up anchor, which was soon done, and we stood out of the Harbour. At noon discharged the Harbour pilot and having secured the boats for sea, we shaped our course with a Coast Pilot in charge. This evening we spoke the American Fishing Schooner *Mary White* from Fair Haven, Me.,[34] bound to Shanendoah [*sic*] Bay. At 8 o'clock this evening we discovered the revolving light on Wm [William] Island.

Friday, August 20. A great many sail came in sight during this day. Nothing of any interest whatever has occurred.

Saturday, August 21. At daylight this morning we discovered land on the Port Beam & at 4 o'clock made the Island of St. Paul[35] on Port Bow, at 8 A.M. we stood between the Island of St. Paul and Cape Breton Island,[36] and at 2 P.M. land was reported ahead on starboard bow, which we soon made out to be the Magdaleen Islands.[37] At dusk we came to with starboard anchor near the Islands. A large number of American fishing smacks are at anchor near us. We have just held communication with one of them.

Sunday, August 22. This morning near daylight Capt. Adams and Lt. Contee[38] left the ship in the 1st and 2nd cutters and boarded several of the fishing schooners. At 7 o'clock we hove up the anchor and got underway, at 9 stopped the engine and spoke the schooner *Ocean Star* of Camden,[39] with 50 bbls. [barrels] of fish on board. We sent a boat to her with our surgeon to render medical aid to one of her sick men. Near eleven o'clock we discovered Bird Islands. They are very small and not far apart. They are moderately high, flatd [flattened] on top and have a white appearance. At certain seasons of the year they are completely covered with Birds, and from that take their name.

Monday, August 23. At 5 A.M. today we spoke the schooner *J. H. Collins* (American fisherman) from Gloucester, Me. [Mass.] and at 9 o'clock we hove to, to speak the schooner *Abigail Brown* from same place. A collision took place in consequence of her drifting into us, the only injury done was the loss of the Main Topmast to the schooner. Sent the 1st and 2nd cutters to offer any assistance that could be rendered. The Boats returned and reported the schooner as having 25 barrels Mackerel on board. At 10½ having hoisted up the Boats, we again stood on our course. About noon stopped and communicated with a Fishing Schooner from Miscou Island.[40] At 2½ we made land on starboard bow, and came to with the starboard Anchor at 3 o'clock. Spoke the English Steamer *Albatross* from Quebec bound to New York.

Tuesday August 24. At 5 o'clock this morning all hands were called to up Anchor, and we got underway and at 6 A.M. discovered the Island of Miscou, and shortly after spoke the English fishing schooner *Wellington* from Prince Edward's Island.[41] 4 P.M. we came to, lowered the 1st & 2nd cutters and sent officers in them to board the fleet of fishermen around us. 16 Sail in all.

Wednesday, August 25. 7 A.M. hove up the Anchor and got underway and stood for a fleet of fishing schooners. At 8 o'clock stopped the engine and boarded a large number of them. At about 3 P.M. we made another fleet, and on our standing for them we saw a steamer come towards us from amongst them, and shortly after we showed our Colors to H.B.M. Steamer *Devastation*.[42] She saluted us by manning her rigging, which we returned. The Captain of the *D.* then came on board and paid a visit to Commo. P. In the meantime the fleet of schooners gathered round the two steamers, not knowing the cause of our stopping. Shortly after the Capt. of the *D.* left and returned to his ship. Our band was then called up, and struck up the old tune of "Yankee Doodle" at the sound of which the men on the schooners climbed their mast and rigging, like so many monkeys, and such cheers as they sent forth I never before heard. It was a truly magnificent scene and cannot be described well in writing. The British steamer then went off like a poor Dog with his feelings wounded and came to anchor off Prince Edward's Island. We went on a little way and dropped our Anchor about four miles from the Island and communicated with the schooners, *All* of which were Americans, & pretty well loaded with Fish (Cod & Mackarel [*sic*]).

Thursday, August 26. Having steam up, at 5 o'clock A.M. we hove up the anchor got underway and started back to New York, after feeding ourselves on fresh fish for nearly four weeks.

Off New York, Tuesday, August 31. This evening at 7 P.M. we made the High Lands of New York; not being able to find a pilot at this hour (9 o'clock) we have come to anchor. I may here state that during the time we have been absent from the States, I have seen but *one* English fishing vessel; it contained but *one* Man, and was in a delapidated [*sic*] state. This now fully convinces me what a small interest the English take in the Fisheries on the North Eastern coast of America. The English there have fishing grounds which they do not make use of themselves and are unwilling that others should use them. Our fishermen who are industrious and enterprising, thinking that that was not the right way to act, intruded on their grounds (within the 3 mile limit)[,] were captured and sold and thus created the fishery difficulties now so much talked of.

Brooklyn, N.Y., Wednesday, September 1. This morning was a lovely one and at 4 o'clock A.M. all hands were called and we hove up the anchor and stood for a pilot boat from which we took a pilot and stood in for New York. At about 9 o'clock passed Sandy Hook and stood up New York Bay. At noon stopped the engine and came to anchor off Brooklyn Heights in the same place we left one month ago.

Friday, September 3. At 8 o'clock this morning all hands were called to Muster, and Otis Austin an Ord'y Seaman (he was tried by a Court Martial before we left New York, for striking an officer, in preventing him from Deserting) was brought forth and his sentence read to him from the Quarter Deck by Capt. McCluney. It was this, "That he should be transferred to the U.S. Rec'g [Receiving] Ship *North Carolina*, to be kept in solitary confinement for one year, the first month to be fed on bread and water and to be disrated to a Landsman."[43]

Saturday, September 4. Today Lieut. Henry Rolando and Gunner J. C. Ritter[44] were detached from the Ship.

Monday, September 6. This morning commenced coaling ship.

Sunday, September 19. Near noon today the United States Steam Frigate *Powhatan*[45] arrived here from Norfolk and anchored near us.

Tuesday, September 28. The last six or eight days have been employed in receiving on board stores for the different Departments of the Ship. At 11 o'clock A.M. The Hon'ble J. P. Kennedy (Secretary of the Navy)[46] with Com[m]odores Shubrick & Newton, Capt. Ringold and a large number of Ladies and Gentlemen visited the Ship.[47] In honor of the visit manned the Yards and saluted the Secretary with 17 Guns. Near 1 P.M. the Hon'ble Secretary and party left the ship to visit the Navy Yard.

Wednesday, October 6. The U.S. Sloop of War *Vandalia*[48] arrived here this morning from the Pacific; she saluted the Broad Pennant of Commo. P. with 13 Guns and proceeded to the Navy Yard. We returned the salute with 7 Guns. At noon the U.S. Sloop of War *Cyane*[49] arrived from Norfolk, Va., anchored off the Battery and saluted us with 13 Guns; we returned it with 7 Guns. This evening the Commanders of the *Vandalia* & *Cyane* visited the ship.

Saturday, October 16. This morning about 11 o'clock A.M. the U.S. steamer *Powhatan* went to sea.

Sunday, October 17. We had Divine Service on board this morning, by our Chaplain the Rev. Geo Jones,[50] for the first time since the ship has been in commission.

Thursday, October 21. This morning we received on board a Draft of Landsmen, 52 in number, from the U.S. Rec'g Ship *North Carolina*. We have now on board 383 souls. One hundred and thirty-three men over our complement, only being allowed 250. The ship is now very much crowded indeed.

At Sea, Saturday, October 23. Having received all our stores and coal on board, we make preperations [*sic*] for going to Annapolis. At noon we got up steam[,] unmoored ship, hove up the anchor and stood out of the Bay of New York, in charge of a pilot, whom we discharged at 4 o'clock P.M. off Sandy Hook.

Sunday, October 24. We had a Muster of the Ship's Company this morning, nothing of any interest during this day.

Off Annapolis, Tuesday, October 26. At 11 o'clock A.M. all hands were called to bring ship to anchor and a short while after we came to about 5½ miles from Annapolis, not being able to go nearer on account of the shallowness of the water. The Fort at the U.S. Naval Academy saluted us with 13 Guns, we returned it with 7 Guns. This evening we received the Schooner *Rainbow*[51] to act as passage boat between the ship and shore.

Monday, November 8. Nothing of any interest has occurred up to the present time. At 12 o'clock today, the Steamer *Engineer* arrived alongside from the town, and Mr. Fillmore,[52] the President of the United States, visited the ship, accompanied by the Hon'ble Secretary of the Navy, the Chiefs of the Bureaus, & the Governor of the State of Maryland.[53] In honor of the visit, manned the yards and saluted the President with 21 Guns. At 3 o'clock the President and suite left the ship, manned the yards again.

Thursday, November 11. This morning one of the Firemen by the name of Murphy, while wrestling, fell and broke his leg in two places.

Thursday, November 18. Up to the present time we have been waiting for the Steamer *Princeton* to come down from Baltimore, at which place she has been for the last four or five months receiving her machinery, but this evening about 4 P.M. the Steamer *P.* was discovered about 8 miles to the North[w]ard of us coming down under steam. A short while after she ran on a mudbank and stuck fast. On perceiving this we were immediately ordered to get up steam, and at 4½ o'clock we hove up the anchor and stood for the *P.* At about 6 P.M. we came up with her and found that she had gotten of[f] the bank. Commodore Perry then ordered Capt. S. S. Lee[54] (Capt. Of the *P.*) to proceed down to Norfolk, and we would follow after. The *P.* kept ahead of us for about half an hour and then stopped. On our coming up to her and inquiring what was the matter, we were told that they could not keep steam enough up to keep going. Commo P. then said that we would go ahead and for her to follow as soon as she could. The *P.* is now at 9 P.M. slowly making her way after us towards Norfolk.

Norfolk, Va., Friday, November 19. This morning at 8 A.M. the *P.* was about 7 miles astern of us. At noon perceiving that the *P.* had stopped, we wore round and stood for her, and accompanied her into this place. We came to anchor at 4½ o'clock P.M. off the Naval Hospital. Soon after, a survey was held on the boilers of the *P.* and they were condemned as unfit for service. At 7 P.M. Commo P. started off for Washington, for what [we] hardly know, but surmise that it is to get some vessel in place of the *Princeton.*

Saturday, November 20. Early this morning we sent all the stores which we had brought round from New York for the *Princeton* on board of her. At 8 o'clock the Broad Pennant of Commo. Perry was saluted by the Battery at the Navy Yard, with 13 Guns. Soon after the *P.* got underway and went up to the Navy Yard, and at noon we commenced coaling ship.

Sunday, November 21. We have been coaling ship all of today, wanting to get the ship immediately ready for sea. I have also been on shore and paid a visit to some of my old friends.

Tuesday, November 23. Commodore P. returned from Washington this morning, and brought news that the Steam Frigate *Powhatan* is to be ordered to return to the States to take the *Princeton*'s place.

At Sea, Wednesday, November 24. We have bid adieu to our native land and the *Mississippi* had head pointed towards an Island far across the waters of the broad Atlantic. Early this morning we had Steam up, all ready to start at a moment's notice, and Captain Wm. J. McCluney, who had thus far the command of the *Mississippi* was detached and ordered to take the command of the *Powhatan* directly on her arrival at Norfolk, and Commander

S. S. Lee was detached from the *Princeton* and ordered to take the command of this ship. At 7 o'clock A.M. we got underway and stood down to Hampton Roads where we came to anchor. At 1 o'clock P.M. all hands were called to take leave of Capt. McCluney. He after bidding the officers farewell and wishing us a pleasant voyage to Madeira, left the Ship, amid the cheers of the officers & men. Capt. McCluney was a popular Commander and left behind him the regrets of all. We discharged our pilot about 4 P.M. off Cape Henry. The following is a correct list of the officers now on board.

Matthew C. Perry	Commodore	E. I. Squadron
Sydney S. Lee	Commander	Stea'r *Mississippi*
Henry A. Adams	" of Fleet	
Alfred Taylor	Lieutenant	
Edmund Lanier	"	
Silas Bent	"	
Jno. M. B. Clitz	"	
Chas. M. Morris	"	
John Contee	"	Flag
Wm. Speiden	Purser	
Danl. S. Green	Surgeon	
Wm. A. Webb	Act'g Master	
L. J. Williams	Passd. Asst. Surgeon	
A. M. Lynah	Assistant "	
Geo. Jones	Chaplain	
Jacob Zeilin	Capt. & Bvt. Major	E. I. S. of Marines
J. H. March	Passed Midshipman	
W. F. Jones	"	
K. R. Breese	"	
J. W. Shirk	Midshipman	
W. McN. Armstrong	"	
Simon C. Mish	"	
Amos Colson	Boatswain[55]	
J. R. Caulk	Gunner	
H. M. Lowry	Carpenter	
Jacob Stephens	Sail Maker	

Jesse Gay	Chief Engineer
Robt. Danby	1st Asst. "
Wm. Holland	" " "
G. T. W. Logan	2d " "
Wm. H. Rutherford	" " "
G. W. Alexander	" " "
E. D. Robie	3d " "
J. D. Mercer	" " "
A. L. C. Portman	Commodore's Clerk
Jas. W. Spalding	Commander's "
Wm. Speiden Jr.	Purser's "
N. B. Adams	Clerk to Capt. Of Fleet
E. Brown Jr.	Act'g Masters Mate
W. B. Draper	" " "
W. Heine	" " "

Officers 41

Petty Officers

Seamen

Or[dinary] Seamen

Lds [Landsmen] & Boys

Firemen

Coal Heavers

Musicians

Marines

Town of Funchal, Island of Madeira,[56] **Sunday, December 12.** We arrived opposite this place this evening about 6 o'clock, after a partly pleasant passage of eighteen days from Norfolk, Va., and are now at anchor a mile or so from the shore. Soon after, the American Consul (Mr. Bayman)[57] with several other gentlemen came on board. We made the Island yesterday evening about 5 P.M. but the sea being quite rough were unable to come in, it also being a dangerous harbour to run into except by broad daylight. So we stood off, and this morning at 7 A.M. we were 60 miles to the Southward of the Isl'd. This town lies in the North Western section, so that we had to go nearly around. On our course we kept about four miles off from the land, but at times could see the houses on shore very distinctly. We also passed several small villages and many beautiful Country Seats. This place has a population of about fifteen thousand souls. Tomorrow I expect to go on shore and therefore when I write up tomorrow night, will be better able to give an account of the place.

Tuesday, December 14. I came on shore this morning about 10 o'clock together with a party of officers & proceeded to the house of Mr. March[58] (a wealthy merchant) and there obtained horses, and started off to view the Country. After proceeding a little way the horse on which I was, not suiting me as well as I would wish (and I not by any means being a good rider)[,] turned back, obtained another one & taking a Portuguese boy for my guide, and started off again, but alone. My outward course was all up hill work, the Island being very steep. I first went up to the Mount Church or Church of the Lady of the Mount, remarkable for its anticquity [sic] and heighth. It is about 6 miles from the town, and over a quarter of a mile high from the level of the sea. I went all through the building and was very much pleased with everything I saw, and after riding about for an hour or so, first along a deep precipice, so near that any shyness on the part of my horse would have precipitated us both into a ravine of five hundred feet below me, then down into this ravine, and when I looked up, I trembled to behold the imminent danger I had a few moments before been in. The shore [sure] footedness of my horse enabled me to proceed in safety. Returning to town, I joined some of the Officers, and we went out to the "Renta[,]" the country residence of the Consul where we were all furnished with an excellent lunch at the hands of Mr. Bayman's Lady. So after enjoying ourselves very much, we returned to the City and prepared for dinner to which we were all invited by Mr. J. Howard March, Vice Consul. At dinner we enjoyed our selves to our hearts content. The streets of this place are all of stone. Carriages are never used[,] the means of conveyance being made by sledges, drawn by oxens, but most of the riding is done on horses. No one rides on horseback without an attendant, who somehow or other keep up with you never mind how fast you choose to drive. The houses are generally made of stone, with large gardens attached to them, which is surrounded by high stone walls. The roofs are made of tiles, which is known to be the case in all warm climates. Some of the houses are very beautiful. The Princess of Brazil[59] is now on a visit to the Island in quest of restoration of her health, with an Idiot child. Her residence is magnificent, being furnished in a most costly manner. The inhabitants are mostly Portuguese and generally an ugly set of people. There are thousands of Paupers who are in a most wretched state. Means are now being made in both England & France for their relief. They are also very industrious, and there not being enough work to employ so many hands, they well deserve the trouble which is being taken for them. Much more is known of this Island than I am able to relate here.

At Sea, Wednesday, December 15. I returned on board ship this morning about 11 o'clock (having remained at Mr. March's overnight). Everything was in confusion taking in coal and provisions, and making other preparations for going to sea. At 3 P.M. a Gun was fired and the Cornet run up. This was to give notice to all persons belonging to the ship to come on board. 6 P.M. everything being ready, we hove up the anchor, bid adieu to our newly made friends of Madeira, and started off for the Cape of Good Hope. Our Good Ship is once again ploughing the mighty deep. Madeira's green clad hills are now in the dim distance, and will ere morning breaks upon us, be as things that are past but not to be forgotten.

In Sight of the Canary Islands, Friday, December 17. Early this morning we made the Island of Palmos on our port bow; about 2 o'clock P.M. we stopped the engine, hove to under the lee of an Island and took ten buckets off of each wheel, secured them and set all the sails that would in any way help us along, so that our noble craft is now quite a fine Sailing Frigate. The North East Trade Winds are now in our favor, and we find that we now log as much under sail as when under steam. This is just as could be wished; were we to have gone on all the time under steam, doubtlessly the coal would give out two or three days before we reach the Cape. We are now not certain that this will not be the case, it depending alone upon the length of time the wind holds as a substitute for steam. At 3 o'clock P.M. we made the High Peak of Teneriffe[60] and other of the Canary Islands, all of which are now in sight.

Saturday, December 18. Near noon today, the Smoke Stack was lowered and laid on Hurricane Decks, and the Main Sail was bent. Several large Fin Back Whales played around the ship this evening, one of them kept company with us for several hours, at one time under the Bow of the ship, at another under the Wheels. Sometimes we would run against him; he would then come up on the top of the water, and blow, and away he would go, for a mile or so not knowing whether we were a foe or no, and again return making a very great show. Flying Fish have also appeared in numbers innumerable, pursued by their enemies, the dolphins, which we also see in numbers.

Sunday, December 19. At 10 o'clock this morning the Crew were inspected at Quarters and we had Divine Service. Our Band played two or three pieces of Sacred Music in which the officers and men joined in & sung. The remainder of the morning passed off very quietly. This evening a squall of wind & rain came up which lasted about an hour, afterwards the sun came out and lit up the heavens beautifully and soon after settled down in the far West in all his glory. Thus has passed the Fourth Sabbath *at sea*.

Thursday, December 23. Late last evening the whole heavens to the southward & westward were light [*sic*] up beautifully, by the Zodiacal lights.[61] It was quite a pretty sight. This morning discovered two sails on our Starboard bow; were unable to make them out.

Saturday, December 25. Christmas day, although at Sea, a merry time we have had. A beautiful and pleasant day it has been too, at half past 9 A.M. the crew were inspected at Quarters, no unnecessary work was permitted, the day being observed as a general Holiday by all on board. The Cabin & Steerage Officers were all invited to a handsome collation served up by the Ward Room Officers, at which several Toasts were proposed and drank. Commodore Perry gave the following; "That we may meet this day, one year hence under as favorable circumstances as we now meet." Others appropriate to the occasion—Major Zeilin[62] rose and proposed "the health of our former Captain, Captain Wm. J. McCluney." Drank to with pleasure; a very fine time we had. This evening at 4 P.M. before the men went to supper, "The main Brace was spliced" the sailor phrase for giving the men an extra "Tot" (cup of grog). The day had been so pleasantly spent, that it has in a great measure taken away our home sickness, though absent ones have been thought of and remembrances of past pleasantly spent Christmas days, thought of with pleasure. And so ends my *first* Christmas day away from home.

Sunday, December 26. This morning at half past ten A.M. all hands were called to Muster and the Captain read from the Quarter Deck General Orders No[s]. 1 & 2, copies of which are herewith annexed.[63] 11 o'clock we had Divine Service; the Band played several pieces of sacred music. Nothing of any account has occurred to mar the harmony which generally reigns on the Sabbath.

Wednesday, December 29. We lost the winds this morning which have favored us for more than a week past, and of course had to go by steam again. At 7 A.M. got the Smokestack up in its place, put the paddles on the Wheels, got up steam and started ahead. The *Mississippi* again under steam. At 11 o'clock saw a Hermaphrodite Brig[64] to the leeward of us. This evening at 5 o'clock sent down lower yards.

2

Volume One: 1853

—⟨⟨⟨⟨⟩⟩—

Saturday, January 1. Last night very near the hour of midnight as the Old Year was about to take its departure, all were sound asleep in their hammocks with the exception of the watch on Deck, when the cry of "Man Overboard" rang through the ship and fell upon the ears of those who slept. Everybody was soon roused up by the noise. The Ship was stopped, the Life Buoys immediately cut away, and a boat well manned was lowered, and in charge of Mr. W. A. Webb (our Master) and passed midshipman Breese[1] (one of the Officers on watch at the time) went in search of the unfortunate Sailor—it was quite dark at the time. The moon which was quite bright a few moments before, had just gone under a cloud. After looking about for nearly a quarter of an hour, they turned back, having considered him as gone to Davy Jones' Locker, when in a moment or so after, the man in the bow of the boat who stood with a lantern in his hand on the lookout—cried out—"look out, or we'll be over him." He spoke just in time; the boat's headway was stopped, and the unfortunate man caught hold of one of the oars and was taken in. During the whole time, he did not utter the least sound that would in any way attract the attention of those in the boat. Poor fellow[,] it came near being all up with him. He is now quite sick, the salt water having gotten on his lungs. His name is Wm. [William] Dry—sullen looking man and seemed always to be half crazy. He was unwell and had gone on the Poop Deck to get a little fresh air. While there he leaned against the ridge rope; his head became dizzy and he fell, fell "overboard." I had just fallen asleep, but was on deck in a moment.

This morning at 5 A.M. the sun rose for the first time in the New Year, but ere he had poured forth his rays one hour another accident happened, which came very near bringing death on a man. One of the firemen by the name of Law, while cleaning a part of the machinery, was caught by the crank and his head jammed into a place about four inches wide. It was truly Providential that he escaped immediate death. The Doctor when he first saw him, gave him up. He soon however came to his senses and is now doing well. His head is very badly out on both sides and looks quite flat. Now after having given a slight shock of two very unpleasant circumstances, I will say a few words as to how the day has been spent. This morning all the Officers were invited into the Cabin to partake of an excellent collation served up there. We had mince pies (the mincemeat of which was made by Miss Perry,[2] Commo. P.'s daughter[,] just before leaving New York and was very nice indeed), Boned turkeys, and many other good things unnecessary to mention, suffice it to say that we enjoyed ourselves very much. Several Toasts were given. Commo. P. gave "Our Friends at Home." Just then the Band struck up "Home Sweet Home;" it really made me feel quite homesick. Just before leaving the Cabin, Purser Speiden rose and proposed the following, "To our Chief Commo. Perry, may the Expedition which he has undertaken be successful." Commo. P. then rose and thanked him and we all left the cabin, having had a very pleasant time. The remainder of the day has passed off very quietly.

Sunday, January 2. At half past ten o'clock A.M. mustered the crew and read the Articles of War. Afterwards had Divine Services with sacred music by the Band. It has been a very pleasant day.

Thursday, January 6. The last few days have been employed in setting up the rigging, and exercising the different Divisions with small arms. This evening 7 boxes of raisins were condemned and thrown overboard, the Purser having called a survey on them as being unfit to serve out to the men.

Jamestown Island of St. Helena, Monday, January 10.[3] Near 6 o'clock this morning discovered the Island ahead, got the ship in trim. At half past ten made this town on our port bow, and saw several strange sail. 1 P.M. spoke a small English Cutter, and near half past two we came to anchor off this town.

The American Consul came on board. At 3 o'clock saluted the Town with 21 Guns, which was returned gun for gun from the Fort on Ladder Hill. The reverberation from the report of the guns among the hills was truly grand. This evening near 5 o'clock I accompanied Passd. Mid. March[4] in the first cutter on board the English Barque *Cuba* to tow her out from under the Lee of the Island. She was laden with wool, bound to London with six or eight passengers on board, among whom were a Priest and two Nuns. One of the latter was quite a pretty lady—we chatted with her for some time, and as the ship passed out our band played "God Save the Queen." She said our people were very kind to play their favorite anthem, and talked so prettily that I hated to part her company so soon. We went about a mile or so from the Island and after wishing them a pleasant voyage got in our boat and returned to the Ship.

At Sea, Tuesday, January 11. We left the Island of St. Helena about six o'clock this evening and are now off for the Cape of Good Hope. We took in 124 tons of coal for which we had to pay $25.20 per ton, and for fresh beef we gave 19¾¢ per lb. This morning a party of us left the ship, and started off on foot to visit the Grave of Napoleon. We left Jamestown about 10 o'clock and ascended the road known as the "left side path" which we found to be a circuitous and fatiguing route for foot travellers. Proceeding onwards slowly (it being very warm) for the distance of about 5 miles, first up and along the side of the Mountain and then down into a beautiful Valley, we came upon the Tomb. It was as still as could be, nothing but the sounds of the chirping of the little birds, as they flew from bush to bush, could be heard. I might well say that the spot was entirely deserted by human beings, for none lived there, save an old woman (colored) and her husband, who took care of the grave, kept the place in order and charged each visitor to the spot twenty five cents admission fee into the Tomb, and to receive such gifts of generosity as the visitors are willing to bestow upon them for their kind attention, and for listening to their long account of Napoleon, which as they had repeated so often before, they could now say without any trouble. Of course our curiosity was so great as to induce us to go down into the grave, which we did five in number. One of our party, who is the litterary [sic] character onboard ship, laid flat down on his back in the grave in the position which Napoleon occupied, his hands folded across his breast. When the old woman saw him, she exclaimed "Please God Massa, you's lain as how the old General did, but you isn't much like him," after which she told us a whole rigamarole [*sic*] of stuff, which is not necessary to mention here, as the circumstances of Napoleon's death are known to everybody. We questioned the old woman in regard to his dress, his manner of walking, together with a great many inquiries concerning the Emperor, all of which she answered very satisfactory. After leaving the grave we went to Napoleon's favourite spring and took a drink, not out of the same cup that he drank out of, but out of one which looked as if it had seen hard service for a number of years. We then proceeded up the Mountain again, until we came to the halfway house w[h]ere we stopped and took some lunch, paying very dear for everything we got. So after quenching our thirst, etc., etc., we went to Longwood where Bonaparte lived and died. We paid fifty cents each to go into the House, called "The Old House at Longwood," a picture of which is herewith annexed. The first room we entered was Napoleon's Billiard Room, the next room was his parlor, but the [one] in which he breathed his last. I stood on the spot where his bed rested. From the wall against which the head of the bed touched, a large stone was taken out (but is now filled up) at the time his remains were taken away, also a plank from the floor on which the bed rested. The next room was his dining room, you then go out of a door to your right into a little yard, and then to your right again, is a room which he occupied as a Bed Chamber. Opposite this was the residence of Doctor O'Harran,[5] his physician, who lived with him until his death. We then walked a little way and saw the fish pond, at which he often amused himself in catching fish. We then visited the New House which was built for him, but it was so long in being built, that he for whom it was built, died before going into it. It is not even now entirely completed. A more extensive description I *could* give of Longwood but smarter heads than mine have been there and books have been written about the place, & it will be useless for me to write in these pages what is known to all the world. Anyhow I think it will not be amiss to write a little about the Historical facts of the Island which may perchance give information to some one.

"The Island of St. Helena was discovered the 21st of May 1502, by Juan de Nova Castella, a Portuguese; in 1645 the Portuguese having abandoned the Island, it was colonized by the Dutch, it was soon after deserted by the Dutch and taken possession of by the English in 1651; it was taken by the Dutch in 1672 and retaken by the English in 1673. Napoleon being a prisoner of the English, was sent to this Island and arrived there on the 15th day of October 1815, and died on the 5th day of May 1821. The Prince de Joinville and Suite, in the fine Frigate *La Belle Poule*, arrived at the Island on the 8th October 1840, from France, for the purpose of conveying the remains of Napoleon to that Country; on the 15th day of the same month the exhumation took place, and on the same day the remains were deposited with funeral honors in the Frigate, which on the 18th sailed for her destination."

After leaving Longwood we started back, stopped again at the "Halfway House" and got back to the City about 2 o'clock, having walked al[t]ogether about 14 miles. I took dinner on shore and returned on board ship about 4 o'clock, having had a very pleasant day, although I now feel very tired and fatigued after my long walk. A gun was fired at 5 o'clock for all Officers to come on board. We got underway at six o'clock and are now away out to sea. The sea smooth, the moon bright, and now into my Hammock to pass away the night.

Cape Town, Cape of Good Hope, Table Bay, Africas, Monday, January 24. At nine o'clock this morning discovered land on port bow. At 12 o'clock made the North Point of Saldanha Bay;[6] half past one, discovered Table Mountain[7] one point on starboard bow; 7½ P.M. standing into this Bay. We spoke an English Mail Propeller coming out of the Harbour on her way to England. At a quarter to eight o'clock called all hands to bring ship to anchor, & at 8½ came to off this Town in 7 Fathoms of water, 13 days from St. Helena, nearly out of Coal. Will remain some days to fill up and take in provisions. Moored ship.

Tuesday, January 25. This morning unmoored ship, got up steam, hove up the anchor & at half past ten got underway and stood in nearer for a better anchorage. At 10.40 let go the anchor in 5 fathoms water, & moored ship. At half past eleven saluted the Town with 21 guns, which was returned gun for gun from the Fort on shore. This evening nearer six o'clock the English Screw Steamer *Mauritius*[8] got underway and stood out to sea, the wind blowing very hard.

Wednesday, January 26. At 7½ A.M. sent up lower yards & top gallant masts. Received fresh beef and vegetables for crew. J[ack]. housed T. G. M's [Top Gallant Masts], wind blowing very strong. Two sails in the offing, a barque with M. T. Mast & F. T. G. Mt. [Main Top Mast & Fore Top Gallant Mast] gone. 11½ commenced coaling ship. 2 P.M. the disabled barque beating up for the anchorage.

Thursday, January 27. All day employed in coaling ship, painting & caulking. At 9 A.M. sent up lower yards. Yesterday evening I visited the Town. The wind blew very hard indeed, was almost blinded by the Dust and Sand, so that I was obliged to remain on shore all night. An English Mail Steamer last night about half after nine broke loose from her moorings and was blown ashore. She got off this morning not much damaged.

Friday, January 28. Today still coaling ship and painting her outside. Received some stores on board in the Pursers Department. This evening at half past seven, the wind blowing very strong, sent down lower yards.

Saturday, January 29. At six o'clock this morning swayed aloft lower yards. During the day 20 or 30 of the Ship's Company went on Liberty. This evening sent down lower yards, owing to the strong wind which sets in at times in certain seasons of the year.

Sunday, January 30. I went on shore this morning to Church, heard a discourse by the Rev. Mr. Newton at Christ Church. After Church together with a few of the Officers, I was invited to take dinner at the house of Mr. Eager[,] a wealthy merchant of this place. We were received by his family in a very cordial manner, and in the evening after dinner we took a walk of about two miles into the country, to the country residence of a son of Mr. E. We enjoyed the walk very much and returned on board ship about sundown.

Monday, January 31. The carpenters and caulkers returned on board this morning and resumed their respective duties. At eleven A.M. sent a boat and boarded the American Ship *Medera* from New York, 17th November 1852, bound to Port Philip Australia.[9] This evening received 6,000 gallons of water on board. I have just returned on board having been on shore for a few hours.

Tuesday, February 1. I have just returned on board ship, having spent a very pleasant day on shore. I left this morning about ten o'clock in company with a shipmate. Hired a horse and buggy and started off to see something of the country round about Cape Town. After driving about three miles or so, we came to Rochester Castle Inn where we stopped and took some refreshment, then proceeded on about five miles further to a little town called Wynburg[10] at which place a Kafir[11] Chief is kept in confinement, having been captured in a late battle. I saw him and one of his wifes, his Counsillor & wife, four in number. The chief's name was Seyolo,[12] his wife Nomise, his counsillor Obeit, and *his* wife Noiant. We made them understand us well as could be, who we were and where we came from and that in our own country we had hundreds and thousands of such people alike in every respect, only speaking a different language. Seyolo is about 6 feet 1¾ inches high, thirty-five or six years of age, a powerful, strong man, very stout and weighs near 200 pounds. When he was captured, he was condemned to death, but his punishment was commuted to imprisonment for life. Nomise his wife (or Naomi she is sometimes called) is 4 ft. in heigth [*sic*], 19 years of age, very thin and puny looking. She is permitted to go out of confinement whenever it suits her, having voluntar[il]y come with her husband. The Chief's Counsillor Obeit is 5 feet 8 inches high, near thirty years of age, very stout and strong. He[,] wishing to be near his Chief, came with him, and is allowed to go anywhere. Noiant is 4 ft. in heigth [*sic*][,] 21 years of age, very well made and a very pretty girl, free and easy in her manners, very quick at catching words and repeating them. She looked not altogether unlike our servant girls do at home, rather a bright complexion. She having followed her husband is allowed the same privileges as he. Seyolo has made a request of the English Government to let him have two more of his wives with him which request I believe has been granted and they have been sent for. It seems strange to me why such people should go to war with white people. They look as if they had not the least grain of sense in the world, but this is not actually the case, as they now seem to get the advantage of the English (with whom they are at war) in every fight they have, although in the end, the English after having expended some 3 or 4 millions of Dollars will exterminate them. After leaving Wynburg we proceeded to Constantia[13] four miles further and were very much pleased with the place. The scenery all the way is exceedingly beautiful, and cannot well be described. Anyone who has never visited this Country would suppose that but one crop of potatoes could be raised in a year, but the difference is this, that instead of one, three are raised annually. It is sunny here now, and [an] abundance of fruit [is grown], namely peaches, pears, plums, grapes, bananas, apples, and many other kinds, also any number of different kinds of vegetables, such as potatoes, cabbages, corn, tomatoes, beans, cellery [*sic*], etc. At Constantia I saw a number of images of Plaster of Paris representing different of the Kafir Chiefs. The principal Chief is Sandilli[14] with a withered leg. If they catch him the war will be ended. £500 have been offered for his head. He is a grand scamp and strong efforts are being made to capture him. Annexed is a picture of Macono[15] who also has given and still continues to give the English a great deal of trouble. At the top of the preceeding [*sic*] page is a representation of two Kafirs fishing, from a drawing lately made at Natal Bay, where the Kafirs are very numerous, and are a great deal of annoyance to the Farmers around about Natal.[16] They are however being dispersed by degrees, and are being driven more and more towards the Kafir country (Caffraria).[17] We came back to the Town about sundown, having stopped at Rochester Castle Inn on our way. Just before leaving the ship this morning all hands were called to muster and General Order No. 3 was read. Late this evening the English Mast Steamer *Sydney*[,] from Sydney & bound to England, arrived with several millions of Dollars on board in Gold Dust. Order No. 3 herewith annexed.[18]

Wednesday, February 2. This morning 7 men deserted from the ship. At 9 A.M. received on board 12 immense bullocks, weighing between five and six hundred pounds each, together with 16 broad[-]tailed sheep, all for sea stock, with a large lot of provender. During the day received stores in the Different Departments of the ship. Also coaled ship all day.

At Sea, Thursday, February 3. Early this morning unbent the sheet cable and started the fires. Sent Wm. Dry O. S. [Ordinary Seaman], an invalid, on board the Barque *Gay Head* for a passage to the United States; sent 80 days provisions with him. By this ship we also sent our mail home. At ten o'clock hove up the anchor and left Cape Town. A heavy swell set in as soon as we rounded the Cape, which is now rolling the ship to & fro, and dashing things from one side of the ship to the other.

Sunday, February 6. At eleven o'clock today called all hands to muster and read the Articles of War. 11½ o'clock performed Divine Service.

Monday, February 7. This morning sent down top gallant yard. A great number of Porpoises have been gambolling [*sic*] around the ship during this evening.

Thursday, February 10. This morning inspected the crew at Quarters and exercised the Divisions at the Great Guns. At half past one wind blowing ahead strong, sent down lower yards.

Friday, February 14. At 7 A.M. a sail was reported on starboard bow. At half past ten o'clock the engine was stopped on account of the breaking of the screw of the rock shaft. At this time the sail reported in the morning came up with us and proved to be upon speaking her, H.B.M. Steamer *Styx*[19] under sail 13 days from Simons Bay, C. G. Hope, bound to Mauritius. At 11 o'clock[,] having fixed the screw, started the engine and stood on our course.

Sunday, February 16. This evening a little before 8 bells (4 o'clock and the supper hour of the Ship's Company) expended 15 gallons of water, 5 gals. Whiskey, 2 gals. of Lime Juice & 20 lbs. of Sugar, which was made into a little beverage called Punch, and served it out to the Crew; they enjoyed it very much, it being a sort of extra.

Port Louis, Isle of Mauritius,[20] **Friday, February 18.** We anchored in this harbour about two hours ago, made the land this morning at half past nine; ahead & on Starboard Bow, at 12. (noon) Brabant Point[21] on the Island, bore true North. At two o'clock standing in for this place, swayed aloft lower yards, bent the cables. 5 o'clock hoisted the Jack and fired a gun for a pilot. At half past five fired the second gun and at 6½ o'clock stopped the engine and received a pilot on board. Started ahead and near seven P.M. came to. Have moored Ship, will remain but a short time to take in Coal. The weather here is exceedingly warm & quite suffocating; at this hour there is hardly a breath of air stirring.

Saturday, February 19. At ten o'clock today, H.B.M. Steamer *Styx* arrived here and anchored ahead of us. The American Consul and the Captain of the *Styx* visited the ship. At 11 o'clock saluted the Town with 21 guns, with the English Ensign at the Fore, which was returned from the Fort on shore with an equal number. The Screw Steamer *Mauritius* arrived near noon from Cape Town. She left the[re] about ten days before we did, but gave out of coal, having had quite a rough passage. This evening I visited the town in company with Father and Dr. Green.[22] We got a carriage and rode out to see something of the country, visited the tombs of Paul & Virginia,[23] obtained a small piece of the Monument of each, together with a few flowers, which are numerous and beautiful. To reach this place you follow the main road from the city for about 7 or 8 miles, when you turn into a bye road, and stop at a neat little cottage, behind which are the tombs spoken of, a very pretty spot. We also visited the Old Church at which it is said Paul and Virginia attended, a very ancient building it is, and it is also now in use. From there we went to the Botannical [*sic*] Gardens, which are quite pretty and a visit to them is well worth the time of anyone. After se[e]ing a good deal of the country, we returned on board ship about Sundown.

Tuesday, February 22. Yesterday evening I rode out to the country seat of Mr. Ferneyerugh, a wealthy merchant, who invited me to remain under the shelter of his roof for the night, which I did, and spent a very pleasant evening, & returned on board ship this morning. At eight o'clock A.M. hoisted the American Colors at the fore and mizen [*sic*] masts, in commemoration of its being Washington's Birthday (annaversary [*sic*] of). This evening a large party of Ladies came on board to see the ship (Officers encl[u]ded). I became acquainted with them, and being a Ladies gallant, escorted [*sic*] them through and around the vessel. They all expressed themselves highly pleased, thanked me for my kind attentions to them and also made me promise to call and see them before we left—which at the earliest opportunity I shall take great pleasure in doing. At five o'clock the Screw Steamer *Mauritius* left this Port and sailed for the Is. of Ceylon.

Wednesday, February 23. This evening about two o'clock, nothing particular requiring my stay on board ship. I went on shore, procured me a guide, whom I requested to direct my steps towards Champleur at which place a family by the name of Keating resided, and who were among the party who came on board last evening and to whom I showed the most attention. After a walk of a quarter of an hour or so I arrived at the house. They were very glad indeed to see me, and treated me in the best kind of manner. It so happened that this was the evening on which the Government Band played at the Champ de Mars[24] (the same as at home, the music at the Capitol.) I not caring particularly to remain at the house, suggested to the Young Ladies the idea of going to hear the music. They consented, soon put on their Hats, (Bonnets) and off we started, Two Young Ladies of the family together with Miss Moran (on a visited [*sic*] to the family) and myself. Well, we heard the music through, and were about to return to the house, about a mile distant, when distant thunder was heard and in a few moments on came *one* of *the* rain showers so frequent at this season of the year. I was in a pretty fix, with no umbrella or anything in the shape of one. We however took shelter under some trees, hoping that it would soon pass over, but, not so, as bad luck would have it. It lasted longer than any shower had ever before, but behold! What comes? A carriage drove down the road and stopped before where we were standing. In it were two Gentlemen who knowing that rain was anything but agre[e]able to Ladies, immediately jumped out and politely offered their carriage. We thanked them and very willingly accepted it, and having gotten in, we drove to the house and were well satisfied with having gotten off from a good drenching. Dinner was served up at 7 P.M. (French hour of dining) in fine style. After dinner I heard from one of the Ladies, some very delightful music on the piano. I have just returned on board ship (9½ P.M.) having notwithstanding the unpleasantness of the weather, spent a very pleasant evening. At 6 P.M. H.B.M. Steamer *Styx* left this port for the Isld. Of Ceylon.

Thursday, February 24. This morning the French Consul visited the ship. He remained but a few moments on board; saluted him with 9 Guns, French Flag at the foremast.

At Sea, Friday, February 25. At seven o'clock this morning cast of[f] the chain moorings and secured ship by hawsers, hove up the anchor at 8 A.M.[,] Discharged Geo. Beckford O. S. in disgrace, and sent him on shore. At nine o'clock let go the moorings, and got underway. At 9½ Discharged our pilot and started the engine ahead fast: with all fore and aft sails set. We are off for the Island of Ceylon.

Saturday, February 26. Today the purser called a survey on, and the following articles were condemned: 59 lbs. cheese, 262½ lbs. raisins, and 48 gallons beans.

Sunday, February 27. At half past ten o'clock this morning inspected the Crew at Quarters, and at 11 A.M. performed Divine Service.

Tuesday, March 1. This morning at half past nine o'clock went to General Quarters and exercised until 10½, when all hands were called to muster, and in the presence of the officers and crew, the Captain read General Order No 4, which is annexed.[25]

Thursday, March 3. Large schools of porpoises have been gambolling around the ship at different times today. This evening the crew were divided into three watches.

Friday, March 4. During the day we have had a remarkably smooth sea. The different Divisions of the ship's company have been exercised at target firing.

Saturday, March 5. This evening near four o'clock a sail was reported two pts. on port bow. She showed English colors, took her to be the Steamer *Styx*. Sent up lower yards. Today General Orders No. 5 & 6 were entered in Log—copies are here an[n]exed.[26]

Monday, March 7. Yesterday morning after muster we had Divine Service. Today killed the last of the twelve bullocks taken on board at Cape Town.

Thursday, March 10. This evening a little after sundown made the Light of Point de Galle Island of Ceylon,[27] half point on port bow.

"Point de Galle," Island of Ceylon, Friday, March 11. We arrived at this place this morning at eight o'clock, took a pilot on board at 6 A.M. 15 miles from the land[,] having made it last night. We lay off and on the land during the night. All of today the ship has been crowded with the Natives (Singhalese) who brought off precious stones, jewelry, work boxes, shells and many other things for sale and trade. They seem eager to take silk handkerchiefs in trade, a great many of which were exchanged by some of the officers. Some were completely taken in, having paid a large price for rings, which proved to be brass, and the sets in them nothing more than glass. Their work in tortoise shell is beautiful, and the Elephants made of black ebony are excellent ornaments for the Mantelpiece. Elephants [*sic*] teeth are very numerous. Out of them are made beautiful paper weights, boxes, knife handles, card racks, etc. The Island is covered with cocoanut trees, and the cocoanuts[,] the principal fruit[,] are innumerable. Bananas, pineapples, oranges & lemons are abundant.

Sunday, March 13. This morning I took a long ride into the Country, to the Country residence of the American Consul, Mr. Black,[28] a distance of about seventeen miles. The drive was along the seashore, but on both sides of the road were cocoanut trees which shaded us from the scorching sun. While in the country, I walked a short distance to see a Buddhist Temple. Having never seen one before I was quite anxious to see this, although I expect to see several more on our travel to China. I am now on shore at the Hotel, and intend remaining here all night. I have spent a very pleasant day, but not exactly as the day should have been passed.

Monday, March 14. We finished coaling ship this evening and got the vessel in pretty good trim. A party of Ladies together with a number of Buddhist Priest[s] and some Natives came on board. Our Band played many pretty tunes and all seemed pleased with their visit. This morning the Capt. of a Siamese Man of War lying in the harbour came on board. He seemed very much pleased and liked the appearance of the Ship.

At Sea, Tuesday, March 15. We got underway from Point de Galle this morning at eight o'clock and are now on our way for "Singapore." The weather is fine and we have a tolerable smooth sea.

Sunday, March 20. This morning discovered the Island of Nicobar[29] on port bow. Near half past seven o'clock A.M. saw a very large sail standing along the Island. This evening made the North Eastern Point of the Island of Sumatra[30] on starboard bow. It has been a rainy and disagre[e]able day, so that we have been unable to have Divine Service as usual.

Tuesday, March 22. About half an hour ago a light was reported to be right ahead. In a few minutes we came up to it and found that it was in a small boat, with a smaller one in tow. The persons in it were four Malays. They apparently hailed us, but we could not understand what they said. They had but one sail in the boat, made of Bamboo leaves. We fired a blank cartridge at them to make them heave to; they[,] however[,] stood farther off, where-upon another was fired, and lowered the dingy, which was sent after them in charge of Mr. Colson,[31] our Boatswain. We also changed our course and stood for the boat. The dingy returned and reported that it was a Canoe (large one) from one of the Islands in the Straits, bound to "Pulo Penang" or Prince of Wales Isld.[32] with fruits and mats. There were four men in the ca-noe and were tolerably frightened; none of them spoke any English, so that we could not get any information from them in regard to who they were and where they came from, except by signs. We then left them to pursue their voyage and we stood on our course. It is now a few minutes after nine, the moon shining bright, with a sail in sight and the ship running slow.

At Anchor in the Straits of Malacca,[33] Wednesday, March 23. This evening near four o'clock, discovered two points on port bow what was supposed to be a rock, which after standing for it proved to be the trunks of trees. At 5 P.M. saw four rocks on the starboard bow. At half past six o'clock stopped the engine and came to with the port anchor in 38 fathoms water. The Straits about here are so filled up with rocks that it is dangerous to run at night.

Thursday, March 24. At half past six o'clock this morning called all hands and hove up the anchor, and soon after started the engine ahead. Near 9 o'clock made Perciller Hill and the Light Boat on port bow. At half past eleven o'clock stopped the engine to wait for a small boat from the Light Ship to come along-side. We received from it a package of letters to take to "Singapore." Near 1 P.M. we passed an English frigate in tow of an English Man of War Steamer. The frigate saluted us with 15 guns; we stopped the engine, lowered the boats and returned the salute gun for gun. During this evening we have passed several large American Clipper Ships, Homeward bound. We showed our colors to them. We are now standing along the Island of Malacca.

Singapore, Island of Singapore, Friday, March 25. A little past noon today stopped the engine and took a pilot on board. By him several of the officers received letters from their families at home. At half past three stopped the engine again and came to in this harbour, We are lying about two miles from the town. There are some ten or twelve Chinese Junks in Port, the first I have ever seen. There is also an American Ship here (the *Dolphin*); she will sail for the United States in a few days. The weather is exceedingly warm, and everything in a state of tranquility.

Saturday, March 26. About eight o'clock this morning saluted the town with 21 Guns which was answered from the shore by the same number. At 11 o'clock the American Consul, Mr. W. W. Shaw,[34] visited the ship. Commodore Perry visited the officials ashore. On landing he received a personal salute of 13 Guns, which was returned by this ship gun for gun. This evening at four o'clock, commenced coaling ship.

Saturday, March 26. Last evening I went on shore, and in company with two or three of the officers rode out to the country seat of Mr. Whampoa,[35] a wealthy Chinese Merchant. We were very kindly received by him, and remained at his house overnight. This morning from the gateway at the entrance into Mr. Whampoa's residence, I took a view of the once splendid residence of Mr. Ballestier (the late Minister from the United States to Birmah [Burma] and Siam).[36] It is now a grand pasture ground owned by Mr. W. who has also very extensive property beside[s]. Have been coaling ship all day.

Monday, March 28. About four o'clock this evening the Lieut. Governor of the Port, together with several English Officers, came on board. On their leaving, saluted the Governor with 13 Guns.

At Sea. Tuesday, March 29. Having steam up, this morning at 10 A.M. hove up the anchor, started the engine and stood out of the Harbour of Singapore in charge of a pilot. Near three o'clock P.M. discharged the pilot off White Rock Light House about 40 miles from S . . . . .e [*sic*].

Wednesday, March 30. Early this morning discovered a small Island on the starboard beam, shortly after saw several others on the stbd. bow, and also passed a sail.

Sunday, April 3. This morning at eleven o'clock read the Articles of War and had a General Muster of the ship's company; afterwards performed Divine Service.

Monday, April 4. During today the weather has been quite hazy, and a considerable heavy head sea on.

At Anchor in the Ladrone Passage,[37] **Wednesday, April 6.** From four to eight o'clock this morning we were passing through an innumerable fleet of Chinese fishing craft. About half past ten discovered high land on port bow. Near eleven stopped the engine and sent the 2nd cutter in charge of an Officer to board one of the fishing boats, to try and obtain a pilot. She returned alongside without one, we then took her in tow and started ahead. Soon after sent her again to board one of the fishing boats; she returned with no better success than before. Started ahead and near half past four made the Ladrone Islands on the starboard bow. As we stood in for the Ladrone Passage spoke a Chinese junk, hailed her for a pilot [and] the people on board showed us some rice—probably did not understand us. At seven o'clock P.M.[,] not being able to obtain a pilot, we came to Anchor in about 7½ fathoms water and then fired a gun.

Victoria, Hong Kong,[38] **Thursday, April 7.** Half past five o'clock this morning got underway and stood in towards Macao, and near nine o'clock we came to Anchor in Macao outer roads. Sent the 1st cutter, with Lieut. Bent[39] and the purser to communicate with the U.S. Naval StoreKeeper in regard to obtaining supplies for the ship. Several Merchant vessels were at anchor in the inner roads, among them an American barque. At noon the boat returned with the U.S. Naval StoreKeeper (Mr. De Silver).[40] About half past one called all hands to up anchor. Soon after the storekeeper left, we hove up the anchor and started ahead fast in charge of a pilot. Just before getting underway, the Capt. of the Port of Macao with several Portuguese Officers came on board. This evening at half past five o'clock called all hands to bring ship to anchor. Soon after, made out the numbers of the U.S. Sloops of War *Plymo[u]th* and *Saratoga*, and Store Ship *Supply*. The *Saratoga* and *Plymo[u]th* saluted with 13 guns each; a few moments after six we came to anchor in the harbour, and returned the above salute with 7 guns. Officers from the different ships came on board to pay their respects and also to receive letters from their friends at home. We brought out a good lot of them. Several of my old friends have just been on board. There is also in the harbour an English and French Vessel of War. We received complimentary visits from the Commanders of them.

Friday, April 8. Last night sent an order on board the *Plymo[u]th* for her to shift her position so at daylight she hove up her anchor and dropped it again about a table's length astern. At eight o'clock A. M. we saluted the town with 21 guns, which was returned gun for gun from the Battery on shore. Soon after let fall the foretop sail and saluted the French Flag with 13 guns, which was returned with the same number from the French Commodore's ship, *la Capricieuses*.[41] At 9 A.M. the English Frigate saluted the Commodore with 13 guns, which we returned gun for gun. Soon after communicated with the squadron by signals. About half past eleven o'clock Comm. Perry visited the French Admiral's ship. She let fall her foretop sail and saluted him with 13 guns. The *Saratoga* hoisted the Broad Pennant of Commodore P[,] let fall her foretop sail and returned the salute gun for gun. At noon he visited the English Frigate *Spartan*. She let fall her foretop sail and saluted him with 13 guns. The *Saratoga* returned the salute in the same manner as before. At half past twelve Comm. Perry visited the town. On landing he received a salute of 13 guns, which was returned by the *Saratoga* with the same number. This evening the English Commodore-in-Chief visited the ship. Saluted him with 13 guns, which was returned by the English Frigate with the same number. At sunset transferred 10 men to the U.S. Sloop of War *Plymo[u]th* and five men to the U.S. Store Ship *Supply*. {High firing today}

Saturday, April 9. This morning rec'd fresh beef and vegetables for the crew. Near ten o'clock the U.S. Sloop of War *Plymouth* got underway and went to sea. She has been ordered up to Shanghai Soon after the Capt. of the French Frigate visited the ship. At 11 o'clock the American Consul[42] came on board; received him with a salute of 9 guns. Near noon the Governor of Hong Kong returned the call of the Commodore. On his leaving, hoisted the English Flag and saluted him with 17 guns. This evening received stores in the Purser's Department and transferred 8 men to the U.S. Sloop of War *Saratoga*. I have been on board the *Supply* to see some of my old friends, and also went on shore to take a look around.

Sunday, April 10, 1853. Today at Eleven o'clock had Divine Service on board, Hymns played by our Band and sung by the Officers and men. After dinner today allowed some of the men to go on libberty [*sic*]. They all returned at four o'clock. The English mail steamer arrived here about an hour ago (8 o'clock P. M.).

Monday, April 11. This morning I had the pleasure of receiving letters from home, the first since leaving the States, very gratifying indeed, all well and good news (dated Jany. 17). This evening a mail steamer left. General Order No. 7 entered in Log today, copy annexed.[43]

Tuesday, April 12. This evening a large number of Ladies and Gentlemen came on board to witness a Dramatic performance by the Thespian Corps formed on board by the Crew. The visitors are now at 12 o'clock (midnight) just about leaving. The performance was very good and all were much pleased (introduced to Miss D).

Wednesday, April 13. This morning the *Saratoga* stood out of the harbour. She has been ordered over to Macao there to await our arrival.

Roads of Macao, Thursday, April 14. Early this morning a pilot came on board, and having steam up, we hove up the anchor, got underway and stood out of the harbour of Hong Kong, and about half past ten o'clock came to anchor in this place. Found the *Saratoga* here. Today General Order No 8 was entered in Log; copy is here annexed.[44]

Friday, April 15. This morning commenced coaling ship, and allowed a number of the men to go on liberty.

Saturday, April 16. Near 9 A. M. the U.S. Sloop of War *Saratoga* got underway and stood out of the harbour. She was ordered to proceed up to Whampoa[45] to await us. This evening the liberty men came on board. Confined ten of them by order of the Commodore, for disorderly and outrageous conduct on shore.

Sunday, April 17. This morning early the U.S. Store Ship *Supply* was discovered at anchor near us. She having come into the harbour about one o'clock last night. We had Divine Service on board today at eleven, nothing of interest has occurred during the remainder of the day.

Whampoa Reach, near Whampoa, Monday, April 18. At daybreak called all hands and hove short on the starboard cable. At six o'clock Commodore Perry came on board. We tripped our anchor and stood up the Tigres River. Near half past seven one of the Bomb Boats in tow of us swamped. We stopped the engine, lowered a boat, rescued the Chinamen and brought the B. Boat alongside. We then righted her, bailed her out and left her in charge of her crew. This boat had in her an [*sic*] hundred Piculs[46] of salt, which the Chinamen were trying to smuggle up to Canton, where they could sell it at a high price, but in this they were frustrated. Their boat leaked, the salt

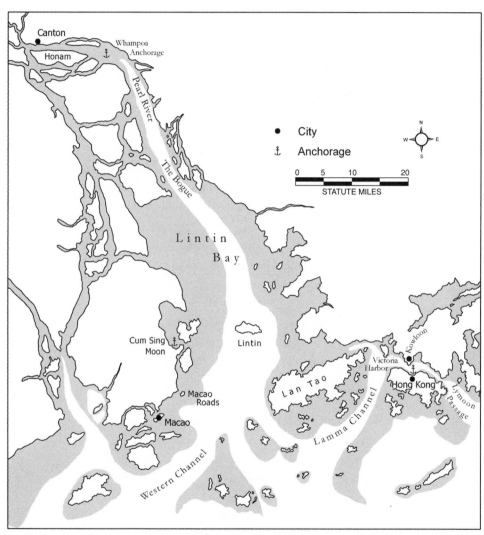

Map 1. Pearl River and the approaches to Canton. Adapted by Alexander Paul Nohe from *OLD BRUIN: Commodore Matthew C. Perry, 1794–1858* by Samuel Eliot Morison. Copyright © 1967 by Samuel Eliot Morison. By permission of Little, Brown and Company. All rights reserved.

became wet and heavy and occasioned the swamping. This evening at four o'clock, we passed the *Saratoga* at anchor ten miles below this place waiting for the tide to set her up. At half past six o'clock we came to anchor here and moored ship. There are a great many ships here, only one American, the *Refuge*. She leaves for the United States in a few days.

Tuesday, April 19. At 8 A. M. today Commodore Perry and suite left the ship for Canton. At nine o'clock the *Saratoga* hove in sight and at eleven she came to anchor ahead of us, but further down the River.

Near Whampoa, Thursday, April 21. Yesterday morning I hired a Fast Boat (near 9 o'clock) and together with four of my Mess Mates, Adams, Armstrong, Jones & Spalding, went up to the great City of Canton. We were three hours going up. The scenery along the Canton River was exceedingly beautiful and picturesque, forts at intervals on either side, but it was hardly perceptible that they were at all fortified, having from three to four guns (small) each. We passed divers Chinese junks and sampans, the former going along in a most slovenly manner. They never, even in a fair wind[,] are able to go over three knots an hour, or four at the extreme. The bows are so broad and flat that it takes as much wind to force one of them of 300 tons as it would to force an American ship of 3000 tons and more too, and this appears to be the way with everything they do. They think their way is the best and will not be learned any other. But to continue, we arrived at Canton about twelve o'clock & put up at Scow's Hotel. The only place of resort and a poor one to boot. We ordered tiffin to be got ready, which was served to us in a little while after, composed of ham and eggs, roast chicken, potatoes, etc., all of which would have been very nice, had they been cooked in a *nice* or eatable manner. It made me quite sick to eat, but the rest of the party went into it right heartily. After tiffin we went out to see what there was to be seen. The principle streets are Old and New China streets. I believe we went into every store in each street. On entering, it was How do, "Pi-sing," how do "Uk-chong," or "Keang-qu" or "Sam-Chun," or I may say, without mentioning any more Chinese names, it was how do, whatever name was over the door of the Shop, and then, what hab got sell, well me got great many things, me make you see shawl, (the first question always put to anyone by them)[.] No John, me want see Fan, (or anything one wanted)[.] He will show you what you want, and you ask him how much for it. He will say a price—say six Dollars, me give you three Dollars, he will say, Ny-yah, how can do, me mak-e loose (and then they take out their books and counters to find out the real price)[.] Me take four dollar half, no me give you but three dollar. Let me see your dollar, you show him your dollar, and after looking at them for a few minutes, the temptation is so great, that he will say, marse-qui (very good), me take, & the general rule is[,] I think, in dealing with the Chinese, to offer them about one half the amount they ask you and never buy more than one article from one store for if you do, for the second article they will ask you about six times its value, and then if you give them one half that price you will get completely taken in. By buying one thing from one shop, you are very apt to get a good bargain, they selling you the first article very low and under its value, expecting on the second to fully compensate themselves. In the evening, I was invited to dinner by Mr. Moore, one of the Firm of Wetmore & Co.[47] Merchants. This could not have happened better, for I could never have eaten of the Dinner which would have been set before me had I returned to the hotel, as I afterwards heard it was composed of an animal which I had in the morning seen lying dead from one of the windows, and some soup made from another animal, together with other things too disgusting to mention. While at Mr. Moore's I had the very best of everything that money could buy, it was quite late when we got up from dinner, and I was about to return to the hotel, to pass over as I expected a restless and sleepless night, when I was requested by Mr. M. to occupy a room which he had already prepared for my reception. Of course I complied with his request with pleasure, and thereby obtained a delightful night's rest, and rose this morning with the lark, having though caught an exceedingly bad cold in my head. After breakfast I went round to the hotel to see how my companions had fared and rested. The former I have mentioned before and about the latter, no sleep, not a wink, for the Musquitoes [*sic*], says one of them, Oh! Cricky, how the m . . s . . s . . s [*sic*] did bite. And such appeared to be the sentiment of all by their countenances, although not saying so, being envious of my good luck in having had a good dinner, a good nights sleep and free from all musquitoe [*sic*] bites, and an excellent breakfast this morning. We then took a walk around the town (did not however see the walls of the City) until near two o'clock, when we got in our boat and came down to the ship. Got here about an hour ago (6 P.M.) having had a Jolly time, firing crackers and sending off Rockets. The Chinamen must have thought that we were a set of demons just let loose. We are twelve miles below Canton and two miles below Whampoa. The only obstacles objectionable in going up to Canton are the Pirates, who attack you in broad day light if they think you have anything valuable. We however got clear of them, having gone well prepared with pistols & swords. I have heard that the boats plying between this place and Canton pay a regular monthly tax to these Pirates, to allow them to pass up and down the river without molestation. If a fisherman goes one month without paying, they board him, and if he then does not make retribution, they take all his nets and cut them up. These acts are disgraceful and a stop by some means or other ought to be put to them. We expect to leave this place tomorrow for Macao.

Macao Roads, Friday, April 22. This morning quite early made preparations for getting underway. About nine o'clock, Passed Mid[shipman] W. F. Jones was detached from this ship and ordered to the *Saratoga*, 9 men were also transferred to her. At half past ten we got underway from Whampoa Reach and stood down the river. This evening at 6½ o'clock called all hands and came to anchor in this place, found the *Supply* still here, in company with the French Frigate *La Capriceuses*.

Saturday, April 23. Today commenced coaling ship. This evening the French Frigate got underway and stood out of the harbour. Sent the Band on shore by order of the Commodore.

Sunday, April 24. At 10 o'clock today inspected the crew at Quarters and at eleven we had Divine Service, nothing of much interest.

Monday, April 25. Still coaling ship. At eight A.M. the store ship *Supply* got underway and stood out of the harbour. She is ordered up to Shanghai. Near 9 o'clock the Sloop of War *Saratoga* hove in sight, and about ten o'clock we received letters from home, brought by the mail of yesterday and bearing date Feb'y 2nd, 1853. This evening at 4 P.M. the *Saratoga* came into the harbour and is now at anchor quite near us.

Tuesday, April 26. At 7½ A.M. the Barque *Caprice* arrived from Whampoa. We received 21 Coolies from her; she then stood in and came to anchor in the inner harbour. This evening we transferred eight coolies to the *Saratoga* for the *Caprice*.

At Sea, Wednesday, April 27. This morning at nine o'clock, hove up the Anchor, got underway and stood out from Macao, with Mr. De Silver, U.S. Naval Store Keeper, & Lady, on board for passage to Hong Kong. We passed through the Nantow Passage and at 2½ P.M. we came to anchor in the Harbour of Victoria H.K. Mr. & Mrs. De S. then left the ship. We rec'd. a tank alongside and filled up with water. At half past four o'clock hoisted the Cornet and fired a Gun. Received Capt. Herber on board as coast pilot to Shanghai, then hove up the anchor and stood out of the harbour. At a quarter past seven, stopped the engine, discharged the harbour pilot, and started ahead fast.

Thursday, April 28. At daybreak we passed through a fleet of fishing boats; at nine o'clock the wind being very strong dead ahead[,] sent down lower yards.

Friday, April 29. During the day we passed by several junks and fishing boats. About five o'clock this evening discovered the Excew Islands three points on port bow.

Sunday, May 1. Not such a day as last year presented to us, but a disagreeable one. We were prevented from having Church. About ten o'clock made a Steamer on port beam, and this evening the English Steamer *Bombay* passed us. Discovered land on port bow, beam & quarter.

At anchor in sight of Chusan Islands,[48] **Monday, May 2.** At half past six o'clock this evening we came to anchor, the water not being high enough for us to cross the Chusan Bar.

Tuesday, May 3. Called all hands at daybreak, hove up the anchor, & started ahead fast. Passed to the Westward of the Islands and stood for the Yan Tse Kiang [Yangtze] River.[49] At half past ten stopped the engine and took a river pilot on board, & at a few moments after eleven stopped again and came to anchor. The water on the first bar above Chusan[50] not being at a sufficient heighth to allow us to pass.

Shanghai, North China, Wednesday, May 4. At early daylight called all hands and made preparations for getting underway. At half past four o'clock hove short, near 5½ A.M. hove up the anchor, started ahead & stood in for the mouth of the Yan Tse Kiang. About half past seven crossed the shallowest part of the outer bar, least water 18 ft. 6 in.[,] very foggy. Land in sight along on port beam. Passed a number of fishing boats. At 10½ sent up top gallant masts, standing up the River for Shanghai. At half past eleven passed Woo Sung[51] on our way up. 12½, standing up the Woo Sung River, made out the numbers of the U.S. Steam Frigate *Susquehanna* & U.S. Sloop of War *Plymouth* at anchor off Shanghai, which we returned by showing ours. The *Susquehanna* saluted the Commodore's Flag with 13 guns. At half past one o'clock we came to anchor off this town and returned the *Susquehanna's* salute with 7 guns. H.B.M. Brig *Lilly* saluted the Commodore with 13 guns, which the *Plymouth* returned with a like number. The American Consul (Mr. Cunningham)[52] visited the Ship; received him with a salute of 9 guns. At five o'clock we hove up the anchor, drifted down abreast of the Souchow Creek,[53] and moored ship. The Mail Steamer *Bombay* came in port.

Thursday, May 5. This evening about three o'clock H.H.M. Steamer *Hermes* arrived here from Nankin [Nanking],[54] she having gone up to that port to take the English Minister. In both going up and coming down the river she was fired into by the Rebels. The latter time she fired back upon them (for further information papers of tomorrow will show). About four o'clock I went on shore to view some races which were to take place. The last race (the horses being ridden by Chinese) was quite amusing indeed, although a description is not necessary. Today General Orders No. 9 & 10 were received[,] copies of which are herewith annexed.[55]

Friday, May 6. Today commenced scraping ship outside, getting ready to paint.

Sunday, May 8. At 10 A.M. mustered the crew & read the Articles of War. At 10½ had Divine Service. This evening the Steamer *Bombay* went to sea.

Monday, May 9. This morning at 10 o'clock the Commander-in-Chief & Suite left the Ship with his Flag. Manned the yards, hauled down the broad pennant and saluted it with 13 guns. Hoisted the Coach Whip.[56] A quarter past ten the broad pennant was hoisted on board the *Susquehanna* and saluted by that ship and the *Plymouth* with 13 guns each. This evening commence moving the Commodore's goods and chattels on board the *Susquehanna*.

Tuesday, May 10. Today transferred several men to the *Susquehanna*, also three Acting Master's Mates[,] (Brown, Draper & Heine, Daguerreatypist [*sic*], Telegraphist, & Artist),[57] with the Commodore's Clerk, and the whole of our Band. This evening received on board the whole of the *Susquehanna's* Band. At 3 o'clock P.M. the English Brig *Lilly*[58] went to sea. Last evening a large Ball was given on shore by the American Consul. Most of our Officers were present, together with the officers of the *Susquehanna* & *Plymouth* and the English Steamers lying in the Harbour. This evening sent on board the *Susquehanna* a number of things belonging to the Artist's, Daguerreatypist's & Telegraphist's Departments. I went on shore for a short time this evening.

Saturday, May 14. This morning a party of Ladies and Gentlemen (composing the American Mission to China) visited the Ship. They were very much pleased with their visit, knowing most of our Officers before leaving the States. Among them were the Rev'ds Messrs. Nelson, Pierce & Crawford, the Misses Fay, Baker. Jones & Parks, with the wives of the mentioned gentlemen, quite a pleasant party.

Sunday, May 15. Quite late last evening finished coaling ship. All today it has been quite disagreeable, raining and blowing. Having a bad cold I was unable to go on shore to church as I expected.

Below Woo Sung, Monday, May 16. During the morning received on board six sheep and four bullock, together with other stores and made preparations for leaving Shanghai having heard late last night that the U.S. Store Ship *Supply* had gone ashore on the North Bank and we had orders to go to her assistance. So this evening at half past four hove up the anchor and at 5 o'clock started ahead and stood down the Woo Sung River, and at half past seven we came to anchor a little below the shipping at Woo Sung.

Yangtze River, Tuesday, May 17. At half past six o'clock this morning got underway and ran out of the mouth of the Woo Sung River and anchored. At 3 P.M. took a coal junk in tow, stood down this river and at six o'clock came to anchor again.

Wednesday, May 18. At daylight discovered the *Supply* bearing S.E. distant about five miles. At half past seven we got underway and stood for her and at 10 o'clock came to anchor near the *Supply*. Found that she had gotten off the Bank, sustained no injury and that no assistance was necessary. Soon after we discovered the U.S.S.F. *Susquehanna* standing down the river; we made our number and she came to anchor. At noon when the tide changed, the coal junk[,] which was made fast astern, got afoul of us and partly stove our launch and port whale boat. At 4 P.M. the *Susquehanna* got underway and came down to us. Called all hands to up anchor, lighted it,[59] and drifted down with the tide to take the coal junk in tow. There was not sufficient water to allow us to go to her, so we came to anchor nearby. At five o'clock the *Susquehanna* hove to on our starboard beam and exchanged signals with us, then filled away and stood down the river. At 6 P.M. sent the first cutter to tow the junk alongside.

Thursday, May 19. The 1st cutter returned this morning at one o'clock, and reported that in the first part of the night the junk had drifted in shore and got aground. At 11 o'clock today the *Supply* got underway and came to anchor a little further out from under the lee of the land. About two o'clock sent the 1st cutter again to the junk. She returned without having boarded her as the sea was breaking over and all around her. This evening at 5 o'clock sent the launch and 1st cutter to the assistance of the junk, to stay by her all night and if possible to bring her alongside at the change of tide in the morning.

Mouth of the Yangtze, Friday, May 20. At half past five this morning the 1st cutter and launch returned and said that the coal junk had bilged and was filling with water, and that there was no chance of saving her and thus the loss of 150 tons of coal. At 6 A.M. sent the two boats to take the crew of the junk away. At eight o'clock the boats returned with the crew (Chinamen)[,] some 26 in number. Near a quarter after eight, hove up the anchor and started the engines & stood across the bar of the river. The store ship *Supply* about five miles on stbd. bow under sail. Near 11 o'clock we discovered the *Susque-hanna* at anchor in the mouth of the river. We stood for her and at half past eleven came to anchor in company with the *Supply* near her.

Sunday, May 22. This morning at nine o'clock on a signal being made by the *Susquehanna*, lowered the 1st cutter and sent our pilot on board. Inspected the crew at Quarters at twenty minutes after ten, and then we had Divine Service. This evening sent all the Crew of the lost coal junk on board a fishing boat for passage up to Woo Sung.

At Sea, Sunday, May 23. At eleven A.M. got steam up. Called all hands to up anchor, hove it up and drifted down near the *Supply* & came to anchor and made preparations for taking the *S.* in tow. At noon lifted the anchor and drifted close to the *Supply* & then let it go again. Sent two hawsers to her and made fast. At two o'clock hove up the anchor and got underway with the *Supply* in tow & in company with the *Susquehanna* stood out to sea. At 3½ o'clock made Saddle Island,[60] also a large sail. On getting nearer the strange sail she showed American colours, and proved to be the U.S. Store Barque *Caprice* from Hong Kong. The *Susquehanna* then wore round, spoke the *Caprice* and again went ahead of us. This evening Wm. Keady[,] Ordinary Seaman, had both hands severely injured by being caucht [*sic*] in the top tackle block, while fidding fore top mast.

Tuesday, May 24. This evening called all hands to muster, and in the presence of the Officers and Men, read General Orders No. 11 & 12[,] copies of which are herewith annexed.[61]

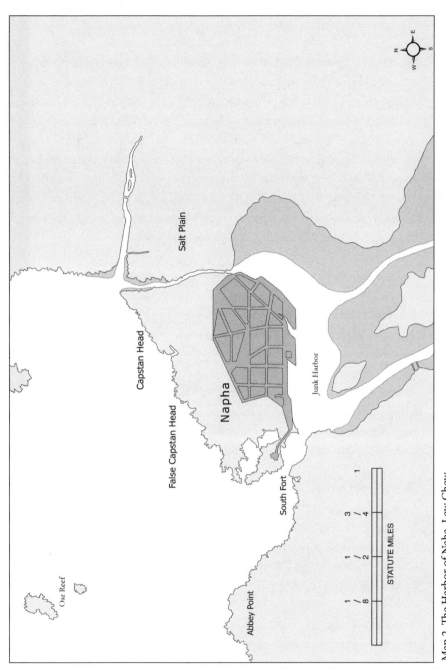

Map 2. The Harbor of Naha, Lew Chew

Adapted by Alexander Paul Nohe based on the 1853 chart by Silas Bent held by the Library of Congress

Wednesday, May 25. About 10 o'clock today beat to General Quarters, exercised the crew at the great guns for an hour or so. This evening the Commodore made signal to us to go to General Quarters, so at four o'clock beat to Quarters and exercised the crew at the great guns again. At a few moments after six made the land from aloft, two points on stb'd. bow. At 6.20 cast off from the *Supply* and slowed down. We then made the land from the deck, got casts of the lead, and commenced standing on and off from the land.

Harbour of Napa Riang [Naha], Loo Choo [Lew Chew, now Okinawa,][62] **Thursday, May 26.** At half past four this morning started the engine ahead fast. At 7 o'clock discovered an Island bearing S.S.E. At 8 o'clock the Flagship on starboard bow, during the early part of this morning[,] made several Islands. About half past eleven made a sail on stb'd. bow. This evening at 3 P.M. lowered a boat and sent Lt. Bent on board the *Susquehanna*. Hoisted up the boat and followed the *Susquehanna* in for the anchorage. A little after three lowered the 1st cutter and barge and sent them ahead to sound. And at ten minutes after four o'clock we came to with the port anchor in this harbour in twelve fathoms water. The two boats sounded round the ship, and found not less than 9 fathoms water two cables length off. Soon after we came to anchor, a boat came off from shore with natives, did not communicate with her[;] the natives made signs to us to go away. We told them to go to the other ship, which they did. At half past six o'clock the strange sail, which proved to be U.S. Sloop of War *Saratoga*, from Hong Kong, came into the harbour and anchored near us.

Naha, Friday, May 27. This morning Acting Master W. A. Webb rec'd the appointment of Act'g Lieut. and was ordered to the *Saratoga* to fill the vacancy occasioned by Lieut. Howells, being condemned by a survey and ordered home. Passed Midshipman David Ochiltree[63] was appointed Acting Master of their ship. Passd. Asst. Surgeon L. J. Williams[64] was ordered to the *Saratoga* as Senior Medical Officer of that ship. This evening I accompanied our Boatswain in the 1st Cutter to drag for shells. We sounded around the outer reef and made several drags; did not succeed in getting anything but a few pieces of coral. The water was so very clear that we could see the coral on the bottom some twenty five or thirty feet deep. This morning five boats came alongside with provisions, composed of 1 bullock, some pigs, sheep (ought to be goats)[,] chickens, etc. We sent them alongside the Flagship. They were there told that no trade could be made with them until the Ruling Prince had come off to see the Commo.

Naha, Saturday, May 28. The storeship *Supply* came into harbour this morning. At noon three boats (native) apparently with men of Rank in them went alongside the *Susquehanna*, and were received with a salute of 3 Guns. It proved afterwards to be the Prince Regent, making a call on the Commodore. At half past two when the Prince left, saluted him again with 3 Guns.

Sunday, May 29. Raining nearly all the day[;] had Divine Service at half past eleven.

Monday, May 30. This morning at six o'clock discovered a barque out at sea and standing in for this place. At 9 o'clock two of our officers, with some from the *Susquehanna*[,] left the ship for the purpose of exploring the Island. At half past nine the barque which was seen came into the harbour and anchored in shore of us. She proved to be the U.S. store barque *Caprice* from Hong Kong, and which was spoken at sea this day last week. Soon after she came to anchor got a hawser to her and hauled her alongside, and commenced immediately to discharge her of her cargo, coal & bread. A little before noon Lieut. Bent commenced the survey of this harbour. I went on shore this evening for the first time and had a long chat by signs with some of the natives. Late this evening rec'd from shore two bullocks and a quantity of vegetables. Arrangements have been made for the natives to supply us with what we want.

Tuesday, May 31. Soon after all hands were called this morning, all the Marine Guard in charge of Capt. W. B. Slack[65] went on shore to drill; they returned at 8 o'clock. During the day a number of the natives came on board. One boat brought off a number of fish.

Wednesday, June 1. Nothing of much interest occur[r]ed during the early part of this day. This evening I went on shore in company with several of our Officers to take a walk. We visited the town and saw what there was to be seen. We had a crowd of the natives following us all the way. The weather was very warm. We returned on board ship about sundown, found that they had finished coaling ship, and the *Caprice* had been cast off from us. She leaves tomorrow for Shanghai and takes our letters.

Thursday, June 2. This afternoon the *Caprice* got underway and stood out to sea. This evening rec'd a bullock and some vegetables for the crew. Part of the crew were allowed to go on board the *Susquehanna* to witness a theatrical performance.

Saturday, June 4. The exploring party returned this evening.

Sunday, June 5. At half past ten today mustered the crew and read the Laws for the better government of the Navy. After which we had Divine Service and some very sweet sacred music by our band.

Monday, June 6. This morning Commodore Perry and suite left the *Susquehanna* for the shore, under an escort of the officers of this vessel, the *Saratoga* and *Supply*, together with Marines and part of the crew of each ship, and two fieldpieces, to pay a visit to the Prince Regent at Sheuti [Shuri],[66] the capital. The Commodore and party returned about 2 P.M. I was unable to go so a description of the visit I am unable to give.

Tuesday, June 7. Quite early this morning the *Susquehanna* made preparatory signal to the Squadron. Armed, Provisioned, and Equipped the Launch, Barge, Gig, First & Second Cutters, and their respective crews, and at 7 o'clock sent them alongside the Flagship to be inspected by the Commander-in-Chief. The boats all returned at 8 o'clock. At ten A.M. the *Saratoga* hoisted the Jack at the Mizen [*sic*], and fired a gun. A Court Martial convened on board for the trial of one of her crew.

Wednesday, June 8. This morning also sent all the boats alongside the *Susquehanna*, armed & equipped, as yesterday[,] for inspection.

Thursday, June 9. At seven o'clock this morning the *Susquehanna* got up steam, got underway[,] took the *Saratoga* in tow and stood out of the harbour. They have gone over to the Bonin Islands.[67]

Friday, June 10. At 9 A.M. hove up the anchor and warped in nearer the shore. Soon after dropped our anchor two ships lengths from the *Supply*.

Saturday, June 11. Early this morning sent the Marine Guard ashore to be drilled.

Sunday, June 12. We had Divine Service on board this morning at eleven and a sermon preached by our Chaplain for the first time. His subject was "Our Father in Heaven." A little before sundown a large sail was seen outside[;] at 8 P.M. a gun was heard in the direction of the sail.

Monday, June 13. At ten o'clock this morning the U.S. sloop of war *Plymouth* came into port. By her several of our officers received letters from home. This evening sent the 1st Division on shore to drill. They returned at sundown.

Sunday, June 19. The last week has been employed in surveying the harbour[;] the different divisions of the ships company have been on shore to exercise with small arms. This morning we had Divine Service and a sermon by the Revd. Dr. B. T. Bettelheim,[68] Missionary to this place. The subject of his discourse was "Strangers," on which he spoke at some length and a good sermon it was. This evening I went on board the *Supply* where I again heard a sermon from Dr. B. which was very good, though not equal to the one this morning. It has been excessively warm all day, the thermometer—92°.

Thursday, June 23. For the last three or four days the men have been on shore for the purpose of scrubbing their hammocks, bedding and clothes. This evening at half past three the *Susquehanna* and *Saratoga* hove in sight. Lieut. Bent went out in the whale boat to pilot them in, and about half past four they both came to anchor in this harbour quite near us.

Saturday, June 25. This morning at eleven o'clock Lieut. Bent and P. Mid. March left the ship in the 1st Cutter for Port Melville,[69] which harbour they intend surveying.

Sunday, June 26. At half past ten A.M. inspected the crew at Quarters and at eleven called all hands to muster and read the sentence of a Naval General Court Martial in the case of Ed. Watson. O. S. attached to the *Saratoga* and the letter from the Com'dr-in-Chief accompanying it. At a quarter past eleven had Divine Service and a sermon by our Chaplain, subject, "Taking the name of the Lord in Vain."

Monday, June 27. "Near Midnight." Three cows and three sheep were presented today to the Prince Regent; also three sheep to Dr. Bettelheim. At six this evening a barque was seen in the offing. Near eight o'clock a large number of the Officers and crew of the different ships came on board to attend a Theatrical Performance by the Thespian Corps of this Ship[;] the theatre broke up about eleven o'clock. After the strangers left, spliced the Main Brace (gave the crew an extra lot of grog). Dr., Madame and the little Bettelheims were present at the performance and were very much amused.

Tuesday, June 28. Near daylight Lieutenant Bent returned from his surveying expedition to Port Melville. At 5 A.M. the barque seen last evening was discovered to be a little outside the harbour and proved to be the U.S. Store Barque *Caprice* from Shanghai. Sent the whaleboat with Acting Master Ochiltree to pilot her in. She came to anchor at half past seven on our starboard bow. This evening near three o'clock a strange sail was reported to be off the harbour. Mr. Ochiltree went out in the first cutter to pilot her in, and near sundown she came in [and] anchored.

Wednesday, June 29. This morning the schooner *Brenda*[70] was hauled alongside of us and commenced discharging her cargo of coal. This evening Mr. Alexander (2nd Asst. Engineer)[71] went in the 1st cutter, with the submarine armour, to examine the *Supply's* bottom. When he returned, reported that she had not sustained any injury.

Thursday, June 30. Nothing of much account has occurred today. We finished coaling ship, the *Brenda* hauled alongside the *Supply* and then alongside the *Susquehanna* to discharge. At sunset she cast off from the *Susquehanna* and anchored astern of us.

Friday, July 1. At noon today the barque *Caprice* sailed from this harbour for Shanghai. These [*sic*] evening I accompanied a few of our officers in the whaleboat and went a long distance up Junk River and on coming back we stopped on board of a Japanese junk. Nothing there seemed particularly to attract our attention, so we soon left and arrived on board ship about sundown.

At Sea, Saturday, July 2. At half past four or about daybreak, called all hands. Bent topgallant sails, sent up and crossed topgallant yards, and a few moments after six o'clock hove up the anchor and stood out of Naha Harbour in company with the *Susquehanna*, *Plymouth* & *Saratoga*. With a fair wind, at seven A.M., we were ordered to take the *Plymouth* in tow. We went alongside of her[,] gave her hawsers and started ahead. The *Susquehanna* took the *Saratoga* in tow. We are now at 5 P.M. on the *Susque*'s quarter, going along nicely.

Sunday, July 3. Last night about 10½ o'clock, carried away the port hawser used in towing the *P*. Roused it in and found that it had parted at her horse blocks,[72] so this morning near five o'clock, veered a breaker astern to the *Plymouth* by a towline[,] with which she hauled in and secured a hawser for the port towline which parted. Today at eleven mustered the crew at Quarters, and read the Articles of War, after which we had Divine Service.

Monday, July 4. The Glorious Fourth and the Seventy Second Anniversary of our National Independence. At meridian in company with the *Susquehanna*, *Plymouth* and *Saratoga*, we fired a salute of 17 Guns in honor of the day. And this evening in order to wet poor Jacks parched lips, spliced the Main Brace.

Tuesday, July 5. Nothing of any interest today. The four ships still in company.

Wednesday, July 6. During this day all the Divisions have been exercised at target firing. The crews of the other vessels have been also engaged at the same exercise.

Thursday, July 7. The different Divisions have also today been exercised at target firing and we have been twice to General Quarters.

Op[p]osite the Town of Oragawa [Uraga][73], Bay of Jedo [Edo]. Near Jedo [Edo], Japan, Friday, July 8. Discovered several Islands early this morning and at eight o'clock there was very high land on port bow and beam. About one o'clock Captains Kelly, Walker[74] and Lee, of the *Plymouth*, *Saratoga* and this Ship, went on board the Flagship in obedience to a signal from the Commodore. At half past one the Captains returned to their respective ships. About half past three we cast off the *Plymouth*[,] and the *Susquahanna* cast off the *Saratoga*, and the four vessels stood with a fair wind for this place. We all came to anchor at half past five in very deep water. As soon as we anchored a number of Japanese boats came alongside. Several of them attempted to board us; called away the First Division of Boarders and repelled them. They[,] after making a great many signs, and endeavouring without success to put on board of us the usual implications to Foreigners to depart, left us and went towards the shore, w[h]ere they must certainly have all come to the opinion that we were a queer sort of people. From our ship we observed that a large number of these boats gathered around the *Susquehanna*. One of these boats containing some High Functionaries,[75] and perhaps a little more bold, went alongside, and were received at the gangway by Capt. Buchanan and some of his officers. Several questions were put to these Japanese Mandarins by Mr. Portman (the Com'd. Clerk), who acted as Interpreter. Among these questions they were asked what the distance was to Edo. They said it was eighteen miles or so, and also whether the water was deep all the way. They said it was nearly all the way. The Japanese then inquired how many ships, guns, and men we had. They were told that we had not asked them such a question as this, so that we could not answer it,

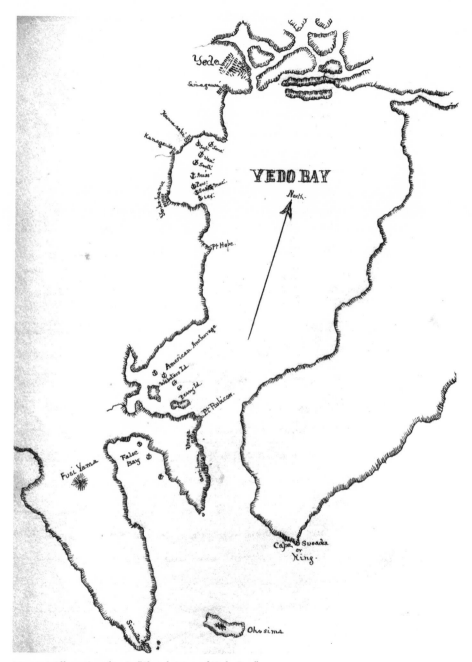

Map 3. William Speiden Jr. "Sketch Map of Yedo Bay"

Library of Congress

and they soon left. Before leaving, however, ten boats surrounded the *Susque-hanna* and the Japanese who were on board being asked by Lt. Contee why these boats came round the Ship, replied that it was Japanese custom. This reply was sent down to the Commodore, who told Lieut. C. to say to them that it was not American custom, and if all the boats were not away in fifteen minutes he would not be responsible for the consequences. They took the hint and soon vamo[o]-sed. About an hour or so after or shortly after six o'clock, another boat contain-ing the Governor of Uraga[76] went alongside the *Susquehanna* and he on being told the object of our visit and that we wished to have some one of high rank to whom to deliver the Letter so that it would reach the Emperor, replied that he was the highest person in authority at this place, that it would be sure death to him if he delivered the letter, but if the Commodore wished he would despatch a messenger to Edo to inform the Emperor of the cause of our visit, that it would take two days for the message to go and the same time to come[,] besides the detention while at Edo. He was told that the Commodore would wait three days for a proper person to come and convey the letter, and if no one arrived in that time, he would go to Edo, land men and deliver the letter himself. I have neglect-ed to say, that before or as we were about coming to anchor, 3 shell[s] were fired from a high point a mile or so distant. As these did not strike anywhere near the ships we supposed they were intended to give notice at Edo of our arrival. Before coming into the Bay the ships were all got in readiness for action.

Saturday, July 9. This morning at half past six Lieutenant Bent and P. Mid. March left the ship in the 1st cutter for the purpose of sounding in the direc-tion of Edo. At eight A.M. the *Plymouth* tripped her anchor[77] and dropped astern of us. The four ships are now in a line so as to bear directly upon the Town. These [this] evening Mount Fusee [Fuji][,] a volcanic mountain, said to [be] 12,000 feet in heighth, and 70 miles distant from this place,[78] was plainly visible. Now at 8 P.M. the wind is blowing very strong from the southard. Nothing of any consequence has been heard from the shore today.

Sunday, July 10. At 11 A.M. we had Divine Service on board. This evening a Japanese boat went alon[g]side the Flagship. The Commodore being informed that there was a boat containing some Mandarins alongside, sent word to them through Lt. Contee that if they came concerning the letter, they would be

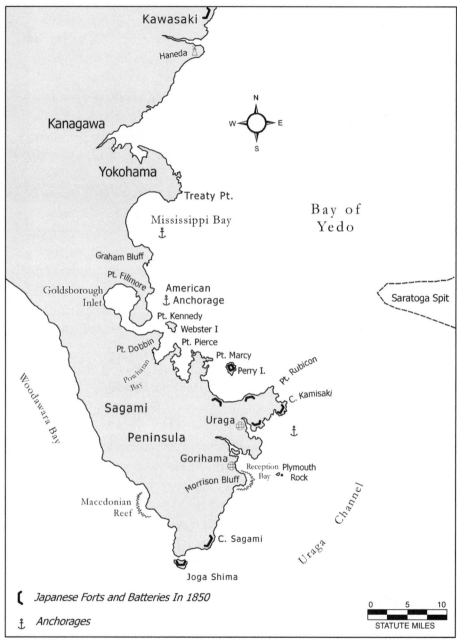

Map 4. Western shore of the Bay of Yedo. Adapted by Alexander Paul Nohe from *OLD BRUIN:*
Commodore Matthew C. Perry, 1794–1858 by Samuel Eliot Morison. Copyright © 1967 by Samuel
Eliot Morison. By permission of Little, Brown and Company. All rights reserved.

permitted to go on board. They said they knew nothing of the letter, but merely came to look at the ship and see the officers. They were accordingly dismissed.

Monday, July 11. At nine o'clock this morning called all hand[s] up anchor. Hove up the anchor and stood up the Bay of Edo with four boats (one from each ship) ahead sounding. We went about 10 miles up, stopping, backing and sounding until two o'clock when we took the boats in tow and stood for the squadron. Just as we were turning round, two White Towers, supposed to be at Edo, were observed. All the way up the Bay about one-hundred Japanese boats kept company with us, some astern and others on each side, and when coming back we observed one of these boats right ahead and laying to. We passed close by this boat and when so closing one of the Japanese spoke out in good English and said, "Do you go back," and then tried to throw us a line by which we might tow him; this we did not do and soon left all the boats far astern. Also while going up the steam whistle was got into operation and blown several times. This seemed to terrify those People exceedingly; they stopped sculling, stood up in their boats and looked with amazement, and seemed to say, "What on Earth would we do next." We came to anchor here in the same berth at 5½ P.M.

Tuesday, July 12. Today near noon several boats kept going backwards and forwards between the *Susquehanna* and the shore. We on board this ship of course could not understand what all this was for. This evening however we heard that after considerable talking and confabbing, the Japanese had consented to receive the Commodore and the President's letter on shore the day after tomorrow, as then there would be a proper person from Edo appointed by the Emperor to negotiate with us. Coming down, ain't they.[79]

Wednesday, July 13. The surveying party under Lt. Bent started off this morning to survey a small bay on which a very little village is situated and at which place the Commodore is to be received tomorrow. To the small bay the surveying party gave the name of "Reception Bay."

Jeddo [Edo] Bay, Thursday, July 14. At eight o'clock hove up the anchor, started ahead slow and stood for Reception Bay. At about half past eight we came to anchor about a mile from the shore, the *Susquehanna* soon after came to near us. A few minutes after nine four of the ship's boats, the launch, barge, 1st and 2nd cutter, were manned and containing Fifty Men, our Band, the Marine Guard, & sixteen Officers, including the writer, left the ship and went alongside the *Susquehanna* with the other boats of the Squadron, all the persons armed and [illegible] equipped. At half past nine all the boats shoved off from the Flagship and went ashore, where we were drawn up in line to receive the Commodore. When we landed the Japanese to the number of six thousand were drawn up in lines along the borders of the Bay. Their front files extended over a mile, and with their Banners innumerable[,] and blue and scarlet pennants[,] presented a most beautiful, with a warlike appearance. The Japanese had made a wharf of some four yards in length and about one in width of dirt, so that we could easily land without having to beach the boats as would otherwise have been the case. The Commodore shoved off from the *Susquehanna* at ten minutes before ten, and was saluted by her with 13 guns. The officers were drawn up on each side of the little wharf and the men as spoken of above. Presently a White Boat with a Broad Pennant painted on each bow, or otherwise called the Commodore's Barge was seen to near the shore, and in a few moments after or at ten o'clock precisely, three long and loud rolls of some half dozen drums proclaimed that the Great Mogul had landed, and immediately the two Bands struck up "Hail Columbia."[80] Really it made the blood thrill in my veins to behold such an imposing and beautiful sight, and more so when I thought that even I was among that happy (then) number. Listen.

"So long as the sun shall warm the earth, let no Christian be so bold as to come to Japan; and let all know that the King of Spain himself, or the Christian's God, or the great God of all, if he violate this command, shall pay for it with his head."

But lo! We landed and after showing the respect due to our Superior, we fell in, dividing the files of the Marines & Men, marched then all of us, off to the "Ben Bolt Quick Step" to the House built for our reception. We had not far to walk. Arriving at this House, the officers went in, but the marines were drawn up in front to prevent an attack, although nothing of this sort was expected, but it was as well to be prepared. The first room we entered was about 20 feet square. On each side there were paintings on silk of Birds and other things very roughly done. Around this room on mats, with their hats on their laps[,] sat a dozen or so of old Men, but still of some account, with their heads hung down, looked as if their last day had come. On one side of the room there was a large doorway hung all around with silk drapery. This doorway gave full view to a room, about the size of the others, although much better ornamented. On one side were four large chairs intended for the Commodore and staff, who on entering took seats in them. On the other side were three chairs, one was occupied by the Prince of Idzu [Izdu], First Counselor of the Emperor. He was appointed by the Emperor to negotiate with us and I have heard that he ranks the same as our Secretary of State. This person's appearance was very gloomy and downcast, and his expression seemed to say that this was great fun for us but it was anything else for him. Next, a little to his left sat the Prince of Iwami. He accompanied the Prince of Idzu [Izdu], and on his right sat his Interpreter. Besides this one there was another Interpreter, who squatted down alongside a large box, very prettily lacquered, and which was intended to receive the box which contained the President's Letter and the box containing the Commodore's Powers. These two boxes were brought in the room by the Commodore['s] body guard, two negroes, each standing six feet. The Interpreter then jumped up, took the boxes from them, then placed them carefully on the lip of the large Box. He then opened and after seeing what was inside closed them. He then took the cover off from the large box, and placed inside it the two small ones; then replacing the cover, he passed around it a thick silk cord, which he tied on the top, and then squatted down as before. The Commodore then told the Prince, through Mr. Portman, our Interpreter, who spoke to the Interpreter who sat on the floor. He told the other Interpreter[,] and by this rigamarole[81] the Commodore's message[,] which was as follows, reached the ears of the Prince. "That as he supposed it would take some time to give an answer to the Letter, he would return again next Spring to receive it, and that while we remained here he should survey the Bay and endeavour to find a safe and commodious anchorage for his Ships as he would bring a good many more with him." The Prince did not like this much but nodded in assent. He said also "that we would leave in a few days for China by way of Lew Chew, and that if they had any commission[s], he should be most happy to take them." He said he had none, but hoped we would not make known to the Lew Chewans the proceedings of this day. Several other questions passed between them, which were unneccessary [*sic*] to give. After this we bid the Princes good bye, and marched back to the landing place accompanied by several of the Mandarins, The Bands playing the tune of the "Low Back Car."[82] After getting into the boats we proceeded to the respective ships. The Governor & Deputy Governor of Uraga and with the Interpreters went on board the *Susquehanna* and went in her up as far as Oragawa or Uraga (more frequently called). They witnessed for the first time the performance of the Steam Engine and were very much pleased at everything they saw. A few moments after twelve we were ordered by the Commodore to get underway and proceed up as far as we went the other day, which we did. The other ships followed us and we all came to anchor about four o'clock opposite a small Island to which we gave the name of Mississippi Island.

Edo Bay, Sunday, July 15. Lieutenanant [*sic*] Bent and Clitz[83] in the 1st cutter & barge left this morning at half past six to survey the harbour and boats from the other ships also went sounding below us. The *Saratoga* at 10 o'clock got underway and went down to cover the boats and at or near two o'clock the *Saratoga*[,] in working up to her anchorage, missed stays and commenced drifting. She let go her anchor and before it could be brought to she fell afoul of the *Plymouth* and carried away her flying jib booms. At 3 o'clock called all hands and hove up the anchor. Shortly after Commodore Perry and Staff came on board the Broad Pennant was hauled down from the *Susquehanna*[84] and hoisted at our main truck. We then stood up the Bay[,] a boat from each of the ships ahead sounding. We went up about 10 miles, and saw distinctly a large number of junks at anchor, and from the continued going in and out of the junks at this place we felt sure it was the Harbour of Edo, and a little out from the junks we saw a Light House, distant about seven miles. Our eyesights could not have been very good last Monday evening, for nothing could be seen of the two White Towers that we then discovered. We returned to our anchorage about sundown.

Monday, July 16. Nothing of much interest has occurred today. The Governor of Uraga has been several times on board the *Susquehanna*, bringing with him presents of Lacquered ware, and received in return a quantity of choice garden seeds. His acceptance of these presents was sanctioned by his superiors and other presents were made this evening. The Governor when taking leave of the officers seemed to do so with a feeling of deep regret and hoped soon to see us again. I have neglected to say that the small town at which we landed was named Gorihama [Kurihama][85] and that visit was the first time the Commodore showed himself to the Japanese.

At Sea, Sunday, July 17. At daybreak called all hands, and a few moments after five, having steam up, lifted the anchor and went ahead of the *Plymouth* and gave her a towline. At half past five hove the anchor up and started ahead slow with the *P.* in tow; we soon after stopped to wait for the Flag Ship. About 7 the *Susquehanna* started ahead with the *Saratoga* in tow, and we followed after and stood down and out of the Bay of Edo. At eleven we had Divine Service. This evening at half past four, in company with the Squadron[,] half[-] masted our Colours during the Burial of one of the crew of the *Plymouth*. During the latter part of this afternoon saw a number of Whalers.

Monday, July 18. The cry of "Man overboard" [on?] board the *Plymouth* was heard today about half past eleven. Stopped the Engine[,] luffed to and shortened sail. The *Plymouth* lowered a boat and succeeded in picking the man up. We soon filled away and made sail as before.

Tuesday, July 19. This evening about 5 o'clock the *Saratoga* cast off her towlines from the *Susquehanna*; the *Plymouth* also cast off from us. The *Saratoga* is ordered to Shanghai & the *Plymouth* to Lew Chew.

Wednesday, July 20. Quite early this morning the *Plymouth* and *Saratoga* were in sight on each beam. A regular gale is now blowing, the sea running high and the ship rolling heavily, not so much so as the *Susquehanna*[,] at every roll she takes water in the gun deck ports. During the day we sent down lower yards, top & topgallant masts, on account of the great strength of the wind. We also pitched away our head sounding spars,[86] in doing so sprung the jib boom. The *Susquehanna* also carried away her sounding spars.

Thursday, July 21. Late last evening, by a heavy roll of the ship, lost the gig from the stern davits, and this morning about five o'clock, shipped a sea, and carried away the port whale boat. We then got the dingys [*sic*] in board and doubly secured all the other boats. The gale has been blowing very strong all day. We are only able to have the top sails set, and they with double reefs.

Friday, July 22. After midnight last night discovered the light of a vessel, supposed it to be the *Plymouth*. Aforenoon the storm abated a little so that we were able to send up the fore yard and set the fore sail. Frequent rain squalls.

Saturday, July 23. Up to the present time the storm has not abated much. There is a very heavy swell from the southard which makes the ship roll a great deal.

Sunday, July 24. About half past nine today we discovered high land on starboard bow—and soon after passed three small islands and then stood to the southward & westward. At half past twelve one of our men by the name of Hugh Ellis,[87] of Syracuse, N.Y., died. He has been sick for some time past with a violent fever. This evening we made the island of Lew Chew and are now standing along the southern end of it.

Naha, Lew Chew, Monday, July 25. Late last evening[,] not being able to make this harbour, we stood off from the land, and early this morning stood for it again—it being very thick and foggy we did not see the land until 9 o'clock. We then found that we were a long distance to the southward of this place, having drifted a great deal during the night. Near one o'clock we made out the *Supply* at anchor. We then stood in and came to anchor in our old berth in company with the *Susquehanna*—at half past one. This evening at 5 o'clock called all hands to bury the dead, read the Funeral Service over the remains of Hugh Ellis, and sent them on shore for burial.

Tuesday, July 26. Commenced coaling ship today. This evening about five o'clock discovered the U.S. Sloop of War *Plymouth* in the offing; at 7 she came to anchor outside.

Wednesday, July 27. The *Plymouth* got underway this morning early and at 9 o'clock came in anchored.

Thursday, July 28. Nothing of any interest has occurred today, we have been coaling ship and filling up with water.

Sunday, July 31. At eleven o'clock this morning we had Divine Service; this evening got everything ready for going to sea.

At Sea, Monday, August 1. Started the fires and hove short at 6 A.M. Near half past eight called all hands up anchor; at 8½ the *Susquehanna* weighed and stood out of Naha Harbour. We hove up, catted & fished the anchor and stood out also. This morning before we got underway the officers of the different ships went on shore to attend a sale of Lew Chew wares.

Tuesday, August 2. At half past five this evening discovered a strange sail on lee bow. Soon after we followed the motions of the *Susquehanna* and stood for this sail, which at 6 o'clock showed her number and proved to be the U.S. Sloop of War *Vandalia* from Hong Kong. She saluted the Commodore with 13 guns. The *Susquehanna* returned 7. We then took in sail and stopped the engine. The *Vandalia* hove to and sent a boat on board the flagship. At 7.30 we started the engine, made sail and resumed our course.

Wednesday, August 3. Today the *Susquehanna* made signal to us to separate as far as possible within signal distance and keep a bright lookout for the Steamer *Powhatan*, that she has all our letters on board.

Victoria, Hong Kong, Sunday, August 7. This morning at ten o'clock called all hands to muster, read the Articles of War and mustered the crew. At 10½ we had Divine Service. A little before 2 P.M. discovered a large fleet of fishing boats; at 2 land ahead and on both bows. Commenced getting everything ready for going into Harbour. At five o'clock we stood in for the Limoon [Lymoon] Passage[,][88] hoisted the Jack and fired a gun for a pilot. Passed two or three ships. Soon after half past five called all hands to bring ship to anchor, and at six o'clock we came to anchor in this Harbour in company with the *Susquehanna*. Received a complimentary visit from the English Admiral's ship. We expected to find the *Powhatan* here, but no such good luck. She left yesterday for Lew Chew and took all the letters which arrived by the previous mails. This is exceedingly trying but cannot be helped.

Monday, August 8. At 8 A.M. the *Susquehanna* saluted the English Admiral with 15 guns which was returned gun for gun by the English Frigate. Nothing of interest. The Admiral and Commodore exchanged visits and were each received with a salute of 15 guns.

Tuesday, August 9. At daylight all the English men of war got underway and stood out the Cap-sing Moon Passage.[89] At 11 o'clock they came to anchor in sight of us. At 2 o'clock they again got underway and stood out. This evening, a member of the ship's company and most of the officers went on board the *Susquehanna* to witness a theatrical performance by the Thespian Corps of that ship. There were a good many ladies from shore and they appeared to enjoy themselves very much.

Blenheim Reach,[90] **Wednesday, August 10.** Started the fires at four o'clock this morning. At 5½ called all hands up anchor, and a few moments after six got underway and stood out of Victoria Harbour at Hong Kong in company with the English Mail Steamer *Ganges*, and stood through the Capsing Moon Passage, and passed near a French frigate and steamer at anchor. While standing up the River passed the American Steamer *Spark*. At a few moments after eleven passed the Forts at the Bogue[91] and came to anchor in this Reach at a quarter past one. There [were] a number of English and American ships here. The tide is exceedingly strong on account of the late freshet at Canton.

Sunday, August 14. A lighter arrived this morning from Macao with provisions and stores for the different departments of the ship. At 10½ inspected the crew at quarters & at eleven o'clock we had Divine Service.

Tuesday, August 16. The ship swung around this morning to flood tide, the first time since our arrival in this place.

Friday, August 19. Last night about 10 o'clock send [*sic*] our band in the fast night [boat] up near the Steamer *Ganges* and gave the officers a serenade.

Each tune that was played was loudly applauded. The *Ganges* left this morning for Bombay via Hong Kong.

Sunday, August 21. We had Divine Service at eleven o'clock with music by our band. About 7 o'clock this morning a Comet was visible bearing N.W. by W. We also saw the Zodiacal light to the westward.

Monday, August 22. During last night the English Man of War Brig *Lilly* came up the River and anchored near us. This morning we discharged all our Chinamen by order of the Commander in Chief. At half past eleven the *Lilly* got underway. Sent our launch and 1st cutter to tow her bow round. Last evening the Captain of the Clipper Ship *Star of the Union*[92] came on board and reported that the crew of his ship was in a state of mutiny and asked for assistance to put the men in irons. Today we sent to the U.S. Marshall 16 prs. hand irons for the purpose of confinement.

Acows Hotel, Canton, Wednesday, August 24. This morning about ten o'clock I left the ship in our fast boat for this place. On the way stopped on board the *Star of the Union* to attend the trial of her crew for mutiny. Five of them were confined again in irons. 7 were released on condition that they would forfeit all the pay due them and leave Whampoa in the first vessel that leaves. 3 were released to go on board our ship, two of these however afterwards preferred to go back in irons. After the trial, in company with Capt. Lee, Lt. Lanier[93] and Father came up to this place. We got here about a quarter before three o'clock. Ordered tiffin which at four o'clock we went into right heartily. This evening while sitting in my room heard the sound of a gong, jumped up, looked out of the window and witnessed the punishment of a Chinaman for handkerchief stealing.

Canton, Thursday, August 25. Nothing of interest today. In company with Father started off this evening to see the Walls of the City. It soon came on to rain and we were obliged to return to the hotel.

Blenheim Reach, Friday, August 26. At ten o'clock this morning hired a Hong [long] boat and returned to the ship. Got here about half past one.

Saturday, August 27. The U.S. Steamer *Powhatan* arrived yesterday at Hong Kong and today we had the pleasure of receiving our letters from home.

Sunday, August 28. Today I went to the Episcopal Bethel and heard a sermon from our Chaplain. Our band and choir were present & we had some very nice music.

Saturday, September 3. This morning we discovered the U.S. Store Ship *Supply* at anchor near us. At 8 A.M. sent 25 of our marines on board of her, and she got underway and went up to Canton, for the purpose of rendering our merchants at that place any assistance that might be necessary in case of an outbreak at Canton by the Rebels, and should that force be insufficient, men could be sent up at a moment's notice.[94]

Sunday, September 4. We had a general muster of the crew at 10 today. Read the Articles of War & General Order in regard to increase of pay. A copy here annexed.[95] At eleven o'clock we had Divine Service.

Monday, September 5. I again went up to Canton today. We left the ship about 8½. Arrived at Canton near 12 o'clock[,] took a look around and left at 5 P.M. and got safely to the ship at a quarter after nine. Blowing very fresh.

Thursday, September 8. This morning at half past nine I left the ship & made my fourth visit to Canton since our arrival in April last. We arrived at Canton about half past one and left at 5½ o'clock, and have just come back to the ship. We had a head wind and rain to contend against going up. Had a pleasant time.

Friday, September 9. This morning received letters from home bearing date June 30th. All were well, and acknowledged the receipt of our first letters from China. About one o'clock the U.S. clipper ship *Sea Serpent*[96] was taken in tow by an English steamer and went down the river. She is bound for New York. By her I sent a small package home to Ned,[97] as also some letters. Lieutenant Contee and Bayard Taylor[98] have gone home in her. As she passed abreast of us sent the band and gave the folk on board some cheering[,] much, which was loudly applauded.

Sunday, September 11. About one o'clock last night the Captain of a Siamese Man of War came on board complaining of his men being in state of mutiny & that his life was in danger and asked for assistance. So shortly after one o'clock left the ship with 10 marines in the 1st cutter to go on board the vessel. He returned at 4½ o'clock after inspecting the crew at quarters. At eleven we had Divine Service.

Thursday, September 15. This evening about five o'clock lowered all the boats and had a race. The 1st cutter came out best. I was in charge of the 2nd cutter next to last.

Friday, September 16. A little after noon today the American steamer *Confucius*[,] Capt. Dearbourn,[99] came up the river, went up to Canton, returned again and anchored in Whampoa Reach. I went on board of her, found she left the States in April last. She is intended as a tug boat at Shanghai.

Sunday, September 18. Today at eleven we had Divine Service on board and a sermon by our chaplain, and music and singing, by the band.

Friday, September 23. Today we heard a rumor from Canton stating that the Rebels were expected to make an attack on that place. So this evening Capt. Lee left in the fast boat, & Lt. Lanier & P. Mid. Breese in the launch with a field piece for Canton.

Saturday, September 24. At noon today the launch returned[;] the rumor was unfounded. Nothing of interest.

Sunday, September 25. Quite early this morning we hoisted our colors and showed our number to the *Susquehanna* steaming up the river. At six o'clock the *Susque* came to anchor in Whampoa Reach. At half past ten inspected the crew at quarters, and read from the Quarter Deck[,] in the presence of the officers & men, the findings of a Navy General Court Martial, approved by Com. M. C. Perry, of dates respectively: Sep. 1st in the case of Stephen Murray (O.S.) of the U.S. sloop of war *Vandalia*, Jos. L. Chapman of the *Susquehanna*, same date, John Whelan (Boy)[,] September 5th of the *Vandalia*[,] &

Wm Watson (O.S.) Sep 22d of the *Susquehanna*. After reading the above we had Divine Service.

Monday, September 26. Many pleasant feelings were recalled by the remembrance of this day, it being the Eighteenth Anniversary of my Birth. Although not of much consequence, would it had been spent at home near my friends. At 12 M. I extended an invitation to all the officers to give me a call in our mess room. My health was drank by all with a glass of wine. I proposed to Father that he & I should drink to my brother Theodore, hoped he might be spending his time pleasantly, this day also being his Eighth Anniversary.

Tuesday, September 27. Our marines returned today from Canton[,] the *Susquehanna* having sent a guard up to relieve them.

Wednesday, September 28. At 7 this morning the English frigate *Winchester*, bearing the flag of Admiral Pellew,[100] passed up the river in tow of the steamer *Styx*. During the day all the men & band that formerly belonged to the ship were transferred from the *Susquehanna* and her band was transferred to her.

Cumsing Moon,[101] **Thursday, September 29.** Received a pilot on board this morning at 6.20. Got underway from Whampoa, hoisted the Broad Pennant of Commodore M. C. Perry, and stood down the Canton River. The U.S. Ship *Vandalia* standing up Whampoa Reach showed her number[.] At half past twelve we discovered the U.S. store ship *Southampton*[102] standing out of Cum Sing Moon. Exchanged numbers with her. A little after two o'clock she passed near us and cheered ship, which we returned. About half past two we exchanged numbers with the U.S. Steamer *Powhatan* and U.S. Sloop of War *Macedonian* at anchor in this place. A few moments after three we came to anchor and moored ship.

Sunday, October 2. Had Divine Service today at eleven. Music by the *Powhatan* band. Mustered the crew and read the Articles of War.

Monday, October 3. At half past one today the *Macedonian* got underway and made sail to Royals and stood out of the Harbour. She has been ordered over to Hong Kong for the purpose of landing a propeller which was brought out in the *Supply*.

Tuesday, October 4. Last evening we had a performance by the theatrical troupe of this vessel. Several ladies were present and the evening passed off very pleasantly. At one o'clock today dropped the colors to half mast in consequence of the death of Lieut. Jos. H. Adams[103] of the *Powhatan*.

Macao Roads, Monday, October 6. Near half past eight called all hands and unmoored ship. At 9 received from the steamer *Powhatan* the body of Lieut. Adams, accompanied by a number of officers and petty officers. At ten o'clock we got underway and stood out of Cum Sing Moon Harbour in charge of a pilot and at half past twelve we came to anchor in this place. I came on shore this evening and am now at the house of the U.S.N. S[tore] Keeper.

Friday, October 7. About 10 o'clock today the remains of Lieut. Adams were taken on shore in a lorcha,[104] accompanied by a number of our officers and the marine band. The funeral formed at the Consul's and shortly after ten proceeded to the American Burying Ground where the remains of Lieut. A. were interred. A large number of French & Portuguese officers attended the funeral together with the Portuguese band and a platoon of soldiers. At two o'clock started off from the shore in the lorcha with the marine guard. All of them were drunk, and behaved in a shameful manner, fighting, etc. We got alongside about half past four. At twelve today the French frigate *Constantine*[105] saluted the Broad Pennant of Com. M. C. Perry, with 15 guns, which was returned by this ship by an equal number.

On Shore, Saturday, October 8. At 2 o'clock the S.S. Sloop of War *Vandalia* made her number off the Harbour. At 3 she came to anchor between us and the town. I left the ship this evening and will remain on shore tonight.

Sunday, October 9. Still on shore. The day has been quite disagreable [*sic*]. At noon Mid. Armstrong[106] left the ship for Whampoa to take passage to the U. State[s] in the American clipper *Sword Fish*,[107] in charge of a number of invalids. This evening I attended church.

Monday, October 10. Last evening after Church I went to Camoens Cave[108] and from there in company with Capt. Lee, Purser Eldredge[109] & Father made a call on Mrs. Hunter[,][110] an American Lady. After taking tea, we went to Mrs. Nye's[111] where we heard some very pretty music, by the ladies of the house. I returned on board this morning.

Wednesday, October 12. This evening the clipper ship *Sword Fish* came down from Whampoa and anchored near the ship. The Weather being very disagreeable, I jumped into a lighter that took some bread alongside the *Mississippi* and came on shore to the Consuls, where I shall stay all night.

On Shore, Thursday, October 13. The *Sword Fish* left Macao this morning. The American ship *Jamestown*[112] came in and anchored. Soon after she got underway and stood up the River.

Friday, October 14. I returned on board ship today quite early. The *Southampton* came out from the inner harbour and anchored. Condemned today by survey 2 bbls. [barrels] of beef and a number of pounds of cheese. We have rec'd. on board stores and provisions for the Pursers Department.

Saturday, October 15. The Sloop of War *Vandalia* got underway this morning and stood out to sea. She has gone to Lew Chew to relieve the *Plymouth*. Commenced coaling ship. I came on shore this evening and will remain for a day or so.

Sunday, October 16. This evening went to Church and heard a sermon from the chaplain of our ship. After service returned to the consul's, took tea & in company with Father made a call on some ladies. We also went to Mrs. Nye's[;] it being rather late we did not have any singing as expected.

Tuesday, October 18. I returned on board ship yesterday. Shortly after 8 A.M. the *Southampton* got underway and stood out of the harbour. She also has gone to Lew Chew, loaded with coal.

Wednesday, October 19. At eleven o'clock today a French steamer of war arrived and anchored near the French frigate. Sent a boat to her with the usual compliments, and found her to be the *Colbert*,[113] 7 days from Singapore. Today the officers of our ship received an invitation to a party at Captain Endicott's,[114] several I expect will go. I came on shore for that purpose and will remain all night.

Thursday, October 20. I enjoyed myself very much last night. Retired to bed this morning about 3, woke up at 7 o'clock, got breakfast, hired a boat and came off to the ship. Still coaling.

Friday, October 21. Nothing of interest today. Still coaling ship. Rec'd. on board a quantity of bread to take up to the *Powhatan*.

Cum Sing Moon, Saturday, October 22. At twenty minutes past eleven today got underway and stood out of the harbour of Macao, and a little after one came to anchor in this place. The *Powhatan* is the only vessel here. Sent her the bread brought up.

Sunday, October 23. We had Divine Service on board today at 11 o'clock. It has been exceedingly warm.

Monday, October 24. At half past nine the steamer *Powhatan* made signal for a Court Martial. At half past ten she fired a gun[,] hoisted the cornet[,] and a Court Martial convened on board of her.

Sunday, October 30. Nothing of much interest has occurred during the past week. The men have been allowed to go on liberty. At 10 o'clock today we had Divine Service. This evening I went on shore and took a long walk over the hills.

Tuesday, November 8. Last Wednesday morning [October 26] about 8 o'clock I went on board the *Powhatan*. At half past nine o'clock she got underway and stood out of this harbour and near twelve she came to anchor in Macao Roads about 3 miles from the town. Soon after we came to anchor I went on shore to the consul's[;] saw my friends Mr. & Mrs. De Silver, also Father, who were staying with them. They were all very well and seemed glad to see me.

The same evening I went to a little party at Mrs. Sullivan's and enjoyed myself. The next morning the Commodore & staff went on board the *Powhatan* and about two o'clock she stood out of the harbour of Macao. She went up to Whampoa for the purpose of relieving the *Susquehanna*. The same evening I spent at my friend Mrs. Hunter's. On Friday evening [October 28] Little Miss Nye's Birthday was celebrated. I spent the evening at Mrs. Nye's. Our band was there and played for the benefit of some twenty to twenty [five?] little girls (all daughters of the American and English merchants at Canton) who were partaking of a little supper that Miss N. gave on the occasion. All enjoyed themselves very much, as is natural. They began to get sleepy and tired about 8 o'clock, and gradually were taken to their respective homes. It has been a long time since I saw such an interesting little party. Saturday evening [October 29] the band played on the Plaza[;] a great many ladies were out as usual. Many of whom were asked by Mr. Bent to walk up to the Commodore's house and spend the evening, which most of them did, and we had quite a pleasant time, dancing &c. Sunday [October 30] I took dinner with Mrs. Lewis,[115] a very nice lady. In the evening, we went out to walk[;] it soon[,] however[,] came on to rain and we were obliged to go back. Notwithstanding that I spent a pleasant evening. Yesterday [November 7] evening, I again went to Mrs. L.'s and was more fortunate; we had a nice walk on the Campo,[116] around the fort and back and passed another sociable evening. This morning took breakfast with Mrs. Endicott. Had supper about noon, and at a quarter to one started off in company with Lieut. Morris & Mr. Perry[117] and came up to the ship in the schooner *Atalanta*.[118] We arrived here a quarter to four, having made the passage in three hours. I do not know when I have spent such a pleasant week before, and I think it very probable if we remain here much longer, Macao[,] and my friends there[,] will be favoured with another visit from me. The first two days I stopped at Mr. De Silver's, the Consul. He and his Lady left on Friday for Hong Kong. I then took up my lodgings at Ayouks[?][,] our Compradore.[119] Had a very nice room there, and really it seems but a short time since I left the ship. I find all well on board, painting and caulking ship.

Friday, November 11. Nothing of much interest has occurred today. Wednesday evening in company with several of our officers took a long walk. Yesterday evening also we took a walk and returned on board about sundown.

Macao Roads, Friday, November 18. Last Sunday morning I left our ship at Cum Sing Moon and in company with Capt. Lee came down to this place in the schooner *Atalanta*. As we stood out of C. M. harbour passed the U.S. steamer *Queen*[120] (chartered for the purpose of relieving the *Supply* at Canton). Standing in we arrived here shortly after 12 M. Capt. L. returned to the ship the next morning. He told me that I could remain down a few days but be up before the ship should leave. On Tuesday morning as I was getting ready to go up to the ship, I heard that she was to leave that morning for Hong Kong. I made myself quite easy & intended to go over in the mail steamer today to join her. Yesterday evening we expected the steamer *Queen* from Hong Kong in the evening about half past three. I walked down on the Piaza [*sic*] to see if anything was to be seen of her, and what was my surprise, or reaching there, to see our ship at anchor in the Roads and the little steamer standing in for the inside harbour. This could not have happened better. Father came on shore last evening and gave me my letters from home dated Sep. 1st & all well. This morning we hired a pullaway boat and came off to the ship. I find all on board finally well. I have enjoyed myself very much during my stay on shore & have rec'd. a great deal of kindness from my friends Mr. & Mrs. De S., & it would be quite wrong in me if I were to neglect again to mention the kindness of Mrs. L. & Mrs. R. & all my lady friends.

Sunday, November 20. We had Divine Service on board at half past ten. Nothing of interest has occurred.

Monday, November 21. Today about half past nine the Str. *Queen* left for Canton.

Monday, November 28. Last Monday morning I was taken down sick with a violent fever and have not been out of my bed since. Nothing of much interest has occurred during the last week. The *Supply* arrived here on Thursday from Canton. Yesterday the U.S. Steamer *Powhatan* arrived from Whampoa and anchored near us.

On Shore, Wednesday, November 30. I left the ship today forenoon, and have come on shore for a little recreation, having recently recovered my attack of fever. Find all my friends well.

Friday, December 2. Shortly after 8 o'clock this morning the *Powhatan* got underway and stood over towards the Nanton passage. She has gone to Hong Kong.

Saturday, December 3. Today 5 Sally Babbooans,[121] natives of an Island somewhat resembling that name, who were picked up at sea by the store ship *Southampton*, came on board ship to live by order of Commodore Perry.

Sunday, December 4. At eleven o'clock called all hands to muster, read the Articles of War, mustered the crew and then had Church with music, etc.

Wednesday, December 7. It had been proposed by some of the Ladies on shore to have a picnic to the Ringing Rocks[122] the first fair day. This was the first favourable day in all appearances that we have had for some time. The party to go was composed of six ladies and six gentlemen. Preparations were made, and we were all to meet at the Portuguese Custom House wharf. Four arrived there—could see nothing of the other[s]—supposed they had gone over—went over. Saw nothing of them over there known by me, came on to rain, came back, etc., etc., etc.

Thursday, December 8. Today heard from the rest of the party—Miss S. tossed by a Buffalo—caught in the rain—hard time—etc. Do [illegible].

Tuesday, December 13. Yesterday—a picnic to Green Island—8 lad. & 12 gent.—pleasant time—for particulars refer as above—composing party were—Mrs. H[unter]. Mrs. W[illiams]. Mrs. L. Mrs. R. Mrs. S[ullivan]. Miss S[ullivan]. Miss Q Raw Mr. B[ent] Dr. L[ynah]. Mr. B[reese]. Mr. L. Mrs. B[ull]. Mr. W. Purser S[peiden]. Mr. H. Mr. P. Cap. Lee Mr. F. Mr. S[peiden]. Jr.

Hong Kong, Saturday, December 17. We got underway from Macao this day at 12 and arrived here this evening at 5. Brought the Com. over & several ladies.

Macao Roads, Sunday, December 18. We left Hong Kong at 10 this morning and arrived here about sundown. We have come over for the purpose of taking our Minister[,] Mr. Marshall[,][123] to Canton.

Whampoa Reach, Monday, December 19. Last night at midnight Mr. M. came on board & at four o'clock we got underway & stood up the Canton River and at noon passed the Bogue—and at 3½ came to anchor in this place, near the English Steam Prop[eller] *Rattler*.[124] Moored ship.

Tuesday, December 20. At half past one Mr. Marshall left the ship for Canton attended by an escort of officers & the marine guard & band. Gave him a salute of 17 guns.

Canton, Wednesday, December 21. I left the ship this morning and came up to this place to spend a few days. I am stopping at the house of Mr. Moore, where I staid [*sic*] during my visit here last spring.

Friday, December 23. This morning at seven I went on board the steamer *Canton* in company with Mrs. Lewis & Mrs. Ridner[?] and went down to the ship at Whampoa. Passed a pleasant day on board and came up in our barge. Spent the evening at a dinner party at Mr. Nye's, in company with several of our officers.

Whampoa, Saturday, December 24. I returned to the ship this morning with all the officers, men, & marines who went up to Canton on Tuesday last. We brought down $46,000 in silver to be distributed among the other vessels of the squadron. This evening got everything ready for leaving this place.

Hong Kong, Sunday, December 25. At six o'clock this morning hove up the anchor and stood down the Canton River and arrived here at 3 o'clock P.M. I eat my Christmas dinner at Mrs. De Silver's. At one o'clock the officers were invited into the Ward Room to partake of a collation, etc.

Tuesday, December 27. The U.S. store ship *Lexington*[125] arrived today—one hundred and ninety-six days from the United States.

Thursday, December 29. At daylight fired 13 guns with the rest of the squadron, in memory of the late Vice President of the United States.[126] At noon fired 17 guns for the same & at sunset fired 21. The English Admiral, in compliment[,] fired the same. At 11 o'clock the *Supply* got underway and stood out of the harbour.

Saturday, December 31. The store ship *Southampton* arrived from Macao. The last day of the year—it ends quietly. A year hence, hope to be home.

3

Volume One: 1854

—◦∕∿∕◦—

Victoria, Hong Kong, Sunday, January 1. Today at ten o'clock read the Articles of War and mustered the crew. At 11 had Divine Service. Yesterday the Commodore made signal to the squadron that he would be happy to see all the officers on board the Flagship today at twelve o'clock. So today after church, all those who could be spared went on board the *Susquehanna* & paid their respects to the Commander-in-Chief, who reciprocated by giving us a nice glass of Egg Nogg.

Thursday, January 5. The last few days have been employed in finishing coaling ship & getting every[thing] to rights preparatory to going to sea.

Friday, January 6. Last night we had a grand theatrical & Ethiopic Entertainment on board. The ship was beautifully decorated with flags, etc. Each of the messes had a handsome collation set out. The Commodore came on board & came below to take a look at the good things. After looking a few moments at the table which was set in the Steerage Mess, he said in a great gruff voice, "I hope you all hav'nt [*sic*] got any of my wine here!" then a pause and cries of "No Sir," "Of course not," "Sorry you think so"—were murmured out. He then went on deck & said to Capt. Adams, who was standing near—"Why Adams, hang me, if those chaps down in the Steerage hav'nt [*sic*] got a Chicken Salad on their table as large as the Capstan," whereupon Adams said g'g'g-go it Perry. Our guests were about two hundred in number.

Among them were Admiral Pellew and Sir George Bonham.[1] All seemed to be pleased with the performance, after which we had a dance and broke up about one o'clock. One of our marines by the name of Goble,[2] {afterwards a missionary in Japan} who had been on liberty, came on board today, having been robbed and dreadfully beaten by a set of Chinese desperadoes a short distance back of the town.

Sunday, January 8. At ten o'clock called all hands to muster & read the findings and sentences of a Court Martial in the cases of several men in the squadron for disgraceful conduct.

Monday, January 9. The Spanish Steamer *Queen Juan* arrived here today. She saluted the Com. with 13 guns which was returned gun for gun by the *Susquehanna*.

Wednesday, January 11. The Brittish [*sic*] mail steamer *Pottenger*[3] left this evening, with the mail for home. Nothing of interest.

At Sea, Saturday, January 14. Last evening the mail steamer arrived & this morning quite early we were put in possession of letters from home—bearing date Nov. 2d 53. They acknowledged the receipt of our letters from Japan. At 7.40 started the fires, soon after eight o'clock sent our hawsers to the *Southampton* & took her in tow. Boarded the American ship *Copia* of New Bedford from Honolulu in obedience to signal. At 9 the *Powhatan* got underway & stood out of the harbour of Victoria Hong Kong with the *Lexington* in tow. We followed soon after with the *Southampton* in tow. The *Susquehanna* came after us, as we passed the *Winchester* (H.B.M. Frigate)[4] cheered ship. The Admiral saluted the Commodore with 13 guns, which was returned by the *Susquehanna* gun for gun. We discharged our pilot outside the Lymoon Passage and are now bending our way towards Lew Chew with a strong head wind.

Sunday, January 15. Quite early this morning discovered land on port bow and passed a great number of fishing boats. We had Divine Service at 11 o'clock. This afternoon the *Lexington* parted her towlines and dropped astern. The *Powhatan* turned round. Took her in tow again and we stood on our course.

Tuesday, January 17. At half past eight o'clock this morning discovered high land on port bow & beam which we soon made out to be the south end of Formosa[5] & this evening discovered the Island of Great Botel[?] Tobago[6] on port bow & we are now at 8 P.M. standing between Formosa and Tobago.

Wednesday, January 18. This morning about 7 o'clock cast off the *Southampton* and made sail to top gallant sails. The *Powhatan* also east of the *Lexington*. We sent six men to her to assist in taking her into port. We were going along nicely with a fair wind until about one o'clock this afternoon, when the wind hauled round dead ahead and we were obliged to take in all sail and send down T. G. [topgallant] Yards & Masts and top masts. We have now quite a heavy sea on.

Naha, Lew Chew, Saturday, January 21. At seven this morning made land ahead and on each bow, during the forenoon passed several islands. About half past three we discovered the *Macedonian, Vandalia* & *Supply* at anchor in the harbour. We then stood in & at 5.20 came to anchor.

Sunday, January 22. We had Divine Service on board this morning. I went on shore for a walk this evening, met several of my old Lew Chew acquaintances. All seemed glad to see me, especially one by the name of "Usesato," who paid me a compliment by telling me that I looked much younger than when we were here before. I also called & paid my respects to Mrs. Bettelheim.[7]

Monday, January 23. Nothing of much interest today. This morning received on board a quantity of bread from the *Supply*. This evening went on shore and in company with one of my mess mates (Col. S.[8]) took a walk to Sheudi [Shuri], the Capital.[9] This was my first visit to this place, & really I was quite surprised to find so great a contrast with the parts of the island that I have seen and this place. Our walk was quite pleasant and we returned on board about sundown.

Tuesday, January 24. The *Lexington* and *Southampton* came in and anchored this forenoon. This evening attended the funeral of young Crosby[,][10] one of the engineers of the *Susquehanna*. He died this morning at 2 A.M. having been sick but a short time.

Wednesday, January 25. Today for experiment—Baked in the new oven 100 lbs. flour, which yielded 106 lbs. bread—39 loaves, which was distrib[u]ted to the officers messes & to the sick, also to the different ships, a small quantity to each by order of the Commodore.

Friday, January 27. Today is the first time since Tuesday that the boats have been able to go from one ship to the other, on account of a heavy sea, which has been setting into the harbour occasioned by a strong northwest wind.

Sunday, January 29. We had Divine Service on board today at half past ten. I took dinner on board the *Supply*, and after dinner[,] accompanied by my friend Arthur Sinclair,[11] went on shore for a walk. We first went into Bamboo Town, a small town back of Jumae. We went into several houses but as soon as we entered the gate the women & children would scamper away as fast as possible. We walked a little further & on looking round perceived that we were followed by quite a number of little boys and half grown men. I said to Arthur that I thought by a little management we might have a good deal of fun and proposed that we should form a company of soldiers the same as the little folks do at home. He agreed, whereupon I turned round and approached the persons who were following us. Some of them ran away but the majority stood still. I went up to one of these boys about 15 or 16 years of age (who seemed by his appearance and headdress to belong to the higher class of the inhabitants), took hold of his hand & without any resistance on his part, led him into the middle of the street, and by sundry signs, made known to him that I wished him to stand still. He at first hesitated, but finally stood in the position I fixed him. I then went and took another of these boys (about the same age) by the hand and placed him behind the first one, making him at the same time take hold of the foremost one's gown. Then leaving Arthur to take charge of these two, he acting as my adjutant, I went and got another & another & so on, until we had eight or ten of them in a line. I then took the foremost one by the hand, shouldered a stick & marched them off to the music "Boom, boom, de boomely, boom," which they all soon caught & struck up after me. We marched up & down the street several times, and these boys seemed highly delighted. By this time I should think there were some one hundred persons, men, women and children gathered around us. Thinking that I could create greater amusement for our spectators, I disbanded this company & formed another composed of the little children between 5 & 10 years of age—all boys. We had about fifteen or twenty in this party. In forming it, I saw a little individual standing by the side of a man. I went up to it, caught hold of its hand and endeavoured to lead it up to where the rest of the children were standing. It was of no use, for with all my persuasions I could not induce it to come with me. I thought it very queer that it should act thus, as all the others seemed very willing to join in the train. I happened then to look at the little child's face more closely than I had done before, and lo & behold perceived by its headdress that it was a little girl. This was quite enough for me. I immediately let fall her hand & went to look after my company, who I found marching off full tilt in charge of my adjutant. The bystanders (all Lew Chewans) seeing me completely frustrated in my endeavours to get the little girl to join the company, burst forth into a hearty fit of laughter. I soon joined the merry train and brought them to a halt & so to a front face. The whole of the villagers seemed to be there, and I estimated that there were at least three hundred persons, & I saw more women than I have seen during our stay here. Well as I said, I brought my company to a front face, and was about marching them off again, when two men in dark gowns came along and in a moment or so after[,] & nearly before I had time to turn round, my soldiers deserted me. The people all left us, & the place where we were standing & which but a moment before rung with the shouts of laughter of the people, was as quiet as could be. I then walked around the corner, saw some children standing there, & endeavoured to get them to come & march again, but it was all to no purpose. I have no doubt but that the two intruding (I call them intruding because I believe that they were the cause of unceremoniously breaking up our assembly) individuals were government spies, who are greatly feared by the people on account of the despotic state of the government. It being near sundown we returned to our boat & came off to the ship. Really I have not enjoyed myself so much before, and feel quite sorry that there were no officers except ourselves to witness this interesting & amusing scene.

Tuesday, January 31. At half past six o'clock this morning the sloops *Macedonian* and *Vandalia* with the store ships *Southampton* and *Lexington*, got underway and stood out of the harbour. They have gone to Japan where we will join them shortly. Quite early our chaplain & surgeon with two men left the ship to visit the north end of the island on a party of exploration for coal.[12]

Wednesday, February 1. Sent the marine guard on shore to drill. Commenced coaling ship from the depot on shore.

Friday, February 3. It has been known for several days past, that the Commodore intended on this day to pay a visit to the Prince Regent of Lew Chew. Let me state here so as not to confuse any who may read this account, that the actual Prince Regent is nothing more than a small child at present. He of course must have some older person to take charge of the duties devolving upon a Prince. This person therefore who acts in the capacity of the Prince Regent is given that title. At about eight o'clock this morning several officers from each ship, with the bands & marines[,] went on shore to escort the Commodore on his visit. I was fortunate enough on this occasion to be one of the party. The Com. landed at half past eight, got into his sedan chair, which was carried by some six or eight Lew Chewans, then in martial array with the band playing lively tunes we marched to Sheudi [Shuri], the Capital, and arrived at the Palace gates about three miles from the beach at 9½ o'clock. The gates were immediately thrown open & the Com. & officers entered, leaving the marines & bands outside. We were here met by some high officers of the Government who led the way for us & we passed on and entered another gate which opened into a courtyard, then through another gate into a second courtyard, getting into each by a flight of stone steps. After passing through three courtyards we entered a fourth gateway which led into an open space, on one side of which, was the House of Reception. We were here met by the Regent and some of his officers. We then went into the Audiance [*sic*] Chamber where seats were placed for us, with tables in front. The Com. & offs. having seated ourselves, the Prince & his officers seated themselves opposite.

They were dressed in garments of Blue & Green silk, with caps on their heads, and looked very neat. After sundry salutations and introductions, carried on by Mr. Williams[13] on the part of the Commodore and a high Lew Chew officer on the part of the Prince, tea and cake were served up. The Commodore told the Prince that he inte[n]ded leaving for Japan in a few days, and that he was going to leave several sick men here in charge of two officers until his return, & that if during his absence these men committed any violations upon the inhabitants, that they would be severely punished & he wished the Prince to protect them from any injury or insult which might be offered by the people. To all this the Prince assented. The Commodore gave him the different coins of our country amounting to $65 and wished to receive the same amount in coins of Lew Chew. The Prince said that at present he could not give them, but would have them ready against our return. The Commodore then rose and said that this visit to the Palace was an official one, & that he would go and pay his respects to the Prince at his residence. We then left the Palace by the same routine of courtyards and gates, & were joined by the bands & marines outside the first gate. We marched along the main road a short distance and turned a street to our right and found the Prince's residence. Here we were received as at the Palace. In the room where we were received, a dozen or more tables were set out, with all sorts of things served up in the style of the country, & we immediately sat down to partake of a sumptuous feast, for such it might properly be called. Tea was served up, then soup of all sorts. I think there were as many as thirteen different kinds, Chicken soup, Potatoe do., Meat do., Snake do, Birds nest do. (this is considered by the Lew Chewans to be the daintiest dish of any), and others, the names of which I cannot reccollect [*sic*]. Most of the officers eat right heartily. I could not go it, but was quite satisfied with a sup of each. "Sacki" [sake, saki], the native drink, was in abundance. Some twenty-five or thirty different courses were set before us. I have often sat down & partaken of Feasts (otherwise called Dinners), but this quite surpassed them all, not in regard to the nicety of the food, but in the great variety of the dishes. When the Feast was over, one of the Lew Chewan interpreters came round and gave to each of us a piece of red paper (which is herewith annexed) with some Lew Chew characters upon it, and which when translated into English said that the bearer was to receive a Lew Chew Pipe & Pouch, 4 Fans & some Paper, as a present from the Prince.

We folded the paper up, put it in our pockets & thought no more about it. We then bid the Prince goodbye and returned with the bands playing to the beach, where the boats were in waiting for us, and got on board ship about half past one o'clock having had quite a pleasant morning of it. Our road to the Palace led through a beautiful portion of the island, with extensive fields of rice, wheat, tobacco and sweet potatoes, etc., in a thriving condition. The morning was pleasant & the fine uniform of the officers & marines & neat dress of the Seaman never showed to greater advantage, except on the first landing in Japan. Along every valley & hillside and even on the summit of the highest rocky hills were seen crowds of astonished Lew Chewans, running to & fro, with expressions of wonder and amazement. Shortly after we arrived on board the Commodore sent word for all those officers who had escorted him this morning and had received a red piece of paper to sent [sic] it, with their names written on it, on board the *Susquehanna*, which we did, & soon after received back the same red piece of paper, accompanied by a Lew Chew Pipe & Pouch, 4 Fans and some Paper, which were as I said above intended as a present from the Prince Regent. On the road to the Palace you pass through two gateways, which have each five sections or gates like this [drawing of the five-section gate found in photo gallery]. The Prince only can pass through the middle section. The first one on the right & the first one on the left are for the Mandarins only to pass through, and the two others for the people generally. We however all passed through the middle one, thereby placing ourselves on an equal with the Prince himself. Since we came on board the weather has become rainy and disagreeable.

Saturday, February 4. The exploring party returned this evening, bringing with them specimens of coal from the north end of the island.

Sunday, February 5. We had Divine Service today at half past ten and a sermon by Dr. Bettelheim, which was very good. We also had muster and read the Articles of War.

Monday, February 6. Yesterday evening the Commodore made signal to the ships to prepare to go to sea this morning, but it being rainy and squally he thought it best to wait a day longer.

At Sea, Tuesday, February 7. Quite early this morning unmoored ship and started the fires. Shortly after seven o'clock we got underway and stood out of the harbour of Naha, Lew Chew, through the south channel. The *Powhatan* & *Susquehanna* followed us. Soon after we got outside, discovered a strange sail standing for us, which soon proved to be the U.S. Sloop of War *Saratoga* from Shanghai. The steamers all hove to to communicate with her. We received from her 4 bullocks and 3 sheep. At half past one we stood on our course and the *Saratoga* stood in for the harbour of Naha. This evening passed several islands, a great many sperm whale in sight.

Wednesday, February 8. Mr. Robie,[14] one of our assistant engineers, while on duty in the engine room, received a severe injury on the right foot and came near losing his large toe, by being caught by some of the machinery. At noon today passed between the islands of Ou-Sima [O Sima] & Cleopatra.[15] This evening the wind come out from N.W. by N. and made sail to topgallant sails. A sail was seen on starboard bow.

Thursday, February 9. Nothing of particular interest today. We have been going along nicely under sail 8 to 10 knots. This evening parted the fore-weather T. G. [topgallant] sheet, furled the topgallant sail and sent down the topgallant yard. Thought the topgallant mast was sprung.

Friday, February 10. This morning sent down the fore T. G. [topgallant] mast, examined it, found it was not sprung, sent it up again, crossed the yard and set the sail. This evening the wind hauled more ahead. Took in all the square sails and set the fore & aft sails.

At Anchor, Bay of Ha-wat-su, Sunday, February 12. At daylight discovered several islands on starboard bow & beam & the Japanese land on our port bow & beam, with the hills all covered with snow. Last night was bitter cold. In the midwatch last sight of the flagship and *Powhatan*, and discovered them at half past six A.M. about 5 miles ahead. At half past ten[,] while standing up this bay, discovered two vessels at anchor, which proved to be the *Vandalia* and *Macedonian*. The *Vandalia* telegraphed that the *Macedonian* was ashore. We stood for them and twelve m[eridian] the *Susquehanna* anchored. The Commodore made signal for our Captain. When he returned, lowered two of our boats and sent them towards the *Macedonian* to sound. We followed them and at half past two o'clock came to anchor near her. We received towlines from her and at 4 P.M. hove up[,] started the engine[,] and succeeded in getting the *Macedonian* off. We towed her near the flagship, cast off her towlines and at half past five we anchored in 105 fathoms water. The store ship *Lexington* came in from sea and anchored.

American Anchorage,[16] **Edo Bay, Japan, Monday, February 13.** Early this morning I went on deck and saw Mount Fusi [Fuji] in the distance all covered with snow. And the hill tops as far as the eye could reach wore a white robe. At a quarter past seven the *Susquehanna, Powhatan, Vandalia & Lexington* got underway. We hove up and waited for the *Macedonian* to come out to us. She soon came out, we took her in tow and stood after the other ships. We entered the bay about half past eleven, and then had a fine view of the Island of O-ho-Sima [O'Shima], with a volcano on it, in a state of eruption, and a beautiful sight it was. About half past one passed Go-ri-ha-ma [Kurihama], the place where we landed in July last. Soon after passed Uraga off which town we first anchored on our former visit. At half past two called all hands to bring ship to anchor and about this time discovered the U.S. store ship *Southampton* at anchor close under the land. And at 3½ came to anchor in company with the other vessels. While standing up the bay, beat to quarters, loaded and shotted the guns and took down the bulwarks in the way of the forward guns. The bay was crowded with junks. A little before[,] or as soon as we came to anchor, several boats supposed to contain Mandarins went alongside the *Susquehanna* but was sent to the *Powhatan* and received by the Captain of the Fleet. They said that three high Mandarins had come down from Edo, and had gone to Uraga to communicate with us, and they begged that the Commodore would go down there. The Commodore would not consent to go, but said if he moved from here he would go up to Edo. I will here quote something from hearsay in regard to the *Southampton*. Coming up the bay she was closely followed by several boats, which when they came near to her would throw grappling lines aboard for the purpose of being towed up, but whenever one was thrown on board it was immediately cast off. When she anchored Capt. Boyle[17] permitted the Japanese to go on board. They asked him in plain English, what he had come for. He told them he was ordered here by Commodore Perry, and whenever his name was mentioned they would all bow very low. They asked him if he was going on shore and requested him to go to Uraga. He told them that he was not going on shore, and that he was ordered here by Commodore Perry (here they bowed again) and that he would remain here until he came. They then asked him his name and the name of the ship. He said his name was Junius (which they repeated one to the other) and that the ship was called the U.S. store ship *Southampton*. They asked him if he was captain of the ship, whereupon he stood up, folded his arms and asked them if they ever saw Napoleon. They smiled & asked what the men and officers called him. He told them "Capt. Boyle" (this they also repeated one to the other). This conversation occurred on Saturday evening. Yesterday evening the Japanese went again on board the *Southampton* and took with them a chart of the Island very well done. They pointed out a place to Capt. Boyle, where they said, one of our ships had gone ashore. He immediately ordered his launch to be got out, manned and in charge of two officers, sent it to the assistance of the ship. When the Japanese heard this order given they were very much surprised and inquired if he was going to send that night, and wanted to know if he was not going to take the ship also. He told them he was going to send a boat immediately, but was not going himself. They then said that there was a rumor among the people that there was a ship near to the one that was ashore, and that she had sent a boat to her. This morning these same men went again on board the *Southampton* and told Capt. Boyle that the ship which was ashore had gotten off, and that three steamers were there near her. The *Southampton* boat arrived where we were at anchor about midnight. The Japanese who went on board the *Southampton* were very sociable and drank very freely.

Tuesday, February 14. The Japanese officials went again on board the *Powhatan* today. I heard that they were very much pleased with the President's letter, and hoped that the Commodore would fully carry it out, as regarded the feeling of amity which it evinces. They also repeated their request about our going to Uraga and said if the Commodore would not take all the ship[s] they would be glad if he would send one ship there, with a proper officer to communicate with the Mandarins from Edo for Preliminary negotiations and that after that a very high Mandarin (higher than any that had yet come down) would come to negotiate with us. The[y] remarked also, that the President's letter said that we had come for amiable purposes, and they thought it singular that we would never yield to their requests.

Yesterday it was made known to them that we wished to survey the Bay, and wanted permission to erect signal staffs on shore, which would be necessary to accomplish this object & today they said that they hoped we would not commence the survey until after the Preliminary negotiations had all been gotten through with.

Thursday, February 16. This morning at ten o'clock all the boats of the Squadron being manned, armed & equipped, went alongside the flagship to be inspected by the Captain of the Fleet. The surveying party under the charge of Lieut. Maury[18] commenced the survey of the Bay. This evening one of the Mandarin or Official Boats went alongside the *Powhatan* and gave back some buttons which had been given to the Japanese sailors by our sailors.

Edo Bay, Friday, February 17. While the surveying party was absent yesterday, some of the Japanese boats went alongside of our boats, and a trade was made by their giving some radishes and receiving in return some tobacco and bread. Two of the boats that were away today landed on Perry Island [Saru Shima] for the officers to take some observations. They were not disturbed in the least by the natives, the few they met were sociable & friendly.

Saturday, February 18. At nine o'clock this morning the Commodore hauled down his Broad Pennant from the *Susquehanna* and hoisted it on board the *Powhatan*. This evening the *Southampton* got underway, stood up the Bay about four miles and came to anchor.

Sunday, February 19. We had Divine Service today at half past ten. Many of the officers of the squadron came on board. This evening I went on board the *Powhatan*, and happened to be there when the Japanese officials we[re] making a visit. They brought with them[19] a number of presents, among them were eight boxes of sweetmeats, about ten boxes of oranges, 50 chickens, a large quantity of radishes, carrots, parsnips, turnips and different other kinds of vegetables. They were told that we could not receive them unless they accepted something in return. They said certainly, certainly, they knew that was our rule and therefore expected to receive something. They were given in return a quarter of a box of tea and a bag of bread, and in my opinion a very small return for their present. On this occasion also, they pressed the subject about our going to Uraga. They said that they had yielded in every instance to our wishes, and they thought it very strange that our Admiral (meaning Commodore Perry) would never in any instance give way to them. They said that the Mandarin who was at Uraga had with him the Emperor's answer to the President's letter, and that he had full power to treat in regard to anything it contained, and they hoped the Commodore would go there to receive it and negotiate. I understand that the Commodore said he would not go there. The chickens, vegetables, eggs and oranges were distributed to the sick in the squadron, and the boxes of sweetmeats the Commodore gave one to each of the commanders in the squadron—retaining one for himself.

American Anchorage, Edo Bay, Tuesday, February 21. Yesterday morning bright and early, the Japanese Official Boats were alon[g]side the *Powhatan*, for what purpose I do not know, but about ten o'clock the *Vandalia* got underway and stood down the Bay. She however was obliged to return on account of a strong gale of wind setting in the mouth of the Bay. She got underway again today and went down to Uraga with Capt. Adams on board to have an interview with the Official from Yeddo [Edo].

Wednesday, February 22. This being the anniversary of the birth of Washington, at noon the *Powhatan, Macedonian, Susquehanna* and this ship, each fired a salute of 21 guns, in honor thereof. About half past twelve the wind changed to S.W. by S. in a heavy squall, and continuing from that quarter increased to a moderate gale. This evening the wind lulled, leaving it very cold.

Thursday, February 23. The surveying boats which were away up the Bay yesterday were obliged to put on board the *Southampton* and remain there all night. They returned about eleven A.M.

Friday, February 24. At anchor 10 miles above Webster Island[20] and in sight of the entrance to the Harbour of Edo.

Shortly after nine o'clock this morning we had steam up, got underway and stood up the Bay, with a boat from the *Powhatan* & *Susquehanna* in tow. And at twenty minutes after ten we came to anchor about a mile above the *Southampton* or off Point Hope[21] about three miles from the shore.

The two boats, with two from this ship[,] went up the Bay to sound. From the deck we could make out with a glass the beacon off Edo Harbour.

About 12. M. the *Powhatan* and *Susquehanna* came up to us and went ahead. We hove up and followed them for about three miles and then anchored in company. At half past two we all got underway again, followed the surveying boats up about two miles further and then came to anchor in this place.

When we came to anchor, I went up into the foretop and with a spyglass could see the City of Edo, which seems to be about seven miles from us. The harbour in front of the city was filled with junks. The houses appeared to be much larger than any I have seen before. The bay above us was completely filled with junks & small craft, and you [cou]ld hardly turn your eyes in any direction but what you could see a large fleet of boats. Our boats[,] which were up the Bay sounding, have just now at 8 P.M. returned. They went as far as the entrance of the harbour, saw the city distinctly and gave three cheers. There are two or three quite large towns abreast of us.

Opposite the Towns of Ka-wa-sa-ki and Koon-a-ga-wa [Kawasaki and Kanagawa],[22] **Saturday, February 25.** The surveying boats went up the bay this morning with a launch (containing a field piece) from each ship, as protection. They returned this afternoon between two and three o'clock and we find that we are entirely mistaken in regard to our views of yesterday. We find that the town around the point on which we see the beacon and also the entrance is called by the Japanese Sin-e-ga-wa [Shinagawa][23] or the suburbs of the great city of Edo. We know now for certain that Edo is between twelve and fifteen miles from here. The boats went within three miles of the city, the harbour of which was quite filled with junks, but innumerable in comparison to those which I spoke of as being in the harbour of the first supposed city of Edo (Sin-e-ga-wa [Shinagawa]).

They had deep water all the way up, and in the harbour where the junks were, the[y] found over five fathoms water.

The *Vandalia* arrived up today from Uraga. The day after she arrived there, notwithstanding the rough state of the weather—Captain Adams and his suit went on shore, where they were met by the Governor of Uraga (Yezaimon)[24] and some other Japanese officers. They were then conducted to the house of Audiance [*sic*], which was a very large one, capable of containing 500 persons. Here they were received by one Hayashi[,] Daigaku no kami[,][25] who it is said is next in power to the Emperor. Capt. Adams gave this Prince a letter from the Commodore, what it was about, I do not know.

Capt. A. was told by this Prince through the different interpreters, that it had been the custom of the Japanese for many years past to hold no intercourse with any other people than the Dutch, and that with them it was very limited, but that while we were away the Emperor had called a meeting of the principal great men of the Empire, and had taken the vote, whether the Americans should be received and treated as friends or not. They accordingly agreed that the Americans should be received and treated as friends. He said that a high officer had been over to Naga-sa-ki [Nagasaki][26] to tell the Russians who were there endeavouring to make a Treaty, that they could not be received, and must leave Japan immediately.[27]

The Prince also told Capt. Adams that he had the letter from the Emperor to the President, and he wished the Commodore to come to Uraga and receive it, that they had been to a great deal of expense in putting up a house for that purpose, and therefore thought it queer that the Com. was unwilling to come there. Capt. A. requested the Prince to put this down in writing for him to take to the Commodore, which he said he would in a day or so. The Governor of Uraga gave Capt. Adams and two of his suit a present of some lacquered ware and silk, which was very fine indeed. They were treated during their stay on shore with a great deal of civility by the Prince and his officers.

The next day (23d) Mr. Portman, our interpreter[,] went on shore to receive in writing what the Prince had said in regard to the letter to the President. He received [it], and the day after[,] when the *Vandalia* was about getting underway to come up here, one of the Japanese boats containing an officer went off to her and told Capt. Adams that the Prince wished to withdraw the paper he had given, which was returned accordingly[,] and he then said that the Prince would come up to Yo-ko-ha-ma [Yokohama][28] to deliver the letter, and that as there was no house at that place in which the Commodore and his officers could be received in, they would bring the house up from Uraga and erect it at the place mentioned and that it would take five days to do this. This evening Captain Adams and Buchanan[29] in company with some of the Japanese officers went on shore to pick out a place best adapted for erecting the house. Capt. A. speaks of the town (Yo-ko-ha-ma) w[h]ere they landed as being a very small dirty looking place and not even comparing with the towns of Lew Chew. If this be the case, what on earth is it fit for, a decision in future.

Edo Bay, Sunday, February 26. We had Divine Service today at half past ten. This day has been spent very quietly, nothing to disturb the stillness which ou[gh]t to exist on the Sabbath.

Off the Town of Yokohama, Monday, February 27. The surveying boats went off this morning to sound in about this town. When they returned this evening we got underway and in company with the other ships stood in for about two or three miles & came to anchor.

Tuesday, February 28. The *Macedonian* came up about eleven o'clock from the American Anchorage and anchored inshore of us.

Wednesday, March 1. This morning confined four of our men in double irons for drunkenness and mutinous conduct.

Thursday, March 2. Last evening Captain Buchanan of the *Susquehanna* gave a dinner to the Governor of Uraga. Several Japanese officers were present, and quite a jolly time they had. Both Americans & Japanese were in a high state of conviviality.

This evening carried a kedge in shore, hove up the anch[or] and endeavoured to heave her to the berth selected by the Commodore, but were unable to get our position on account of the force of the wind.

Friday, March 3. We hove up today and took our position in line with the other ships.

This evening some Japanese officers came on board, this is the first occasion any of them have been on board. They have been exceedingly anxious to see the ship on account of her formidable appearance, and more particularly so, because we repelled them when they attempted to board us on the evening of the 8th July last. They were very friendly and sociable, and before leaving, two of them, the Imperial Interpreter and Lieutenant Governor of Uraga were quite merry. The Lieutenant Commanding the military at Uraga was also on board. His manners and actions were every way unlike those of the others. He went about the ship prying into every hole and corner, looking in the officers' staterooms, and his ways were anything but agreeable to the officers. The Interpreter to the Governor of Uraga appeared to be a gentlemanly person and conducted himself with a great deal of propriety. He spoke a little English so that we could understand him. The Imperial Interpreter speaks English very well indeed. I obtained from three of them their cards, which I annex for the purpose of allowing those who may chance to peruse this to see the style of visiting cards used in Japan. I gave to one of them my card & told him my name, which he wrote in Japanese and then repeated it to me almost as plainly as I could say it myself. When they left they took our water casks to fill the ship with water.

This evening late we discovered a vessel beating into the entrance of the bay. We supposed it to be the U.S.S. *Saratoga* as she has not been heard of since we spoke her off Lew Chew, and she was ordered not to go into Naha.

Yokohama, Saturday, March 4. The Japanese boats came alongside today and returned the water casks which they took yesterday. After we emptied them into the tanks they took them again. The men whom we sent temporarily on board the *Lexington* on the 18th Jany. returned on board this evening. Quite early this morning Lieutenant Bent went down the bay in the 1st cutter to pilot the *Saratoga* and she is now at 7 P.M. beating in for the anchorage.

Sunday, March 5. This being the first Sunday in the month, at half past ten read the Articles of War and mustered the crew. Two duties, the former falls upon the Captain's Clerk, and I being the Purser's Clerk the latter necessarily falls upon me. And at eleven o'clock we had Church and some sweet sacred music by our band.

Monday, March 6. Shortly after half past twelve today one of our marines[,] by the name of Robert Williams,[30] died of an affection of the brain, which caused paralisis [*sic*] of the right side, occasioned by a blow given him by a Chinaman with a stone while on liberty at Cum Sing Moon.

Listed the ship to starboard for the purpose of caulking below the waterline.

Tuesday, March 7. Nothing of any particular interest has taken place today. It was expected that the Commodore would land but it being an unpleasant day he put if off until tomorrow.

Wednesday, March 8. This has been an important and great day and on which the Second grand landing of the Americans in Japan took place. I was fortunate enough on the occasion of the First landing to be one of those who landed, but this time I was unable to go. However[,] as an account of it will be interesting to me to read at some future day I will give it here, just as it was furnished me by our chaplain.

A great day. We are in a fair way to get through our Treaty business in Japan soon, and entirely to our satisfaction.

This A.M. at eleven the boats began to leave the several ships and to assemble and get their assigned places by the *Powhatan*.

They were all fully armed, some with brass pieces (field) in addition to small arms, and during the early part of the day the ships had been warped so as to bring their broadsides to bear upon the shore at the place of landing. No one expected any collision {*The Japanese had said themselves that they were so well satisfied of our friendly intentions that they would bring out no troops.},[31] but still it was thought better to be prepared for every event.

The boats were 27 in number, and as they moved towards the shore all abreast, filled with marines and armed sailors and officers, made quite a fine display.

We landed and formed upon the beach, at which time (12 o'clock) the Commodore left the *Powhatan* under a salute of 17 guns from the *Macedonian* (in his capacity as ambassador).

The annexed diagram will give some idea of his reception on shore and the place prepared for the meeting. Our own force comprised altogether about 500 persons. It consisted of the Commodore, his escort of 4 or 5 officers from each ship, 160 marines with their officers, 240 sailors armed with muskets, pistols and cutlasses, with officers to regulate them. Three bands of music, etc.

The Commodore, as Ambassador was received on his landing with the usual flourishes of drums, arms, etc., his escort forming a line with uncovered heads. As he passed up, also uncovered,[32] the officers closed into line behind him, and were thus conducted up to the reception room. (As they entered the hall, the Japanese Flag was hoisted in one of our boats, and the field pieces saluted it with 21 guns, and when the Japanese Commissioner was introduced he was saluted with 17 guns.) It occupied the large house which was brought up from Uraga and erected here. It was a handsome edifice of plain boards, and the rooms were hung with purple silk crape [*sic*], except at one end where [there was] a screen of blue silk with orneriel [armorial?] emblazoning on it. It was drawn up but ready to let fall, and so form an inner retiring room.

On each side of the large room were double lines of raised platforms or seats, matted and covered with cloth, and in front of each line another raised and covered platform, on which the refreshments were to be placed.

The Commodore was conducted to his seat at the head of the hall, the five Japanese Commissioners in front of him. The Interpreter on his knees between them. The Chief Commissioner was introduced. He made some polite inquiries about the Commodore's health, etc., and the other Commissioners were separately introduced, each one as this was done rising and bowing respectfully and adding such complimentary remarks. The Commodore was seated all the while, but bowing in return to their salutations.

Then tea was brought in on stands thus [drawing of the stand found in photo gallery] all red Japanned ware excep[t] (a) which was of porcelain. A slice of pound cake and a cake apparently of baked pulverized beans, sweetened, with a large [*sic*] of sugar candy made in stripes of red and white and twisted thus [drawing of the twisted sugar candy found in photo gallery] was laid before each one on Japanned dishes.

The five Commissioners asked permission to retire for consultation, but soon returned and at their request the Commodore, Capt. Adams, Com. Sec'y & two Interpreters (Mr. Portman & Mr. Williams) accompanied them into the curtained recess. The curtains were let fall and they were shut out from the view of the officers.

Before each of us was then placed a low square table of Japanned ware, covered with dishes containing soup (rich & would have been good had it not been sweetened)[,] fish, variety of things like soft cheese of various colors, vegetables in ornamental forms, walnut kernels, etc. They all looked prettily, but the fish and walnuts were about the only things that we could at all relish.

Our Japanese friends seeing we did not fancy the dishes, tried to show us how to do so by taking some of the articles in their chop sticks[,] steeping them in two little cups of a species of catsup, and then putting them into our mouths. Although this improved the taste a little it could not bring us to relish their dinner. Sacki (rice whiskey) was also brought in silver and Japanned pots, and poured out for those who fancied it. In the meantime the ambassadorial business, together with eating[,] was going on behind the curtain, but the outsiders having tasted and then smoked, broke up and went out for a ramble about the premises.

The Japanese attendants showed an unwillingness to have us go from the immediate neighborhood of the building and tried to prevent us doing [so], but on our paying no attention to them they let us have our own way and followed on in excellent humour.

We then went over to their soldiers and still against their will, but without any rising of subsequent ill feeling, we inspected their arms which consisted of bows and arrows or matchlock guns or spears, the official having two swords, one a long and the other a short one, both very sharp. Except their swords, which seem to be more for show than use, their arms are of the most primitive kind, very neatly and handsomely get up, but ages behind the time and of little comparative use in modern warfare. And their soldiers, though today they stood soldierlike, looking straight forward only, and scarcely glancing at us as we passed, had the very reverse of a formidable appearance. One company of them[,] armed with spears, had the long spear handle all covered over with mother of pearl, bits of $^3/_8$ of an inch square. They were very pretty glittering in the sun. We examined their horses, small but tough looking animals. The saddles have a good deal of Japanned and richly inlaid work about them and their stirrups were the oddest I ever saw. Their shape is thus [drawing of the stirrups found in photo gallery] or rather this is in cross section of them, for they are wider than the foot; they are of steel, very heavy and nicely inlaid, some of them with silver.

The day has been beautiful, a bright sun shining, and the air just cool enough to be pleasant. About half past three the conference broke up. The Commodore was led to look at the room prepared for the telegraph and presents, and then we returned in procession to our boats and so all abreast again back to the ships.

The following are some items about the behind curtain negotiations today. We think that the Commodore will get all he can reasonably ask for or expect at this time, that we shall probably have more than one Port open to us for Commerce, and they seem to show every disposition to be accommodating. The Commodore today gave them his paper of requirements and they handed in theirs of what they will concede, but there was not time then to examine either. For a few days now the negotiations will be carried on in writing and then there will be another interview.

We have heard that much of the day was spent in arranging about the burial of our dead marine. The Japanese proposed that we should deliver his body to them at Uraga, and said that they would then take it to Nagasaki and inter it there, but to this the Commodore utterly objected and he finally carried his point. They are to come tomorrow morning to conduct our men on shore to the place for digging the grave, and in the afternoon the funeral will take place. Our marines have subscribed about $40 for a monument over him, and have asked to procure a stone on which they will have an inscription cut on board. The present[s] are[,] we understand[,] to be delivered tomorrow. [Herein is inserted a diagram of the landing.]

While the officers were walking about on shore, the Japanese took great interest in all that concerned their dress and appearance generally, and took occasion to make drawings of their epauletts, pistols, swords and every appendage attached to their persons. The Japanese also amused themselves in recording the officers names in their books, and the names of the vessels to which they belonged. An artist of some merit attempted to sketch some of the officers faces. He succeeded tolerably well, but invariably gave them noses badly proportioned to the rest of the face. A lad of about eleven years of age, who had evidently received lessons in drawing, amused himself in a similar manner. He occupied about three minutes in sketching Father's face and a branch of Japonica in bloom which he held in his hand, and which I annex herewith. Also one of Commodore Perry, taken by another lad. But I cannot say much for the likeness they bear to either, especially the Com. It can be truly said that in giving the Com. that uncharacteristic Imperial mustache, insult has been added to injury.

Yokohama, Thursday, March 9. Yesterday was a great day but this can be said to have been a greater one. We have had a religious service, publicly and with the consent of the authorities who were standing by, and in the presence too of thousands of the population, and this in Japan. Most persons perhaps will remember the inscription on the Monument put up over the massacred Christians at Simbara more than 200 years ago.[33]

"So long as the sun shall warm the earth, let no Christian be so bold as to come to Japan, and let all know that the King of Spain himself or the Christian's God, or the great God of all, if he violate this command, shall pay for it with his head."

I mentioned yesterday that at the interview then, the Japanese were brought to consent to allow the body of the marine Williams to be buried here.

During the forenoon today their interpreters & the mayer [sic] of Uraga, with other officials, came on board and went with our men to show them the spot selected for the grave. In an interview which one chaplain had today with the Commodore, he asked him if he should bury the marine with the usual religious services. "Yes," he said, "exactly as you always do, no more nor less." He asked him what he should do "in case the authorities forbid it and try to prevent me." "Still go on and have your usual service" was his reply. Dr. Williams who was present, said however that there would be no difficulty. Our chaplain did not expect any, but thought it best to have orders that would meet any emergency and so got them.

Preparations were made for an interment exactly after the usual method with a marine. A great many of the officers would have liked to go, and some applied for permission; but it was thought best to give the occasion no unusual éclat, at the same time nothing was to be omitted[.]

After preliminary exercises on board, as is our custom on such occasions, two boats left the ship, the first containing Dr. Lynah,[34] Capt. Stack of the marines and Mr. Jones, our Chaplain in uniform and gown; and the other having the dead body, with a guard of honor, consisting of a sergant [sic], corporal and six marines.

They landed at a spot designated—a quarter of a mile south of the landing place of yesterday and in front of this village, the whole shore being lined with villagers come down to gaze. The Mayor of Uraga, interpreter, etc, received them there. All had expected that on their seeing the chaplain in his official costume and first knowing that there was a Christian Minister on their shore and among them, that there would be a recoil and that they would shrink from him as from something poisonous. But there was no such thing, on the contrary they came up successively and gave him their hand for a shake (they have learned one salutation and seem to be fond of it) and the interpreter pointing to the chaplain's prayer book, asked if it was for ceremonies over the dead, and smiled as before when he told him that it was. The marines were now put into line and received the body with presented arms after which the procession was formed and moved on—they—6 marines with muskets muffled down and fife playing dead march, the chaplain, the coffin borne by four marines, Capt. Stack and Dr. Lynah, hospital Steward [and] 6 or 8 sailors.

Their way laid through the village and the occasion seemed to create quite a holiday among the Japanese. Everybody, men, women and children, running and gaining good places for seeing, and squatting down on the ground till the funeral passed, when they would run and gain another place for observations if they could. The street however along which their road laid was kept entirely clear, and at intervals they noticed fresh boards stuck up with inscriptions probably to warn people from intruding on their way. But the people[,] even women and children[,] showed no fear nor any hesitation in going near them, or in being seen themselves, and some stores which they passed were kept open as usual. The chaplain was often pointed out, being doubtless recognized by his book and gown as the Clergyman of the party, but it was without any exhibition of displeasure on their countenance, but as they would look at any other curiosity.

At the further edge of the village, on a wooded hill at their left was a temple with two different flights of steps leading up to it, and ornamented gateways below. Th[r]ough the further of these gateways, they now saw a Buddhist Priest in his officiating costume, emerge, and perceived that he took his way towards some fresh earth, the grave—a little beyond.

The Japanese had selected for the interment a very pretty spot about a hundred yards from the village and closely adjoining an old burying ground of their own. They found the Buddhist Priest seated there, but he attempted no interference with their religious ceremonies, which the chaplain commenced (all uncovering) as they approached the grave.

The scene at this time was an exceedingly interesting one, even apart from its being the first breaking through of the Japanese settled oppugnation to Christianity. The hills here formed a semicircular sweep and at one end of the semicircle they were standing; at the opposite side on the heights above was the Buddhist Temple. The sides of these hills and the whole sweep of the crest was covered with people, quiet and attentive spectators of what was going on.

Close to our officers stood the Japanese officials, just below the grave the marines were drawn up in line, and by their side on a mat sat the old Buddhist Priest, with a little table before him, on which were a number of papers, etc., with incense burning in their midst.

The Japanese were quiet and attentive, while the chaplain went through the usual service for the solemn burial of the dead.

Then the marines fired three vollies [*sic*] over the grave. As the first volley was given there was a half shout on the hills around, a kind of boyish glee among the multitudes who were computed by our officers at about 2000.

While they were filling up the grave, our officers asked permission to examine the Japanese burying ground, which the officials readily gave, the interpreter also going with them and explaining the several parts.

Against the side of the hill is a range of sculptured stones which he said were their Gods. Some had bas-relief of figures like human beings on them. Across the space were lines of small headstones, some of these also with human figures sculptured in bas-relief on their front, others with inscriptions. These were commemorative of individuals buried below, and when one of the officers observed to the interpreter that the space for each body was very small, he replied that the dead were buried in a *sitting posture*.

The officers then went to the Buddhist Priest, a venerable looking man of about 75 years of age, who was very friendly and showed them his rosary, half of the beads in were glass and half wood, & also his book.

The interpreter opened the papers and showed them their contents, and stated that the Buddhist had come there "as a compliment to Mr. Williams["] (Williams having been the name of the deceased). On the little table in addition to the incense box and some rolls of unknown materials and paper, were also a bowl of cooked rice, a covered vessel of sacki and a small gong. The priest now commenced his ceremonies, sometimes touching his gong, sometimes stirring the sacki, while he thumbed his beads and then muffling his hands in his robe and bowing his head, he read some prayers in a low unintelligable [*sic*] voice. His outer garment was a poncho of very rich brocade silk, covered with fanciful figures.

After putting a head and foot board to the grave with inscription, and covering it in the usual manner, our officers and men left the Buddhist Priest still engaged at his ceremonies and set out on their return, the crowds gathering around as before and all very civil and polite. So with drum & fife playing they returned to our boats & then to the ship.

I was very anxious to attend the funeral but could not as there was a limited number to go. What I have here stated in regard to it was kindly furnished me by one of our officers who went.[35]

Sunday, March 12. We had Divine Service today at half past ten. Tonight—Increase C. Smith,[36] one of the messenger boys, in calling the music for Tattoo fell down the fire room hatch, injuring himself severely.

Monday, March 13. At ten o'clock today, the boats of the squadron containing the articles intended as presents for the Emperor & Empress of Japan, and an escort of officers and marines, collected near the *Macedonian* and shortly after they started for the shore in charge of Captain Abbot. They landed and delivered the presents to the Japanese officials. The boats returned at 3 P.M.

The officials from shore were on board this evening and a meeting was held in the Cabin.

Tuesday, March 14. The Japanese boats brough[t] off our water cask filled with water. Rev. Bittinger,[37] the chaplain of the *Susquehanna* went on shore this morning and started off from Edo. The officials came on board and complained about it, whereupon the Commodore ordered two guns to be fired and the Cornet run up, which was to notify all persons away from their ships to go on board. He also wrote two letters, which were given to the officials, and they were told to go on shore and whoever they should see belonging to any of the ships, to show them one of these letters, which read thus, "That all persons under my command will immediately on the receipt of this, repair on board their respective ships" which was signed by the Commodore, and they were also told to dispatch a courier in the direction Mr. B. had taken and endeavour to overhaul him. It is now nearly nine o'clock and nothing has been heard of Mr. B.

Wednesday, March 15. Mr. Bittenger arrived on board the *Susquehanna* late last night in a Japanese boat. When the order of the Commodore reached him, he was nicely nighted in a comfortable room in a tea house about three miles this side of Edo.

Friday, March 17. Some High Prince came down from Edo this morning in a beautifully decorated barge with silken banners, etc., towed by some twelve or fo[u]rteen small boats.

The Commodore with an escort of officers and marines went on shore to see him. A private interview took place between them, the particulars of which I have not been able [to know?], but we know it was something in regard to the Treaty negotiations. The Com. & party returned soon after 5 o'clock. The Telegraphists,[38] Deguerreotypist [*sic*],[39] Agriculturist,[40] and some Engineers have been on shore for the purpose of putting the instruments of their respective departments in readiness for operation. The Rail Road is being laid and the Engine, Car & Tender is being put to rights, under the superintendence of Mr. Gay.[41] I have not yet had an opportunity to go on shore and see the Locomotive & Car, but our officers who have seen it, say it is a magnificent affair and a perfect piece of workmanship.

Sunday, March 19. Yesterday morning the *Southampton* was hauled alongside and we commenced discharging her of her coal. Continued coaling ship all night and finished about 10 today, having taken in about 120 tons, also all our stores which were on board the *S.*

JOURNAL OF A CRUISE IN THE U.S. STEAM FRIGATE MISSISSIPPI

BY

WM. SPEIDEN JR

VOL. I.

Title Page for Volume One

Anchor

Unknown artist, sketch of "Town of Funchal Island of Madeira"

William Speiden Jr., "Caballero on Horse," January 8, 1853

a rough sketch of the
Grave of Napoleons
from Memory

Anton L. C. Portman, "A Rough Sketch of the Grave of Napoleon"

William Speiden Jr., "The Old House at Longwood—Where Napoleon Lived and Died"

William Speiden Jr., "Cape Town, Cape of Good Hope"

William Speiden Jr., "Bushman," "Malay Woman—Cape Town," and "Hottentot Hut—Algoa Bay"

William Speiden Jr., "Bomb Boat—Cape Town"

William Speiden Jr., "Zulu Fisherman—Natal," "Macono—Kafir Chief," and "Coolie—Cape Town"

Unknown Chinese artist, "Victoria—Hong Kong"

Unknown Chinese artist, "Freight Junk"

Unknown Chinese artist, "Soldiers"

Unknown Chinese artist, "Actors & Sleight of Hand Men & Women"

Unknown Chinese artist, "Imperial Family"

Unknown Chinese artist, "Whampoa Reach"

Unknown Chinese artist, "Sing Song on Flower Boat—Canton"

Unknown Chinese artist, "Canton"

Unknown Chinese artist, "Chinese Beggar"

Unknown Chinese artist, "Chinese Painter," "Governor of Canton with Son and Daughter," and "Chinese Showman"

Unknown Chinese artist, "Macao"

William Speiden Jr., "Chinese Coolie," "Chinese Restaurant—Ambulant," "Woman, Lower Middle Class," "Tanka Boat Girl, Macao," and "Tanka Boat, Macao"

William Speiden Jr., "Japanese Junk"

William Speiden Jr., "Mandarin Boat of Jeddo"

Unknown Chinese artist, picture of city—either Canton or Shanghai

Unknown Chinese artist, "The Bogue"

Unknown artist, "Dr. Lynah and the Bull"

William Speiden Jr., "Loo Choo Woman & Babe" and "Loo Choo Policeman or Spy"

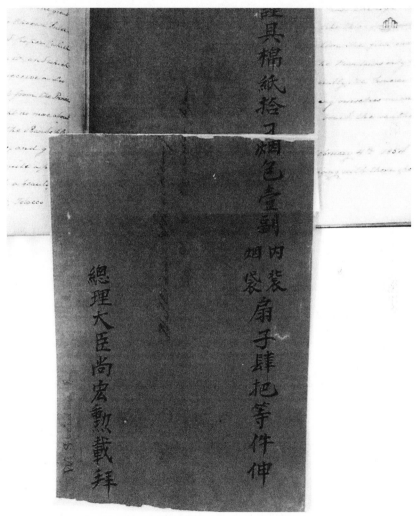

A small drawing of a gateway

Rice paper handwritten in Chinese to William Speiden, USS *Missippi* [*sic*]: "We are happy to present a pipe and fan. From the Prime Minister of the Great Lew Chew Shan Qua Hun."

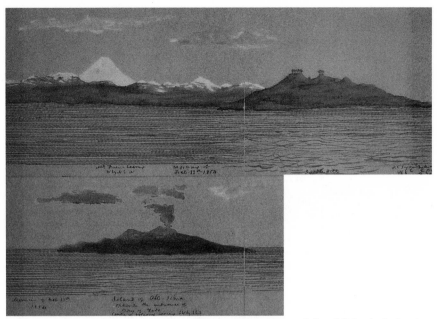

William Speiden Jr., "Mt. Fuji, Saddle Hill, Entrance to Bay at Yedo" and "Island of Oko-sima opposite the entrance of Bay of Yedo," February 13, 1854

Edward C. McCauley, "Japanese Freight Junk"

Unknown artist, sketches of Commodore Perry

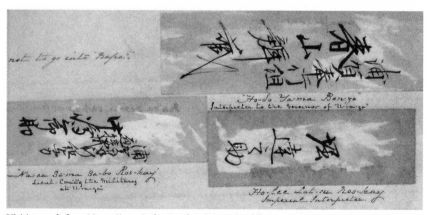

Visiting cards from Na-ca Si-ma Sa-bo Ros-kay (Lieut Com'd'g Lt-c Military at Uraga), Ho-do Ya-ma Ben-yo (Interpreter to the Governor of Uraga), and Ho-lee Lat-su Nos-kay (Imperial Interpreter)

...s .

was brought in on stands thus all red
...of porcelain. A slice of pound cake and

A small drawing of a cup on a stand

...f baked pulverised beans, sweetened, with a lo...
...pes of red and white and twisted thus wa...
...tanned dishes .

A small drawing of twisted sugar candy

...d work about them and their stirru...
...heir shape is thus or rather this...
...they are wider than the foot; they are of ste...

A small drawing of a Japanese-style stirrup

Anton L. C. Portman, "Conference Room at Yokohama Kanagawa. Japan, March 1854"

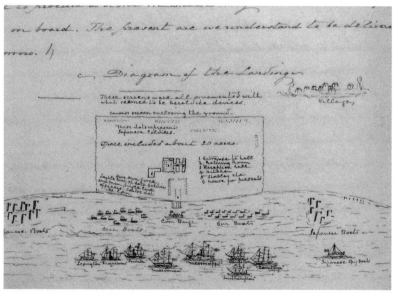

William Speiden Jr., "Diagram of the Landing"

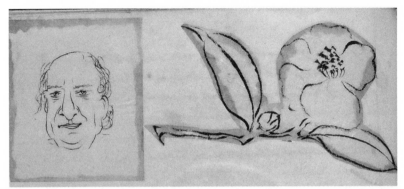

Unknown Japanese artist, "Profile of Purser Wm. Speiden and a branch of Japonica by Japanese lad at the reception at Yokohama," March 8, 1854

Unknown Japanese artist, "Commodore M. C. Perry by Japanese at the reception at Yokohama," March 8, 1854

JOURNAL OF A
CRUISE
IN THE
U.S. STEAM
FRIGATE MISSISSIPPI
BY
WM. SPEIDEN JR

VOL. II.

Title page for Volume Two

Unknown Chinese artist, "Chinese convicts"

Unknown Chinese artist, "Chinese Upper Class"

Unknown Chinese artist, "Chinese worker"

Unknown Chinese artist, "Chinese worker"

Honolulu Oct 1854

William T. Peters (from the original by Wilhelm Heine), "Honolulu," October 1854

W.T.S. from the Original by W. Heine

William T. Peters, "Native Hawaiian—Honolulu"

William T. Peters, "Native Hut—Honolulu"

Unknown artist, "Gambling Table—California House—San Francisco"

William T. Peters, "Saloon—Taboga Island"

William T. Peters, "Native Hut—Taboga Island"

William T. Peters, "Native Men—Valparaiso"

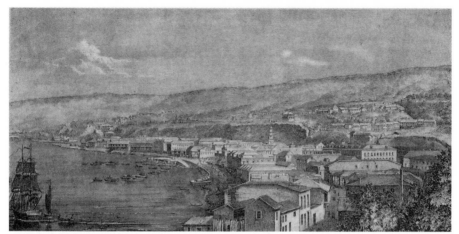

Unknown artist, "Valparaiso"

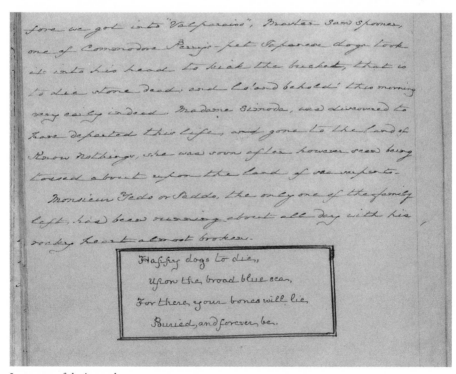

Last entry of the journal

after people are quiet tomorrow night, we will be at "Karkizaki" in a purt at a place where there are no houses near the beach. There we greatly desire you to come & meet us, & thereby carry out our hopes to their fruition." — April 25th.

Superscription on the Envelope, copied from the original.

覧者幸轉呈　大合衆國師艦各大員書　密呈

Wm. Speiden, Jr.

Superscription on the envelope of a letter from two intelligent Japanese, translated "A secret communication to the American Man of War Ships; to go up higher."

This morning early discovered a vessel standing up the bay which this evening proved to be the U.S. store ship *Supply* from Shanghai. She brought us letters of late date as 3d December from home. All well, and we are all well on board. Here we are in Japan, the most distant portion of the world from home, but still we can hear from our friends in a little over three months. The *Supply* anchored about 4 P.M. We were unable to have church this morning on account of coaling ship.

This evening I went on board the *Supply*[,] saw my friends there who were quite well. They left Shanghai on the 1st of this month, and had quite a rough time.

Monday, March 20. The *Southampton* and *Vandalia* got underway this morning and stood down the bay. They have gone to survey the harbour of Tehmu-de [Shimoda],[42] one of the towns which the Japanese have prepared to open to us.

Friday, March 24. Early this morning the steam frigate *Susquehanna* left this port, she has gone to Hong Kong—took our letters for home. We expected that the Treaty was to be signed today, but it was postponed until some day next week.

This morning was set apart to receive the presents of the Japanese in return for those sent out by our Government and delivered last Monday week.

The Commodore and his escort of officers and marines left the *Powhatan* about half past ten o'clock this morning and went on shore, where they were received by the Japanese Commissioners. The presents, which were seven large launch loads of rice together with several large boxes containing lacquered ware, etc., were delivered by the Commissioners and received by the Commodore, who ordered the rice to be sent on board the *Supply* and the other articles to the *Powhatan*.

After the delivery and reception of the presents was gotten through with, the Commodore and officers were led out into an open space by the side of the Reception House, w[h]ere some fifty or sixty giant-like men were assembled and who performed some wonderful feats of strength, fighting, wrestling, etc. Only one officer was allowed to go on shore from each ship. I was not able to go[,] it not being my turn, nor have I yet been on shore, but as soon as the Treaty is signed, we shall all be able to go on shore whenever we please, and we would have been able to have gone some time since, had it not been for the indiscretion of the Chaplain of the *Susquehanna*.

Monday, March 27. I am almost at a loss to know how to commence to narrate the circumstances of this day, but to come at once to the point, the Commodore intended giving a Banquet to the Japanese Commissioners, who came off this evening and went on board the *Macedonian*. They intended had it been smooth and pleasant to have come off in their barge, but it being quite rough, they came off in one of the Government boats, which are so much alike that you are unable to distinguish whether one contains a person of some note, or another. As these boats neared the *Macedonian* the officers on board of that vessel discovered that the foremost boat contained the Commissioners (we were ordered to salute as soon as they got abreast of our ship, but they not coming off in their barge[,] we were unable to tell what boat contained them). The distinguishing pennant of this ship was hoisted (this being the signal to let us know that one of the boats contained the grand functionaries) and we immediately let loose our battery and saluted them with 17 guns. The *Powhatan* at the same time hoisting the Commissioners flag at the fore and main.

On board the *Macedonian* the men were exercised at General Quarters. Commodore Perry's barge was sent to the *Macedonian* to take the Commissioners to the *Powhatan*.

All of our officers had received an invitation from the Commodore to attend the Banquet —which most of us did, I went for one. When the Commissioners left the *Macedonian* she saluted them also with 17 guns. When they arrived alongside the *Powhatan* the Commodore and all the officers who had been invited were assembled at the gangway to receive them. The Marine guard was drawn up and three rolls of the drum given in compliment, and a salute of 17 guns was fired by her also.

They were shown around the ship and witnessed the working of the engine, steam having been got up for that purpose. The four Commissioners, a Prince and two interpreters with the Commodore and Captains then went down into the cabin to partake of a collation set out there. Tables were also set out on deck for the Commissioners escort and the officers.

A great many toasts were given, some of which have not escaped my reccollection [*sic*]. One of the officers of the *Powhatan* rose and proposed "the health of the Emperor of Japan," which being drank, one of the Japanese officers by the name of "Nam-mo-ra" arose, and in plain English, sung out, "the health of the President of the United States." Then "the health of the Japanese Commissioners" was given, and in return by "Nam-mo-ra," "long life and health to Commodore Perry," all attendant with the usual Hip, Hip, Hip. Hurra etc.—"The Ladies of Japan, may it not be long before we make their acquaintance." One of the Japanese rose and gave, "the health and happiness of the Ladies of the United States." And many others were given by both Americans and Japanese. A toast which Father gave, I may as well put here, it was this—"California and Japan, next door neighbours, may they soon step in and spend the evening with each other."

After sitting at table about an hour and a half, the Commodore came up from below with the Commissioners and proposed that they should all go forward and hear the Japanese Olio Minstrels[43] (a band of Ethiopians on board the *Powhatan*) who by their comical acts while playing and afterwards dancing afforded immense amusement for the Japanese, who kept in one incessant roar of laughter, being all a little tinged from the effects of "*old tom*" alias cherry cordial and Champagne, etc.

I noticed one of the Commissioners who had taken over his allowance, throw one of his arms around the Commodore's neck, rest his head on his epaulette and laugh and chat at a great rate. Really it was an amusing sight.

After listening to the Minstrels for some time, one of the Commissioners, whose head braces were not set up quite so taut as the others, rose and proposed that they should leave, which after thanking the Commodore they did, and on leaving were saluted by the *Saratoga* with 17 guns.

Really the whole thing from beginning to end was no doubt a remarkable circumstance, and we all hope that the Americans and Japanese will soon be on lasting terms of friendship with each other, and I truly believe that the new era which is now about to take place in the History of the Japanese Empire, will be one in which far more greater changes will occur than we have at this time any reason to anticipate, and that too before many years have passed.

I have been able to procure the names of the Commissioners which I shall give on the day of the signing of the Treaty.

——Card of the Japanese officer who gave the toasts.[44]

Tuesday, March 28. There was another meeting on shore today between the Commodore and the Commissioners. We have heard that they have consented to open two ports to us, and [in] a year or so will open two or three more. One of the two is where the *Vandalia* and *Southampton* have gone to survey. The Commodore heard today from them, and they report favorably concerning its capacities of being a good harbour. The other port is on the Island of Mats-mai [Matsumae].[45] Our whalers when they go into the Japan Sea (where the whales now resort) have to pass very near it, and therefore it will be an advantageous harbour for them, as they can put in there, obtain supplies and make repairs, instead of having to go several hundred miles to the southard for the same purpose.

Wednesday, March 29. At daylight, discovered that the *Vandalia* and *Southampton* had arrived during the night and anchored, the *Van* a short distance down the bay, and the *South* in the anchorage.

Friday, March 31.
  "Signing of the Treaty between the United States and Japan."
  "Two Ports to be opened for Intercourse."
  "Names of the Japanese Commissioners."
  "Commodore Perry for next President of the United States."

About twelve M. several boats of the squadron containing a few select officers—two from each ship, went on shore, with the band of the *Powhatan* and her marine guard.

I on this great occasion was one of the few who landed. When we arrived on the beach, we drew up in line to receive the Commodore, who landed at a quarter past twelve and we then proceeded to the House of Reception. As soon as we entered it, the Commodore and staff went into the Audience Chamber for an interview with the Commissioners, & the rest of the officers remained in the Banquet Hall. A feast was then set before us, something after the style of the Lew Chewans. After this was through with, those who wished went out and took a short walk around the premises. After the Commodore and Commissioners had been in private confab for some two or three hours, the conference broke up and we then heard that during the interview the long desired Treaty was signed, which is one of Amity and Intercourse. Two ports are to [be] opened to us, the names of which were left blank in the Treaty. The Commodore is to decide which ones we will take[;] it is believed that he wishes Sha-mo-di [Shimoda] for a coal depot, and Chak-a-date [Hakodate] for a resort for our whalers.

The Commodore told the Commissioners that before he should leave this place, he intended to run up in sight of Edo and salute the Emperor. They tried to raise some objections to this, but he told them they ought to have objected before the Treaty was signed. We were unable to gain any other information, as the interview was private.

Will not all the world be astonished to hear of our success in making a Treaty with Japan, and the greater part of it can be attributed to the good and efficient management of our gallant Commander-in-Chief. Let him now be put up as a Candidate for the Presidency, and he will find that many who now run him down, because he does not act according to their own nonsensical ideas, will never rest until they have him placed in the highest position, which can be given by the unanimous vote of the people of the United States.

If Congress does not immediately on their hearing of the Treaty having been made tender to Commodore Perry their entire approval of his conduct, and also give him the title of Admiral, and place him at the head of the list, it will be a gross neglect of duty, which undoubtedly they owe to such a man, and all I have to say inclusion [*sic*] to this, that he would have *my entire* approval, provided he would let us go on shore or else tell these people that he must have some fresh grub for his officers to eat.

While on shore, I saw for the first time, the little Locomotive, Car & Tender which was sent out by our government as a present to the Emperor of Japan; it is a beautiful thing. These and the other presents are to be packed up and sent up to Edo. We left the shore about four o'clock and returned on board ship. Coming off, we pulled around the Japanese Commissioners' barge, which is quite a fine affair, all dressed up with silk and beautifully decorated with banners.

The following are the names of the Japanese who carried on the Treaty negotiations.

Hayashi Daigaku no Kama, one of the Chief Councillors of the Empire—
    Third in Rank.

Ido,[46] Prince of Tsus-sima (the Islands lying between Corea and Japan.[)]

Izawa,[47] Prince of Mima-saki[,] a principality of Nippon.

Udono[,][48] Member of the Board of Revenue.

Matsusaki Michitaro[,][49] Is 5th, but not a Commissioner.

Sunday, April 2. Today at half past ten, read the Articles of War and mustered the crew, and then had church. Several officers from the different ships were on board.

Monday, April 3. Lieutenant Silas Bent was detached from this ship today and ordered to the *Powhatan* as Flag Lieutenant.

Tuesday, April 4. The U.S. sloop of war *Saratoga* got underway this morning about 9 o'clock and commenced beating out of the harbour. As she passed us cheered ship[,] had our Band up and played "Home Sweet Home." The *Saratoga* is bound home. She takes Captain Adams to the Sandwich Islands—bearer of Despatches to the Government.

As she passed the *Powhatan*, saluted the Commodore with 13 guns, which was returned by the *Powhatan* with 9 guns—all the other vessels cheered ship. By her we sent our letters. 1 to Mary[50] & 1 to Ned. By Lieut. Goldborough[51] I sent a small bundle to Ned.

Thursday, April 6. Made a present to the Japanese today of one of our 12 Pounder Howitzers, with boat and field carriage and equipments.

American Anchorage, Edo Bay, Monday, April 10. Yesterday evening the Commodore told some of the officials who were on board the *Powhatan* that he intended going up in sight of Edo today. They begged him not to stop there; he told them he would not. As the Imperial Interpreter was leaving the *Powhatan* he told Mr. Portman that he was going on shore to tell the authorities that the Commodore was going up in sight of Edo, but was not going to stop there, and if after this the Commodore broke his word by anchoring there, he would have to rip himself open.

Shortly after eight o'clock this morning we got underway and stood up the bay towards Edo in company with the rest of the squadron, and with two Japanese boats in tow, some of the officials being on board to go up with us—and all prepared to commit Hare Kari [hara-kiri] in case the Commodore should anchor.

We got in sight and had a view of the City about half past twelve, and then turned back and stood in for Yokohama, where we were ordered to go and get the *Lexington* off shore, she having gone ashore while getting underway this morning. We came to anchor about a quarter past two, ahead and outshore of her. Sent our hawser to her and succeeded in getting her off, kept her in tow and stood down the bay after the other vessels, and near five o'clock came to anchor with the squadron in this place.

Tuesday, April 11. The *Macedonian* got underway this morning at half past six and stood down the bay out to sea. It is believed she has gone to the Bonin Islands to obtain fresh vegetables for the squadron.

Friday, April 14. The *Supply* and *Powhatan* (store ships) stood down the bay this morning shortly after six o'clock. They have been ordered to Shimoda where we will join them in a few days. Yesterday & today coaling ship and receiving provisions in the Pursers Department.

Monday, April 17. The *Vandalia* and *Lexington* left this morning for Shimoda. This evening we rec'd. orders to prepare to sail at early daylight tomorrow.

Shimoda, Tuesday, April 18. At a quarter past three A.M. called all hands and commenced heaving in. At 4.35 got underway and stood down the bay of Edo, in company with the *Powhatan*. At half past eight in the mouth of the bay the Island of Oo-sima [O Shima] in sight on port bow, passed it about 12 M. and soon after made land on both bows. About two o'clock discovered the *Vandalia* and *Lexington* at anchor outside the harbour. The *Powhatan* stood in for the anchorage and anchored about three o'clock. We anchored near the *Lexington* at 3.15 and at half past three we got underway again and stood further up the harbour and came to anchor again above the *Powhatan* in 5¼ fathoms water and in about the best berth in the anchorage.

This is quite a small harbour but a very pretty place, with high hills nearby, surrounding us which are richly & beautifully cultivated. The town which looks to be a good sized one is estimated to contain about 20,000 inhabitants. I have not been on shore yet and of course can say nothing about the place. The harbour is open to the south west, and should the wind come from that quarter it will be likely to get up quite a heavy sea & swell and make it very unpleasant. At other times vessels will lay quiet and safely at single anchor. The harbour is well capacitated to allow 8 or 10 vessels to swing clear with 40 fathoms of chain out. 12 to 15 can be accommodated if properly moored and as many as thirty—if moored fore and aft. In the case however of the latter number there would hardly be sufficient room allowed when getting underway.

The *Southampton* and *Supply* are here also. After we anchored some of the Government boats came off and communicated with the flagship.

Wednesday, April 19. This morning warped closer in shore and moored ship. Commenced coaling from the *Lexington*.

Friday, April 21. Commodore Perry and suit went on shore to return an official call of the Governor. Two or three of our officers joined the party, among them was Jones,[52] our Marine Officer, who as he attempted to land, made a misstep and went overboard, and was obliged to return to the ship, which caused the following wit of one of our officers.

~ *Cross questions—hard words & their results* ~
1st Part
To obey or not to obey is the question. One said, "none but legal orders he'd obey." "Would you not jump overboard if ordered so to do" said Jesse Gay, "Not I for one," said Jones, & to back it up, angrily said, "No, I'll be *hanged* if I do" ~

2nd Part
Jones visits the shore attached to the suit of the Commander-in-chief.
Hurry hurry is the word—
Quick quick to land is here preferred.

So up sprang Jones to lead the way
    When overboard he tumbled in the Bay.
On pleasure bent he approached the shore
    In the suit of the gallant Commodore
But sad to say his pleasure was prescribed—
    In jumping to the shore he fell outside
Both wet & cold he hastes on board the *Mississippi*
    And disappointed much told all his mournful ditty.

A Court Martial convened on board for the trial of two of our men for desertion.

Shimoda, Saturday, April 22. General permission was given today by the Commander-in-Chief for officers to land, and they are not to go beyond a prescribed limit of ten miles.

A number of officers from each ship visited the town. Accompanied by my friend A.L.C.P. [Anton L. C. Portman],[53] I started off to see some of the novelties which are to be noticed in Japan. The people were glad to see us and crowds followed us, as we passed through some of the principal streets, went into several of the Temples, some of which were highly decorated. One of them was a Temple of Offerings, in which were hung in appropriate places, scenes of shipwreck, locks of hair, which had been placed there by persons who had been saved from shipwreck, they having vowed that if they returned in safety, they would cut off the tuft of their hair and offer it to their God. This is considered by them as doing great pennance [*sic*]. There were also representations of numerous diseases of which persons had been afflicted and recovered.

We passed through the town and took a long walk into the country, four or five Japanese officers following us, who were continually stopping, rubbing their legs and making sundry signs for us to turn back or stop. We completely tired them out, not being used to walk as fast as our accustomed rate.

The scenery along the river of Samodi [Shimoda] on the banks of which we walked for some distance, is very picturesque. We returned into town about half past twelve and then went into several of the houses which are neat & clean. The streets are well laid out, and the people[,] both men and woman[,] entirely free from the restraints which characterize those we saw at Yokohama and also at Lew Chew. We saw some quite good looking girls, from 8 to 15 years of age, who were as fond of being looked at as they were to look at us. Passing along one of these streets, we were joined by three officers from the *Vandalia*. We noticed a young and quite a pretty girl going along ahead of us and at intervals turning round to look at us. She presently stopped at the door of one of the houses, which was opened and presented to our view the faces of four or five more girls quite as pretty and good looking. On seeing us they did not seem to be at all astonished, and stood still until we reached the door, when someone suggested that we should go in, which we did, but expected that they would run away, but no, they all came in and sat down near us on a raised platform, covered with matting.

Two or three of the party who had watches, took them out and showed them to the young Japanese Ladies, who were very much amused at the sight of them. One of the officers who had a good deal of jewelry about him, several rings on his fingers, took them off and with his breastpin handed them to one [of] the young ladies, who placed them on her person in their appropriate places, then stood up, looked at herself and laughed at a great rate, and really I never saw anyone look so much pleased as she did with all this finery about her. We sat but a few moments, which were passed much to our amusement as well as theirs, & then got up[,] shook hands (they are very fond indeed of this salutation) with them all around and with much bowing, and other Japanese graces[,] left the house, came down to the landing place and got on board ship soon after one o'clock.

The married women black their teeth with iron rust which is considered to be a mark of fidelity, but which makes them look very disgusting.

The single ones leave their teeth as nature gave. They probably clean them, as they looked nice and white, and the young ladies appeared to be very fond of showing them. I believe that there is no place which abounds more with children than this, and all of them good looking & merry boys & girls.

Sunday, April 23. We had church this morning at eleven o'clock, and were going to have a sermon, but just as the chaplain had given out his text, signal was made to furl sails, & the church service was broken up.

I went on shore this evening and took a walk through the town. It came on to rain, but the Japanese who followed me soon provided me with an umbrella. Went into several of the houses, the people were very sociable and seemed glad to see me.

Monday, April 24. I went on shore this morning by order of the Captain, to take a list of the fresh provisions required by the different messes of the ship. I left it with one of the Japanese Officers who said that they would be off tomorrow. We are coaling ship from the *Lexington*, & rec'g. water from shore by Japanese lighters.

Tuesday, April 25. Accompanied by one of my messmates, Col. J.W.S. [James Willett Spalding], went on shore this evening for a walk, went about five miles into the country along the Shimoda River, which is quite a pretty stream of water about forty feet wide. We had a pleasant walk and came on board at sundown. The Japanese brought of[f] today all the provisions required with the exception of the eggs and some of the potatoes.

Wednesday, April 26. At half past ten, called all hands to muster, and read the findings and sentence of a Navy General Court Martial in the cases of James Welsh (Sea[man]) and Nathaniel N. Parsons, the former is to forfeit all the pay and subsistence due him, the latter is to forfeit all the pay and subsistence due him and be confined in irons on bread and water for a fortnight.

Tuesday, May 2. Discovered a large sail outside this morning and at five P.M. the *Macedonian* came in from sea & anchored. She left Bonin Islands on the 28th ult[im]o. Has brought turtles for the squadron.

Saturday, May 6. On Wednesday morning received on board from the *Macedonian* five turtles for the crew and one for each of the officers messes. We are now every day feasting on turtle soup & steaks.

Thursday noon the *Lexington* was towed out to sea by the boats of the squadron. She has gone to Lew Chew to await us.

Yesterday evening I went with our boatswain in the 1st cutter to haul the seine. As we passed about two cables length from the *Powhatan* saw one of her men while furling sails fall from the foretopsail yard to the deck. His name was Parish[54] and the poor fellow lived but two hours after this sad accident. We were not successful in getting many fish but had quite sufficient for a nice mess for breakfast. The *Macedonian, Vandalia* & *Southampton* left this morning for Chackadade {Hakadati} [Hakodate][55] where we will join them in a few days.

This evening attended the funeral of the man who was killed yesterday; it was quite an interesting occasion. He was buried in a Temple yard back of the village of Cacasaki. Hundreds of the inhabitants gathered around the body as it was landed on the beach, and followed it to the place of interment. Several of the Japanese officials were present and followed after the procession of our officers and men. The crowd kept perfectly quiet while our chaplain read the prayers for the burial of the dead. Several of the Buddhist Priests were there also, but did not perform any of their religious ceremonies over the body during the few moments we remained on the spot after our service was over. The officials on shore somehow or other heard that the man was killed and came off this morning to know if we should not want a place for him to be buried. They were told that we should, and they accordingly selected an elevated spot by the side of the Temple mentioned above.

Sunday, May 7. After reading the articles of war and mustering the crew, we had Divine Service.

Some few nights ago a Japanese boat containing two men came alongside. We could not understand exactly what they wanted. They pointed towards Edo and indicated as much that they came from there. We sent them alongside the *Powhatan.* Mr. Williams our interpreter had some conversation with them and learned that they were two respectable citizens of Edo—that they had heard and read a great deal about our country, and had a great desire to go and visit it—that the Japanese laws forbid any Japanese leaving his home to travel abroad. They wished so much to go that they had determined to escape and get on board one of our ships in the hope that we would take them to America. They stated that they were at Yokohama for some time, waiting [for] an opportunity to get on board, but such a strict watch was always kept over them that they dared not make the attempt. They heard however that our vessels were coming to this place and expected we would stay but a few days and then leave for good, and believing that this would be the real case of things, they had that day pulled all the way from Yokohama (in consequence of which, not being used to sculling in boats, they [*sic*] hands were all blistered and sore) in order to reach us before we should start. They were told that they could not remain on board (as they desired to remain[,] stating that we might put them anywhere in the ship we pleased). And having shoved their boat off as they got on board the *Powhatan* they were set ashore in one of her boats. A day or two ago a note addressed in Japanese was thrown into Capt. Lee's gig while on shore. The note was sent to the Commodore and when translated was found to have been written by these two men. In it they gave an account of themselves, all of which was in accordance with the statement they made to Mr. Williams a few nights before.

A day or so ago also one of our officers was standing near the landing place waiting for a boat, when two Japanese, who from their dress, he took to be gentleman, came up to him, took out their pens & papers, pointed to the vessels and indicated as much that they wished him to write down their names, which he did, and after that, they commenced examining the buttons on his coat & vest and appeared to be exceedingly interested in his dress. One of them presently looked around to see if anyone was looking at them and immediately thrust a Japanese note into Mr. Spalding's (this is the name of the officer) breast and made signs for him to keep quiet and not take it out. He to oblige them allowed it to remain until they left him. This note proved to be a facsimile of the one which was thrown into the boat.

Last evening some officers who were walking back of the town accidentally came upon a small house, by which a guard was on post. They looked inside and found a large sized cage in which were confined two men, who were recognized as being the same men who came on board this ship. This got to the ears of the Commodore, and this morning he sent Lt. Bent and Mr. Williams on shore to inquire about the matter and see these men. They went to the place but the men were gone and had[,] as they heard[,] been taken off to Edo. These are all the particulars we have been able to learn. It is very probable that these poor fellows will in accordance with the laws of this country suffer the penalty of their crimes with the loss of their heads. The direction on the note was, "A secret communication to any American man of war, to go up further."

Tuesday, May 9. Yesterday morning Lieut. Bent and two or three other officers from the *Powhatan* went on a hunting excursion and did not expect to return until this evening. They however got back into the town late last night, and their not wishing to come off to the ship at that time of night (11½ o'clock) went into one of the temples (in which the Japanese have placed several rooms at the disposal of the Commodore) to pass away the night. They had been there but a few moments when about an hundred soldiers with their officers, and one of the interpreters, all carrying lanterns, came to the temple and requested our officers to go on board ship. They refused to comply with the request, whereupon several of the Japanese left and came off to the flag ship and requested the Commodore to order these officers on board ship. He said he would do no such thing, that the treaty was in force and they might remain on shore as long as they wished. They then went back to the temple and endeavoured to make them leave by force, and their annoyances became so great that Mr. Bent and the others were obliged to load their guns and pistols and tell these Japanese, if they[56] did not immediately desist, they would suffer for their insults. Seeing that our officers were not to be trifled with, the Japanese desisted, and the interpreter, Tatsu Noskay,[57] began to bow and scrape and ask pardon for his conduct, but asked them again to go on board ship, which Mr. B. positively refused to do. Seeing that their insults, persuasions, etc., could not make them go, the Japanese left the Temple but kept a watch around it all night. This morning Mr. Bent came off and told the matter to the Commodore. He sent him again on shore with Mr. Williams and some marines to inquire into it. The Prefect said that he knew nothing of the matter, that it was done without his order and the only excuse they could give was that the interpreter, Tatsu Noskay, was under the influence of liquor and on his asking pardon for his conduct the matter was settled.

Friday, May 12. About 4 o'clock this evening one of our men by the name of Michael Henderson (Lds.) [Landsman] fell from the main topsail yard, striking in his descent the main rigging, which broke his arm in two places, and threw him out from the ship's side into the water. He was picked up by Jas. Collins Sea[man], who jumped overboard after him. Although this unlucky accident happened to the poor fellow, he is doing well.

At Sea, Saturday, May 13. Got underway this morning at half past six and stood out of the harbour of Shimoda in company with the steamer *Powhatan*. We passed around the south end of Oo-sima [O Shima] about noon.

Hakodadi [Hakodate] Matsmai [Matsumae], Japan, Wednesday, May 17. We arrived at this place today about ten o'clock along with the *Powhatan* [and] find the *Macedonian*, *Vandalia*, and *Southampton* here. Our passage was a pleasant one. We saw a great many whales, had land in sight nearly the whole time. We lay to last night in the Straits of Sangar.[58] This [is] a magnificent harbour and will accommodate a great many vessels. There are between one and two hundred junks at anchor inshore of us. The houses appear to be much larger than any we have heretofore seen.

Friday, May 19. Yesterday the Commodore sent word on shore that he wished some of [the] officials to come off and have an interview on board this ship. The Commander-in-Chief came on board at 11 A.M. and was received with the usual honors. About noon, three Japanese boats, containing the Governor and some other high officers[,] came on board, and an interview was held in the cabin. We hear outside but little of the conference, which amounts principally to this—They say that they have heard nothing of the treaty, and thought we had come with evil intentions and the inhabitants, chiefly believing that to be the case, had most of them packed up all their goods and were leaving the city and going into the interior. Mr. Williams[,] our interpreter[,] informed them everything concerning the treaty, showed them some papers which had been sighned [*sic*] by the Imperial Commissioners and other things which it was thought necessary in order to convince them of the amicable feelings which were now existing between the Americans and Japanese, made by the Treaty signed on March 31st 1854.

They were told by order of the Commodore that this was the day on which the Treaty was to go in force, that the officers of the squadron would be allowed to go on shore tomorrow, and he wished the Japanese officers not to follow them about wherever they pleased to go. They replied that this was immaterial to them but that if their officers and our officers were allowed to go together, it would be the means of assuring the inhabitants that our intentions were friendly instead of[,] as they supposed[,] to do them harm and reassure them as to what we had told them & thereby cause them of their own accord to return to their homes.

The weather was quite unpleasant and prevented the Japanese from leaving until late this afternoon. They were in the meantime shown around the ship and seemed very much pleased with what they saw and the attentions shown them.

Thirty pounds of bread and a pound and a half of tea was distributed among the sailors who composed their boats' crews. Of this they were very proud and expressed many thanks, and all of them (6 in number) were very gentlemanly in their bearing and whenever anything was handed them to look at they always returned it with a low bow; this however is not uncommon, but characteristic of all Japanese.

Saturday, May 20. I have been on shore today and was the second person who landed in the town from this ship. The landing place is quite a good one, and agrees exactly with the description given by Capt. Ricord of the Russian Navy, who was here in 1813 endeavouring to affect and at last affected the release of Capt. Golownin & some of his officers and men who were captured in 1811 at Kunashier, having been enticed into the garrison at that place in the belief that they were to have an interview and while in the garrison their vessel the *Diana*[59] was fired into and obliged to put out of that harbour and Capt. G. and his companions were surrounded, bound hand & foot, brought to this place, then carried to Matsumae, and finally brought back to this place and released to Capt. R.—this however is giving an account of which is well known.

After landing with a few officers, besides several Japanese officers following us—I took a walk about the city. A short distance from the principal streets is a Buddhist Temple. We went into it, and it is the handsomest one I have ever seen in Japan; it is very prettily decorated and had some very fine carved cornice work about it, emblematic of their Gods, etc.

Coming back to the landing place we went into several of the stores and were able to buy anything we wished. The streets are much wider and neater than those at Simoda [Shimoda]—the houses larger and everything on a grander scale. The population is estimated to be about 60 thousand, that is when they are all at home, under the late panic two-thirds of the people have been away, but are returning by degrees. They already begin to understand us a little better and things will soon go on swimmingly.

The things you buy, you pay the owner of them. This is generally the case, but as it was different at Shimoda, I make this remark. There, if you went into a shop, saw any article which you might wish to purchase, then put your name on it, and go to a sort of custom house in the end to get it, and pay three and sometimes four times as much as the shopkeeper actually charges for it. This will be different however when we return there. Our dollar is equal to 4.800 cash and a mace[60] (this is a string of cash, equal in China to 8 cents) contains 100 cash so when you wish to ascertain the cost of the articles, the shopkeeper shows you as many mace as the articles are worth and by calculating, you pay him accordingly.

Things appear to be quite cheap, but there is no telling how long this will last. We returned to the ship about 2 P.M. having had quite a pleasant time.

Tuesday, May 23. Yesterday the authorities of this place laid a complaint before the Commodore, stating that the officers had come on shore, gone into their stores, pulled their drawers open, broken open boxes, endeavouring to find something they might like, and if they did find anything, would throw down some money, take the articles and walk out. Some even had taken the articles without paying anything for them Buying swords (stating the people let the officers have them through fear; that it was not allowed in Japan to sell arms) and also that they had gone into their temples and desecrated them by playing cards in them.

This morning the captain sent for all the officers to come into the cabin and told us this complaint which the Japanese had made. He said that he was ordered by the Commodore to inquire of all the officers of this ship, and see if any of them had committed any of the above faults. One of our officers only had purchased a sword. He was ordered to make a written statement of how he bought and what he paid for it, etc. Two or three had been guilty of playing cards, not however in the temples but in an adjoining building. They were also ordered to make out written statements. These statements with a general report from the Capt. were submitted to the Commander-in-Chief. The swords had to be given back, and those who played cards were not to be allowed to leave the ship without further orders from the Commander-in-Chief. It seems instead of the officers being guilty of rum[m]aging in the stores [it] was found upon examination to have been done by some men who were allowed to go on shore from the *Powhatan*.

Signal was made this morning that no communication was allowed with the shore for the present.

Wednesday, May 24. The officers were allowed to go on shore again today. A bazaar at the landing place has been opened, where we can now purchase any articles the Japanese might have for sale. The prices however were marked on each article and so there could be no mistake about paying the Japanese the proper price for their goods. Some very pretty lacquered cups, saucers, etc., were purchased at very moderate prices.

The storeship *Southampton* left here this morning. She has gone to Volcano Bay[61] to make a survey of it, and will probably join us at Shimoda.

Friday, May 26. Today about noon lowered our colors to half mast, with the rest of the squadron, while the body of one of the crew of the *Vandalia* was taken on shore to be buried.

Sunday, May 28. We had Divine Service this morning at half past nine. This evening I attended the funeral of another of the crew of the *Vandalia*. He was buried in a very pretty spot in the S. West end of the town, nearby was a small temple. In it was a large figure of the Virgin Mary, and [it] looked more like a Catholic sepulchre than a Buddhist Temple. The chief officials of the place were present and looked on with quiet amazement while the service of the burial of the dead was read by our chaplain. The Japanese have already commenced to put a very nice railing around the grave of the first man that died and it will be a nice place for a graveyard.

Tuesday, May 30. Last evening I attended a concert of the Japanese Olio Minstrels on board the *Powhatan*. A large number of the Japanese were on board and seemed highly pleased.

The fishing party have been away twice today and succeeded in getting quite a number of fish[,] salmon, trout, etc., which was very nice.

Wednesday, May 31. The *Macedonian* and *Vandalia* got underway this morning and stood out of the harbour. The former vessel has gone to examine some islands between this and Shimoda and will join us there. The latter vessel has gone to Shanghai to relieve the *Plymouth* and has taken our letters for home.

Shimoda, Wednesday, June 7. In company with the *Powhatan* we got underway on the morning of 3rd inst. and stood out of the harbour of Hakodati Matsumae. We had been underway but a short time when a thick fog came up and we were obliged to turn round and stand for the entrance of the harbour where we came to anchor. Shortly after nine the fog cleared off and we got underway again and stood out to sea through the Straits of Sangar. The same evening we discovered a sail standing [to] the southward and eastward, which we supposed to be the U.S. storeship *Southampton*. On Sunday we had service as usual. Mustered the crew & read the rules and regulations for the better government of the Navy.

We arrived here today at 1 P.M.—the *Supply* still here. Our passage down has been a tolerable pleasant one. Yesterday however was quite a disagreeable day, strong head wind and heavy sea. Early this morning we had a peep at our old friend Mt. Fuji—towering high into the heavens, with its top all covered with snow, and seemed as if it stood there as a protecting friend for all the hills around. It was a beautiful sight and we were able to see its top when we were one hundred and twenty miles from its base.

The weather is quite pleasant here, sufficiently warm as to make white clothes quite comfortable.

Monday, June 12. On Thursday last at half past eleven, the launch, 1st & 2d cutters, Ariel & gig —with the *Powhatan*'s 1st cutter (to assist our boats) containing their full crews—with 25 seaman as infantry and 24 artillery men with 2 howitzers, 39 marines, and a band of music, with officers in charge, left the ship in company with the boats of the *Powhatan*, with her marines, band, seamen & officers[,] and went on shore to receive the Commander-in-Chief. Four officers of this ship jointed his suite—he left the *Powhatan* at 12 M. precisely—and we saluted him as Ambassador with 17 guns. The Commodore had an interview with seven Princes, five of him [whom?] were the Treaty Commissioners. We have heard nothing that took place.

The Commander-in-Chief with his suite returned soon after four o'clock. Capt. Lee[,] in charge of the infantry, bands and marines, walked along the beach from the landing place to abreast of the ship where the boats were in waiting and brought them off. On Friday morning commenced coaling ship[62] from the *Supply*.

The *Southampton* arrived in the harbour on Saturday morning. She was hauled alongside the *Powhatan* and they commenced discharging her of her cargo.

On account of the disagreeable state of the weather yesterday morning we were prevented from having church. In the evening the *Macedonian* came in from sea and came to anchor a short distance astern of us.

Corp'l Riley left the ship this morning for Yokohama to assist in bringing the remains of [Robert] Williams (marine) late of this ship, to this place for interment.

Tuesday, June 13. The five Salibabooans which were picked up at sea by the U.S.S. *Southampton* and came on board this ship while we were laying at Macao, were today transferred to the *Macedonian*. She is expected to sail shortly for Manila via Formosa. From Manila, the Salibabooans will be able to reach the island to which they belong. The poor fellows appeared to be very sad when they parted with the ships company, who were nearly all at the gangway to see them over the side.

Thursday, June 15. The body of Williams[,] the marine, was today brought down from Yokohama and sent on shore for interment.

Saturday, June 17. Commodore Perry yesterday gave an invitation to Commissioners to come on board this ship to a performance of the *Powhatan's* Japanese Olio Minstrels.

The ship was beautifully dressed up with flags. The Commissioners (7 in number) came on board at 6 P.M. last evening with a large number of other Japanese officials. The concert commenced at 7 P.M. The minstrels performed about two hours—much to the amusement of the Japanese. The

Commodore had a collation set out in the cabin. For the Commissioners, who after the performance (judgeing [*sic*] from their appearance when they left at 10 o'clock) partook of the viands very freely. Quite a nice time, we had of it. The Commodore left a few moments after ten.

Nothing of much interest today. Received several men from the *Powhatan*.

Monday, June 19. The Commodore with his retinue of servants, etc., came on board last evening. We hoisted the Broad Pennant this morning, which makes us once again the flag ship.

Wednesday, June 21. The Japanese today returned our flags which were on the buoys in the harbour, and on which they have put their own national flags.

Friday, June 23. At 12.40—unmoored ship, hove up the anchor, got underway and stood outside and came to anchor in the mouth of the harbour. The *Powhatan* also came out a short distance. Three of our mess—[Walter F.] Jones, [K. Randolph] Reese & [Samuel W.] Williams were ordered to the *Macedonian* on special duty.

Saturday, June 24. The Japanese this evening brought off a number of birds & dogs, a present to the Commodore.

At Sea, Sunday, June 25. Quite early this morning got underway and waited off the mouth of the harbour of Shimoda, Japan[63] for the squadron to come out. At half past six the *Powhatan* came out with the *Southampton* in tow, the *Macedonian* being towed by Japanese boats. A gang of our men were on board the *Supply* to assist in getting her underway. The wind was sitting very strong into the harbour, so that the *Macedonian* & *Supply* were unable to get out, so they came to anchor. We received our men from the *Supply* and stood out to sea, in company with the *Powhatan* towing the *Southampton*.

Thursday, June 29. At daylight discovered land ahead. During the first part of the morning passed several islands. At 12 M. stopped the engine off the Island of O Shima and sent the 1st cutter & gig in charge of Lt. Maury & Actg. Lt. Webb. Went ashore for the purpose of ascertaining if there were any sort of a harbour to a town which [was] put down on a Japanese chart. The boats returned at half past three & reported the town to be a small one, with no harbour.

The natives (Lew Chewans) gave us a few[64] chickens and some potatoes. In return we gave them some pork & bread. At 4 o'clock started the engine and stood along the land, stopping at intervals to sound.

Friday, June 30. Stopped the engine today at 9 A.M. Capt. Boyle of the *Southampton* came on board; he received orders to proceed to Hong Kong. A letter bag was sent. We had but a few moments notice that the ship was going to sail and therefore only had time to write but a very few lines home. Capt. Boyle returned to his ship; she cast off from the *Powhatan*, made sail and stood to the N*d* & W*d*.

At 10 the Lew Chew Isld. (Great) in sight ahead. At 3.45 discovered a strange sail on port bow, standing towards us. She no sooner saw us then she changed her course & stood away. We altered ours and stood across her bow, a gun was fired for her to heave to; she then stood off further. We changed our course so as to cut her off, another gun was fired. She then wore round and stood for us, and hoisted English colours. Lowered the 1st cutter & gig and boarded her. Found her to be the English ship *Grt. Britain* from Shanghai bound to London. The Capt. of her said he thought it was all up with him when he first saw us, thinking we were the Russians, informing us at the same time that England and France had declared war against Russia and knowing that the Russian squadron were somewhere in these waters he took us for them. He sent the Commodore some late papers, and then stood off with his mind greatly relieved.

We are now at 8 P.M. in sight of the land with the port of Naha—Lew Chew about 30 miles off; as it is too late to run in tonight we will lay off and on.

Naha, Lew Chew, Saturday, July 1. About half past six this morning we discovered the *Lexington* at anchor in this harbour. We stood in and came to anchor at 8.50. We hear quite a lot of news here. A few days after we left for Japan the Russian Squadron were all in the harbour, their men were given liberty and behaved themselves well. They made a short stay and went off. No one knows where. Since the *Lexington* has been here her crew have been on shore. One of them was killed, by whom it is not known. Evidence seems to be against the Lew Chewans. We will have more particulars in a day or so. The Regent sent off as a present to the Commodore 1 bullock, 2 hogs, 2 goats, 150 eggs, 80 catties[65] sweet potatoes & 6 water melons.

Sunday, July 2. We had Divine Service at 11 A.M. and a sermon by the Rev*d*. Mr. Morton[,][66] an English missionary stationed at this place (he came here during our visit to Japan) to relieve Dr. Bettelheim. Dr. B's wife & children left in the *Supply* in February last for Shanghai. Dr B. remained for the purpose of teaching Mr. Morton the language. Mr. M. has with him his wife and a little boy. They appear to be very pleasant people.

This day I close this book, I know that there are a great many mistakes in it, such as misspelt words, words left out & tautology. I have endeavoured to please myself. I do not know how it will please others, hope, well.

FINIS

Wm. Speiden Jr.

4

Volume Two: 1854

—⁓—

Naha, Lew Chew, Monday, July 3. Commenced coaling ship from the depot on shore—with native boats. Jno. B. Smith & Geo. Scott were brought on board, prisoners from the *Lexington*.

Scott, it has been found out, was concerned in the affray which led to the death of Wm. Board,[1] by some of the Lew Chewans. Investigations are now being made by the authorities to find out the murderer.

Tuesday, July 4. When all hands were called this morning, "spliced the main brace." At eight o'clock hoisted the American Ensign at the fore and mizzen, in honor of the day. At eleven all hands were called on the Forecastle and the "Declaration of Independence" was read by Henry Smith—Gr. Mt. The "Star spangled Banner," sung by Hugh McEver—C.H. "Hail Columbia" played by the band. Recitation, "America my native home," by McEver, and "Yankee Doodle," by the band.

At Meridian fired a salute of 17 guns & at supper time served an extra Tot, to old Jack, by order of the Commodore.

Wednesday, July 5. A Court Martial convened on board the *Powhatan* for the trial of Geo. Scott, and 3rd Asst. Eng. LeRoy Arnold.[2]

Thursday, July 6. This evening sent on shore, a sergeant, corporel [*sic*] and twelve privates, in charge Capt. Tansil[3] [to] take possession of the Ameku

Dera[,] a place formally [formerly] used as a hospital for the squadron. This step was taken by the Commodore to intimidate the authorities, and cause them to make stronger efforts to find out the murderer of the man, Board.

Friday, July 7. Preparations were made this morning to land all the marines and one howitzer and take further possessions. A few moments after twelve, the Regent came on board with his suite, bringing with him a man who had been found guilty by the Laws of Lew Chew of being the murderer.

An interview was held in the Cabin between the Commodore and Regent, which lasted until half past two, and we then heard the result.

This man being found guilty was brought off and delivered over to us to do with him as we pleased. The Commodore told the Regent, that under the aggravating circumstances which caused the Lew Chewan to commit the murder, he would allow the authorities to punish the prisoner in the same manner as if he had murdered one of his own people under the same causes—which would be, as they said, Banishment to some uninhabited island for life.

At three the Regent returned to the shore, taking with him the murderer, whose hands were fastened behind him with a piece of rattan and was led by a rope fastened to his hands, and had a guard of four Lew Chewans over him. The poor fellow looked as if his time had come, and seemed greatly relieved when he found himself being taken away from the ship.

This evening the marines gave up the place they had taken and returned on board ship.

Saturday, July 8. Before noon today called all hands to muster and read the sentence of a Court Martial in the case of Mr. Arnold, Eng—he was afterwards detached from this ship and ordered to the *Powhatan*.

Sunday, July 9. We had Divine Service today at eleven o'clock, and a sermon by the Revd. Dr. B. J. Bettelheim.

Tuesday, July 11. This morning a number of agricultural implements were sent on shore as a present to the Prince Regent. At 1 o'clock, Commodore Perry and suite paid an official visit to the Regent, escorted by the marines

& band of this ship and the *Powhatan*. A compact was made between the United States & Lew Chew, and was signed. Herewith is a copy.[4] At sundown the Commodore and suite returned.

Wednesday, July 12. Sent ashore today to the Rev. Mr. Morton a present of some agricultural implements and some provisions.

Received from the Lew Chewan authorities a large bell, a present to our Government.

Thursday, July 13. Finished coaling ship today. During the day quite a number of Japanese junks have sailed from this place.

Friday, July 14. This evening Commodore Perry gave an entertainment to the Regent, before which we had an Etheopic Entertainment by the "Nightingale Minstrels" of this ship. Nearly all the Officials from shore were present besides a great number of the native[s]. Mr. Morton and family were also on board—a nice time we had. Annexed is a Programme of the Etheopic Concert.[5]

Saturday, July 15. The U.S. storeship *Lexington* sailed today for Hong Kong. Sent our 1st cutter to assist in towing her clear of the reefs.

Sunday, July 16. We had a sermon today by the Rev. Mr. Morton, English Missionary to this place & successer [*sic*] of Dr. Bettelheim.

At Sea, Monday, July 17. Good bye to old Lew Chew and may I never see thee more. At half past five this morning we got underway in company with the *Powhatan* and stood out of the harbor of Naha, Lew Chew. The *Powhatan* was ordered to proceed over to Ning Po & Amoy[6] and about 11 o'clock we lost sight of her. Dr. Bettelheim left Lew Chew in the *Powhatan* for passage to Hong Kong. Having a head wind this evening sent down topgallant masts & lower yards.

At anchor in the Lima [Lymoon] Passage, Friday, July 21. Nothing of much interest has transpired in the last few days. We have had beautiful weather, with the sea as smooth as a mill pond.

At a quarter past two P.M. we discovered land, and soon after took a pilot on board, and at half past nine[,] not being able to run into Hong Kong, we came to anchor in this place.

Victoria, Hong Kong, Saturday, July 22. At five o'clock this morning we got underway and stood through the Hong Kong passage for this place, and a quarter before eight we came to anchor in this harbor. We find here the Sloop of War *Plymouth*, Surveying Brig *Porpoise* and store ship *Southampton*, also the English Frigate *Winchester* and the usual Merchant Fleet.

The *Plymouth* saluted the Broad Pennant of Commodore M. C. Perry, with 13 guns. We returned it with 9.

A boat from the *Winchester* came alongside with the usual compliments.

At Meridian, hoisted the English flag at the fore, and saluted the town with 21 guns, which was returned gun for gun from the Fort on shore.

The U.S. Consul[7] and Governor of Hong Kong visited the ship. Saluted the former on his leaving with 9 guns, and the latter with 17.

We had the pleasure today of receiving our letters from home, latest dates were April 16th. All well.

Victoria, H.K., Sunday, July 23. H.B.M. Frigate *Winchester* went to sea this morning. At noon arrived the English Frigate *Spartan* from a cruise after pirates. Allowed a number of the crew to go on liberty on board the different vessels.

Blenheim Reach, Tuesday, July 25. At 6 o'clock this morning we got underway and stood out of the harbor of Victoria, H.K.

Coming up the river we passed the U.S. Surveying Schooner *J. Fennimore* [*sic*] *Cooper*,[8] bound up. We came to anchor at half past two. The Sloop of War *Vincennes*[9] is at anchor in the American Reach.[10] While below at Hong Kong we heard that the Rebels were expected to attack Canton, and we have come up for the purpose of sending assistance to the American residents at that place. This evening sent No. 3 howitzer, with crew, up to Canton in charge of Lieut. Clitz.

Wednesday, July 26. The U.S. Steam Tender *Queen* arrived down this morning from Canton. Sent on board of her two howitzers and 40 men, also thirty marines under charge of Capt. Tansil. Commodore Perry and suite also went on board and at 9 the *Queen* got underway and proceeded up the river. At meridian the *Vincennes* went down the river to Macao.

This evening the U.S. Surveying Steamer *Jno. Hancock*[11] passed us bound down to Macao.

Thursday, July 27. The *Fennimore Cooper* arrived here today and anchored near us. Sent the 1st & 2d cutters to Canton. This evening Commodore Perry and suite returned to the ship.

Victoria, H. K., Friday, July 28. At eleven A.M. we got underway, took the *Fennimore Cooper* in tow, and stood down the Canton River. About half past four cast off the *Cooper*; she made sail and stood in for Macao Roads. We passed through the Capsingmoon [Cum Sing Moon] Passage and at 7½ o'clock anchored in the harbour.

Victoria, Saturday, July 29. This morning sent the stones which we brought from Shimoda, Japan, and Naha, Lew Chew—as specemins [*sic*] for the Washington Monument—to the *Plymouth*. Also sent on board of her the birds and dogs[12] which were presented by the Emperor of Japan to our Government, with Y. D. Reeves—Lds. [Landsman]—to take care of them to the United States.

This evening the *Plymouth* got underway and left the harbor bound home. As she passed us cheered ship—she saluted Commodore Perry with 13 guns, which we returned with nine.

Received stores on board today for the different departments. The *Hancock* arrived tonight from Macao.

Macao Roads, Monday, July 31. Commodore Perry this morning visited the English Frigate *Spartan*. On leaving he was saluted with thirteen guns. At half past one we got underway and stood through Green Island Passage[13] for this place.

Passed the French Frigate *Jean D'Arc*[14]—cheered ship, lowered the boats and saluted the Admiral with 15 guns, which was returned with an equal number. A little before 7 P.M. we came to anchor, the *Vincennes* at anchor inshore of us.

On shore, Macao, Wednesday, August 2. I came on shore yesterday morning, and last evening attended a very pleasant party at Capt. Endicott's—our Band was there, besides a number of our officers. I met nearly all my old friends, and had a very nice time. I stopped last night at the Union Hotel with Father.

This morning Capt. Lee gave me charge of the band to take off to the Ship, in our Compradore's [*sic*] fast boat. It was blowing very hard indeed. I however got the bandsmen in the boat (half of them were beastly drunk) and started for the Ship. Capt. Lee at the same time, with several of the officers, in the Ship's fast boat, started. I did not much relish the idea of going to the Ship in such a small boat, with seasick bandsmen, blowing terrifically to[o]. After getting out some distance, I found that instead of nearing the ship we were blown farther off. I then told the Chinaman who was steering the boat, to look and see where the other fast boat was. He immediately answered, "She have go back shore sir." I then said—["]John you go shore too,["] for I well knew that if the ship's fast boat had given up the attempt to reach the ship, there was no use in my trying to do so in a smaller boat. When I reached the shore, or at least the anchorage for the fast boats, I took a Sampan and went alongside the ship's fast boat and reported to Capt. Lee the circumstances, gave the bandsmen in his charge and told him that I was not going to risk my life by attempting to go off again, and so saying, came ashore, found Father at Mr. Goodridge's, where we are both now stopping. After putting on a dry suite [*sic*] of clothes[,] for I got ringing [*sic*] wet, I told my tale to Father, and he told me his, which was that he had started to go off with Capt. Lee, but on getting back to the anchorage he had come to the same resolution that I did and accordingly got into a sampan to go ashore. On getting to the beach, one has to be very alert, and jump at the right moment. Father however jumped too quickly, and went, went where? Overboard, and the sampan passed over him. Fortunately the water was shallow and he got out safely with only a good ducking. This would have been all well enough, but unfortunately, one of his lady friends, looking from her corridore [*sic*] beheld this laughable accident befall him. It caused many a good laugh.

This evening Captain Lee managed to reached [*sic*] the ship, and she was soon after underway and went up to Cum Sing Moon.

Cum Sing Moon, Friday, August 4. In company with a number of our officers I left Macao this morning and came up to this place in the steamer *Hong Kong*. We had to remain several hours on board of her before a boat from our ship was able[,] on account of the heavy sea, to come and take us aboard.

This evening the weather has moderated a little. Sent up the topmasts and lower yards. They were sent down on the way up here.

Saturday, August 5. The Steamer *John Hancock* arrived today from Hong Kong. The weather has been rainy & disagreeable.

Sunday, August 6. The *Hancock* left the harbor this morning at 11 A.M. Mustered the crew and read the articles of war, also the finding and sentence of a Court Martial in the case of Jno. B. Smith Sea[man]—(Bad conduct at Lew Chew) which was carried into effect. This evening allowed 15 men to go ashore. At sundown all of them returned with the exception of Jno. Lobson Qr. Gr. [Quarter Gunner]. Two of the crew swam ashore and back, smuggling liquor. A number of men from the *Vincennes* came aboard on liberty.

Macao Roads, Thursday, August 10. Yesterday morning at a quarter past eleven our ship got underway and stood out of Cum Sing Moon harbor, and about a quarter before two, came to anchor in the Roads. I came on shore this morning and am now stopping at Mr. Goodridge's with Father, having a pleasant time. The *Fennimore Cooper* went to sea this morning.

Blenheim Reach, Friday, August 11. Returned on board early this morning. At 7 o'clock we got underway from Macao Roads and stood up the Canton River. At Meridian passed the Bogue, and at 2 P.M. came to anchor in this place.

Commodore Perry and suite left in our fast boat for Canton. Sent the 1st cutter armed as an escort to him. At four o'clock a heavy squall came up, accompanied with rain, thunder and lightning. The lightning struck the mainmast and ran down the main conducter [*sic*], doing no injury. One or two vessels in the American Reach were also struck, and two others without ballast were nearly capsized. Several Chinese boats sustained some considerable damage. At Bamboo Town[15] several houses were blown down, and the roofs were taken off of several others.

When the squall first came up, I was on my way up to Bamboo Town, in the 2d cutter, with our carpenter, going up on some business. We got thoroughly drenched, and were obliged to put in shore and take shelter in a small house built on the water, where we expected every moment to be carried away.

Saturday, August 12. The U.S. Steam Frigate *Susquehanna* arrived here today from Shanghai. This is the first time we have seen her since she left Yedo [Edo] Bay on 25th March last.

The *Hancock* passed us this evening bound up to Canton.

At anchor in the Canton River, below the 1st Pagoda, Monday, August 14. The last two or three days have been employed caulking ship. Yesterday sent the 1st & 2nd cutters to Canton. Today they returned, bringing down the marine guard, which has been up there to protect the American merchants. At half past three P.M. we got underway and stood down the river in company with the *Susquehanna*. At 5½ we came to anchor in this place and the *Susquehanna* continued on down.

Victoria, Hong Kong, Tuesday, August 15. At half past ten this morning the steamer *Jno. Hancock* arrived alongside from Canton. Com. Perry and suite with all the men who were up at Canton came aboard and we then got underway and stood down and came to anchor in this harbor near six o'clock.

Found the *Powhatan, Vincennes, Porpoise, Southampton* & *Lexington* in Port, besides several of the English Squadron.

Tuesday, August 22. During the last week we have been receiving provisions and stores on board for the different departments, allowing men to go on liberty, watering ship and lots of other things unnecessary to mention.

The *J. P. Kennedy*[16] (store ship of the surveying squadron—condemned) got underway in tow of the *Hancock* and went up to Canton.

This evening the Hon. R. McLane,[17] U.S. Commissioner to China, came on board to pay his respects. Hoisted the American Ensign at the fore & saluted him with 17 guns.

Macao Roads, Thursday, August 24. Yesterday forenoon, Mr. McLane, our Commissioner to China came on board for passage to Macao. At noon we got underway and came over, came to anchor at half past five. Com. Perry & Mr. McLane went on shore. Today crew employed scraping ship outside and setting up rigging. I came ashore this morning, and am again stopping at Mr. Goodridge's house. Mr G. went up to Canton with us on the 11th inst., and left the house in charge of Mr. Moses.[18] Father is here also and we are both enjoying ourselves very much.

Victoria, Hong Kong, Monday, August 28. At 10 A.M. yesterday Monsieur de Bourbillon [Bourboulon],[19] Minister Plenipotentiary from France, & Mr. McLane with Com. Perry came on board. Saluted the French Minister with 17 guns. Shortly after 10 we got underway and came over to this place and anchored a quarter before three o'clock. Mr. McLane & Mr. de Bourboulon went on shore. We find that the sloop of War *Macedonian* and store ship *Supply* have arrived during our absence.

Saturday, September 2. On Tuesday morning last, the clipper ship *Shooting Star*[20] was hauled alongside and we commenced discharging her of her coal. The same day Sir John Bowring,[21] Governor of Hong Kong[,] came on board. Hoisted the English colors and saluted him with 17 guns. Yesterday we finished coaling from the *Shooting Star*.

This morning Mr. McLane, U.S. Commissioner, went on board the *Powhatan*. She saluted him with 17 guns and then got underway and went over to Macao. At half past three the *Supply* got underway for the United States, cheered ship.

Monday, September 4. Shortly after 11 o'clock today, the Steamer *Susquehanna* got underway, took the *Southampton* in tow and stood out of the harbor. The *Susquehanna* saluted the Commodore with 13 guns, returned it with 9 guns— she cheered us, as also did the *Southampton*, returned the cheers.

They have gone to Japan on their way home, the *Southampton* filled with coal for the former vessel and us. At half past one we shifted our berth nearer in shore. Received a lighter of coal and commenced coaling ship from the store house.

Saturday, September 9. The steamer *Hancock* with the *Fennimore Cooper* went to sea this morning. This evening the U.S. store ship *Lexington* left for the United States.

Monday, September 11. Shortly after eleven o'clock today Commodore Perry and Flag Lieut. Bent left the ship to take passage home in British Mail Steamer *Ganges*,[22] via overland route. At 2 P.M. the *Ganges* got underway. We saluted Commodore Perry with 17 guns.

Hauled down the Broad Pennant and hoisted the coachwhip. It was intended that we should have gone to sea, but disagreeable weather prevented.

At Sea, Tuesday, September 12. At half past two this morning started the fires, and at a quarter past six got underway, with pilot on board and stood out of the harbor of Victoria, Hong Kong, through the Lymoon Passage.

The *Vincennes* & *Porpoise*[23] also underway. We are now fairly out to sea, with quite unpleasant weather, ship very deep, and not making over four knots. Summing up thoughts to see if I have any regrets at leaving China. I find I have none whatever, far from it. I am truly glad we have left. There are some few there that I should like and hope to see again, the majority of the foreign residents in China are a regular snobby sett [*sic*], put on a great many airs and are much above in their own estimation, their proper position. In mentioning Foreign Residents, I allude more particularly to the English.

The last we saw of the Pig-tail Celestials was our Pilot—Ashing, who after being paid his $30—Pilotage—left us at 8 A.M., with such a chin-chinning, beating of gongs, firing of crackers and guns. I find am wrong in stating that Ashing was the last of the "Glorious assemblage of Celestial Spirits"—for we have one of them on board whom I am going to take to the United States; he is now a waiter in our mess and we find him quite as useful as he is ornamental.

Shimoda, Japan, Thursday, September 21. We arrived here today at two o'clock, having made the passage in nine days and a few hours, having made the land quite early this morning. The *Susquehanna* and *Southampton* are both in the harbor, our passage up has been generally pleasant, with the exception of the first three days out from Hong Kong. The 2nd day out we passed the surveying steamer *Jno. Hancock* and surveying schooner *J. Fennimore Cooper*.

As we were entering the harbor, one of the Japanese pilots, who had been appointed for this port, came out to us in a small boat with an American Flag hoisted on a staff, close alongside a staff on which was the Japanese Custom House Flag. This looked very odd as one can well imagine; he came on board, but did not seem to understand what he had come for, as he stood still and stared at everything around him. We had no need of a pilot, as the entrance to the harbor was perfectly familiar. The *Susquehanna* is coaled and ready for sea.

At Sea, Sunday, October 1. At half past nine this morning, called all hands to muster, read the Articles of War and mustered the crew, after which performed Divine Service.

At a quarter before two we got underway with the *Southampton* in tow, and started to go out of the harbor of Shimoda. We were obliged however to back ship a little in order to clear Centre Island, and in doing so, fouled the *Southampton*, stove one of her quarter boats, and stove in our starboard head bulwarks. Let go an anchor, at 2.15, hove up and started again, parted the hawser, anchored again and sent another hawser. After a good deal of trouble, at three o'clock we managed to get out. Directly we got outside made sail to double reefed topsails, and at sundown cast off the *Southampton*.

The *Susquehanna* left Shimoda last Sunday morning for Honolulu; as she passed by us, cheered ship. On Friday morning the Lieutenant Governor of Shimoda, Is a Sintshiro,[24] & suit[e] visited the ship. Received him with the band & marine guard. Captain Lee gave him an entertainment in the cabin, and when the old fellow left, his head appeared to be wool-gathering.

Yesterday morning sent the band on shore to play for the Japanese. As soon as the band commenced playing, the people all rushed from their houses with one accord, and thousands followed it round the town. It was quite a pretty sight and all the inhabitants were very much pleased. Several of our officers were on shore, who did not know the band was coming, and they noticed every now and then some of the little children come up to them and blow with their hands, and make all sorts of signs, imitating the musicians, and they did not understand what the little rascals meant until they heard the band play; how on earth they found out the band was coming, no one could tell, as it was only known on board but a few moments before the band left. While on shore they went into the Temple yard and played a few tunes for the Lieut. Governor; he treated them to tea & grapes. While in the yard a large quantity of grapes were brought in, a present from the people.

Our visit to Japan this time has been an exceedingly pleasant one. The people were more friendly, and everything seemed to have undergone a great change. They were more willing to sell to us, and even came out into the streets and invited us by signs to come into their stores. A bazaar was open in the Temple during the whole of our stay. I went on shore nearly every evening, called on my old friends, who were exceedingly glad to see me. One of the families, Dr. Watanabe Tayarn and his wife, "Phfsar," became very fond of me, and would not let me go away without accepting some little token of remembrance.

The last of the officials who were on board, as they were leaving for shore, and as we stood out of the harbor of Shimoda, waved their handkerchiefs and hands to us in regular civilized style.

Directly we got outside the harbor, the wind began to blow very strong.

Honolulu, Oahu, Sandwich Is.,[25] **Tuesday [Monday], October 23.** We arrived here today twenty three days from Shimoda, Japan. We discovered land quite early this morning. A number of native boats came out to meet us. We find in the harbor the steamer *Susquehanna*, the sloops of war *Portsmouth* and *St. Mary's*,[26] an English and French frigate, besides a large number of whalers and merchantmen.

We are thankful to be once again safely anchored in port, after experiencing what we have in the run over from Japan. The greater part of our passage has been very unpleasant.

On the 7th inst. we experienced a cyclone, or in other words, a storm which you seldom read about. It used us up considerably, we had a most awful time and never expected to reach port again. The sea was so heavy and the ship rolled so, that one of the large bow guns was capsized on the deck. A greater part of our port wheelhouse was carried away, lost the port whaleboat & port dingy. All the head rail was stove in and the head bulwarks pretty well smashed. The gale lasted most furiously for about three hours. The barometer fell to 29.7"—lowest. You could scarcely hear yourself talk on deck, and all felt greatly relieved when we found it moderating.[27]

The next day we had a strong wind directly after us, carried away our fore topgallant mast, saved the yard and sail, and lost the main topgallant sail during a squall. Notwithstanding the disagreeableness of the weather we made the passage over in a day and a half[,] less time than the *Susquehanna*. She had beautiful weather all the way.[28]

Tuesday, October 24. At eleven o'clock today in company with a number of our officers, and officers from the other vessels, I attended a presentation to the King of the Sandwich Islands, King Kamehameha III.[29] His Majesty's black self did not appear to be in the most agreeable humor to receive visitors, for he had but slightly gotten over an accustomed good spree, which he had been on for a week past. There was nothing of much interest attending the visit, only I have it to say that I paid my respects to a King.

Friday, October 27. Yesterday morning at 9 o'clock, we hoisted the Hawaiian Ensign at the fore and saluted the town with 21 guns, which was returned with an equal number from the Fort on Punchbowl Hill.[30] At noon the Governor of Honolulu[31] visited the ship. At 3 P.M. his Majesty—King Kamehameha III—visited the *Susquehanna*. She, with the *Portsmouth, St. Mary's,* & the English & French frigates, hoisted the Hawaiian Flag, manned yards, and saluted him with 21 guns each. After leaving the *Susquehanna*, His Majesty visited the *St. Mary's* where he got gloriously tight. A large ball was given last night on board the *St. Mary's* and a nice time we had.

Monday, October 30. At half past one today the *Susquehanna* got underway and stood out to sea on an excursion with King Kamehameha on board. At half past three she came in to the entrance of the harbor, the King left her under a salute of 21 guns; she then stood out to sea, and off for San Francisco, California. The King on his return, on passing by the different men of war in the harbor[,] was cheered.

Sunday, November 5. At 10 today mustered the crew and read the Articles of War, after which we had Divine Service. A number of Ladies and gentlemen from shore attended.

This evening discovered the U.S. Store Ship *Southampton* in the offing.

Monday, November 6. This morning at half past nine, performed the burial service over the body of Private of Marines Wm. Miller, and send [*sic*] the corpse on shore for interment, escorted by a Corporel's [*sic*] guard. The *Southampton* came in today and anchored.

Wednesday, November 8. At ten o'clock today the American Commissioner Mr. Gregg visited the ship, received him with all the honors and a salute of 17 guns. Between ten and eleven the following officials visited the ship, viz., French Consul General of the Hawaiian Islands, who was saluted with 13 guns—the Peruvian Consul, with 9 guns—Danish Consul with 9 do— Bremen Consul, with 9 do—& American Consul[32] with 9 do, all of whom were received with all due honors. At eleven the Governor of Honolulu & suite, accompanied by the Minister of Foreign Affairs and Minster of Finance, visited the ship.[33] Hoisted the American Ensigns at the fore and mizzen, and the Hawaiian ensign at the main and fired a salute of 17 guns. A large number of Ladies and Gentlemen were on board. Beat to quarters and inspected the ship. Saluted the Governor and suite on leaving with the same number of guns as was given when they came on board.

At Sea, Thursday, November 9. We have just left Honolulu, a place I should desire soon to visit again. I have left some very dear friends. I have never visited a place where I enjoyed myself so much and spent such an agreeable time, and my regrets at leaving are far greater than the pleasure I enjoyed while there.

Arrived there we did on the 23rd of last month, and left the harbor this morning at 9 A.M.—sixteen days stay, actually sixteen, but it has appeared to me like a short week. Every evening I went on shore and visited different friends that I had made. From three to five o'clock was the usual time I visited the shore, and returned on board between ten and twelve—generally an absence of seven hours, but that seven hours never appeared to be longer than three or four spent on board ship. What cause it can be attributed to, I hesitate to say.

The family where my visits were most frequent during the latter part of our stay was Mr. A. . . . ,[34] Prime Minister to the King. The attraction there of course being the female portion of the family. It is unnecessary for me to give names or description of those or the one proper to whom I refer, for the impressions are too well laid in my mind ever to be rubbed out, and I know it will be no gratification to anyone else to know. I made an agreeable acquaintance with many others, the kindness of whom will ever imprint their names on my memory.

I saw nothing of any great interest during our stay. I took several rides into the country, one evening on horseback in company with Sam—a [Samia?]. This ride used me up considerable. We were from the day we arrived until two days ago employed coaling ship, and repairing damages received by the cyclone of the 7th ulto.

"Stone House" was the last place I saw with the spyglass, having kept my eye upon it until such objects as a house became quite invisible to the naked eye as well as to the glass.

We are now off for San Francisco with a head wind, going between six and seven knots.

San Francisco, California, Tuesday, November 21. At daylight this morning discovered land on both bows, at eleven o'clock made a pilot boat under the land and soon after received a pilot on board and stood in for the Golden Gate.[35] At half past eleven discovered the steamer *Susquehanna* lying off the city, exchanged numbers with her. At one o'clock we came to anchor in this harbor, near the *Susquehanna* and surveying steamer *Active*.[36]

We have had quite an unpleasant passage over from Honolulu. On the 16th inst. we encountered quite a severe gale. Barometer 29.45". We had to stop several times during the passage over to tighten the key of the crank pin.[37]

Find no letters from home, too bad.

Wednesday, November 22. On shore—Several Ladies visited the ship today and a great many gentlemen. Made the acquaintance of Mr. T. O. Larkin[38] and family. I am now staying at his house. This evening took a long ride all over San Francisco with Tom Larkin. Enjoyed the drive very much. I do not find San Francisco to exceed my expectations, although it is a great city, for so short a time since it was first settled.

Among the Ladies on board this morning was Mrs. Hooper[,] an old friend of Father's. Called at her house this evening.

Thursday, November 23. Again on shore; went on board this morning after breakfast, came ashore in the 3 P.M. boat—met Father in Jackson St., talking to Mr. Larkin. He handed me two letters from home, good news, which makes me feel in good spirits. Went to the Bacchus Minstrels[39] tonight, very much pleased.

Benicia,[40] California, Friday, November 24. I returned on board this morning having spent a very pleasant time on shore.

About half past eleven Lieutenant Governor Purdy[41] with a party of Ladies came on board, received him with a salute of 15 guns with the usual honors. At 12.10—called all hands and hove up the anchor and made a circuit around the harbor of San Francisco. At one o'clock Lt. Gov. Purdy and party left the ship. Started ahead fast with a pilot on board and stood up for this place. At 4 P.M. we anchored off this town in the Straits of Carquinez,[42] abreast of the Pacific Mail Steam Ship Company[']s Works.[43]

At Sea, Saturday, December 16. At 1 P.M. today started the fires, hoisted the Jack and received a pilot. At 2, fired a gun and hoisted the Cornet, for all persons attached to the ship to come on board, and at half past three hove up the anchor, got underway and stood out of the harbor of San

Francisco, California. At twenty minutes past four, discharged our pilot outside of Golden Gate.

It is necessary now to give some account of our stay in California, as by my remarks before, the ship has arrived at Benicia and has just left San Francisco without my mentioning what occurred between times.

The day of our arrival in Benicia Father went on shore, and took passage in the steamer *Queen City*[44] to Sacramento, for the purpose of paying a visit to my Aunt and Uncle[45] at that place. The next day I received a message from him, directing me to meet him at the landing place of the steamer on Monday evening (27th ulto.) and be all ready to continue down to San Francisco with my uncle. I was at the boat according to appointment, and found Father and Uncle Clement standing at the gangway. I went on board and shook hands with them. Father then asked me if I was all ready to continue down. I told him yes, he then bid us good bye and went on shore and returned to the ship. I then went up into the Cabin of the *Queen City* with Uncle C. He introduced me to the Captain, Capt. Barclay. After talking with him a few moments, he politely presented me with a ticket for passage to San Francisco. We arrived there about half past nine the same night, and instead of going on shore to a hotel we concluded to sleep on board the boat that night. We however went up town to a restaurant and got a light supper of oyesters [*sic*], for which we were charged the small sum of four pasos [pesos]. After taking breakfast on board the boat next morning, we went on shore and walked up to Wilsons Exchange,[46] where we took a room. My Uncle[,] feeling a little unwell, laid down, and I went off to take a walk. While out I met Tom Larkin. He asked me how long I intended remaining down. I told him three or four days, whereupon he insisted on my going and stay[ing] at his house, which invitation I accepted with pleasure, and which added considerable to the pleasure of my visit.

The intention of my Uncle's going to San F. was to meet his wife, my aunt, who had been staying for a short time in San Jose. He had previously sent her a despatch, telling her to meet him on the 29th, in San F. On Wednesday the 29th we accordingly went down to the wharf at which the San Jose boat usually stopped. At the hour at which she generally arrived, found the boat had arrived, went on board and inquired of the Clerk if Mrs. Coote had come up from San Jose. He told us that no lady of that name had come up, and that all the Ladies who did come up, were with gentlemen and had all gone on shore. We then walked out to Capt. Gray's, where my Aunt generally stayed when in San F., but found that she had not been there, and then of course came to the conclusion that she had not come up. After walking back to the hotel with my Uncle, I went to the telegraph office to send a despatch to San Jose, to inquire what time she intended coming up. The clerk[,] as soon as he read the message, told me that there was a Lady of that name down on board the steamer *Guadaloupe* very uneasy about her husband. I thanked him and ran round to the hotel and told Uncle Clement this, and said that I would run fast down to the boat, [and] see Aunt Sarah as quick as possible, so that she should not be kept in an uneasy state any longer than was actually necessary. I found her on board the boat, sitting in the captain's cabin. She told me she had laughed and cried and cried and laughed, until she did not know what to do. In a few moments Uncle C. came down to the boat and things were soon set right.

We remained in San Francisco until Friday evening (1st inst.) when we went on board the steamer *Willhamet* and took passage up to Sacramento City. We arrived there after midnight, the distance being 120 miles. Went on shore the next morning. I took a room at Jones' Hotel, and my aunt and uncle went to their own house.

That day with my uncle took a long ride into the country, went some distance up the American River,[47] saw where the gold was first discovered, and saw some Americans digging and washing gold. While out we enjoyed an excellent dinner at Patterson's Hotel, and returned in town about dusk the same evening, having on the way stopped at a beautiful garden where I obtained a pretty bo[u]quet of flowers.

The next morning quite early I was aroused by a rap at the door of my room, and on getting up to see who it was found Father there. All that morning (Sunday) I suffered dreadfully with the toothache & resolved to have it extracted, so went with my uncle to Dr. Thomas,[48] the best dentist in Sacramento. He looked at my teeth and told me that the one which ached was caused by one on the lower jaw being decayed, and advised me to let him plug the upper and extract the lower. The upper was very soon plugged and he started to extract the lower. The forceps were accordingly put upon the tooth, and in attempting to draw it, it broke off close to the gums. I knew how painful it would be taking the roots out, so I told him to administer chloroform, and the roots were extracted without my feeling it, and it was not for several minutes after the effects of the chloroform wore off that I knew it was entirely gone. It was a great relief, and I did not say anything when I saw an X passing from my Porte Monnaie into the doctor's pocket, with the sound of thank you on my ears.

That day Father and I were invited to dine at my Uncle's. It was unfortunate for me for just having had a tooth pulled I could not do justice to a most excellent dinner which we sat down to.

The next day we bid them good bye, and at 2 P.M. left Sacramento in the *Queen City* and arrived down at Benicia about seven o'clock the same evening.

We remained on shore that night, made the acquaintance of Capt. Walsh and family. We returned on board ship next morning, found they had finished coaling ship and were fast progressing with the work on the machinery, it having been necessary to make a new crank pin for starboard engine.

During our stay at Benicia we had a number of ladies on board to visit the ship, nearly every day. A great many parties were given on shore to which the officers were always invited. On Friday evening the 8th inst., a regular Pike County Ball was given at Martinez,[49] a little village across the straits from Benicia. Part of our band were there and a fine time we had. Kept it up until five o'clock the next morning. The same day (8th) Major General Wool,[50] commanding the Western Division of the Army, and suite visited the ship. Hoisted the American Flag at the fore and saluted him with 13 guns. While he was on board inspected the crew at Quarters.

On the morning of the 13th inst. we bid farewell to our friends at Benicia, and at 11.20 hove up and stood down the bay for San Francisco, and at half past two came to anchor in that harbor. Immediately on our arrival commenced filling up with water, and taking in provisions, which we were not able to obtain from the Naval Store at the Navy Yard on Mare Island,[51] five miles from Benicia. Benicia is about 30 miles from San Francisco.

Each day of our stay in San F. we had a number of Ladies and Gentlemen on board, and there were even some came alongside to come on board just as we were getting underway. The wharfs were crowded with thousands of people as we passed out, and such a waving of hats and handkerchiefs we have never seen, and all I have to add in conclusion to these remarks, is, that our visit to California will ever be looked back to with a great degree of pleasure.

While in California we lost 17 or 18 men by desertion and discharged 5 or 6, the term of their enlistment being up.

Monday, December 18. Sunday yesterday was, and at eleven A.M. we had Divine Service. Today Acting Master Jno. Kell[52] was appointed an Acting Lieutenant and Passed Midshipman J. H. March was appointed Acting Master of this ship.

Sold today at auction the effects of the deserters. This evening discovered the light of a vessel on our starboard bow.

5

Volume Two: 1855

—

Taboga Island,[1] **12 miles from Panama N. Y. [Naval Yard], Wednesday, January 3.** At half past six this morning, made Chama[2] and Taboga Is. ahead on port bow. All day yesterday we were standing along the land, up Panama Bay. At meridian came to off this place. We have made the passage down in seventeen days and twenty hours, very pleasant weather with the exception of one or two days off the Bay of Tahauntepec [Tehauntepec].[3] Christmas passed off quietly, as did New Year's day. The night before New Years was as lovely a night as I ever saw. I sat up until seven bells and was just about going to sleep when it struck eight bells, 12 o'clock—and the information of the fact that the New Year had begun. The strains of sweet music was heard, and our band played three of as pretty pieces of music as I ever listened to, and never could it have had a greater effect upon one, and was much inclined to make me wish myself at home. New Year's night we had part of the band on the main deck, & a party of us got together and danced for an hour or so, and had quite a merry time.

At Sea, Friday, January 12. This morning at half past five found us underway standing out of Taboga harbor down Panama Bay.

We had a very pleasant time during our stay there. The day after our arrival, in company with three of my new mates and Mr. Munroe, agent of the P.M.S.S. Co., I went up to the city of Panama in the 1st cutter to see after the letters. Found none from home. We left Panama the same evening and could not form a very favorable opinion of the place, as it was raining nearly all the time. We however visited the Cathedral, where they were holding grand mass in honor of General Herara,[4] a Spanish general who was killed recently at Taboga, just as he had finished quelling a revolution among the people. We also visited the Jesuit's College, which is now in ruins.

We made the acquaintance of the acting American Consul, Mr. Boyd—who we found to be a very clever gentleman, and did all in his power to make our time pass as pleasantly as possible. We also met several Spanish ladies, wives of American merchants in Panama.

Last Friday evening the little steamer *Young American* was launched at Taboga. She went off the stocks beautifully. Night before last a party was given on board the steamer *Panama* by Captain McLain.[5] A number of ladies were there from Panama. They came up in the *Young America*. Just as she got to the entrance of Taboga harbor her cylinder cover blew off into pieces; fortunately no one was hurt. The party passed off very pleasantly.

Yesterday morning, although we were dirty with coal dust, the ladies and gentlemen who were at the party visited the ship. The American and Portuguese Consuls[6] were among them. Saluted them each with 9 guns. At two o'clock the party left and went on board the steamer *Columbus*[7] to take passage up to Panama.

Tuesday, January 16. Discovered the coast of South America today at 11 o'clock. This evening discovered an English steamer inshore of us, showed our colors. This evening one of Commodore Perry's Japanese cats, while playing about on the poop deck, saw fit to jump overboard to take a salt water bath. Kept away for her, lowered a boat and picked poor puss up, but sad to say she was alive and kicking. More annoyance for this. At 4.45 stood on our course.

Valparaiso, Chile, Thursday, February 1. Quite early this morning discovered land on port bow and beam, also saw several vessels. At half past seven discovered a tower resembling a lighthouse, bearing East; bore away and stood for it. At half past nine made the U.S. Frigate *St. Lawrence*,[8] bearing the broad pennant of Commodore Dulany,[9] and the U.S. sloop *John Adams*,[10] at anchor in this harbor. At ten A.M. we came to anchor in 31 fthms. water. Soon after saluted Com. Dulany with 13 guns which was returned with 7 do. Found the store ship *Fredonia*[11] and English Frigate *President*[12] in port, besides a large number of merchant vessels and three Chilean men-of-war. At half past eleven hoisted the Chilean Flag and saluted the town with 20 guns (a mistake, ought to have fired 21) which was returned with 21 guns from the fort on shore.

The American Consul[13] visited the *Jno. Adams*; on his leaving she saluted him with 9 guns.

We were agreeably surprised on receiving letters from home, although of not very recent dates. Aug. 2—all well however, which is a great satisfaction to learn in such a far off distant place.

Friday, February 2. The U.S. Razee[14] *Independence*, bearing the broad pennant of Commodore Mervine,[15] arrived today from Rio. She saluted Com. Dulany with 13 guns, which was returned gun for gun.

Saturday, February 3. At 8 A.M. the *Independence* hoisted the Chilean Flag and saluted the town with 21 guns, which was returned from the fort on shore with an equal number.

Sunday, February 4. Yesterday morning I went on shore for the first time since our arrival here. Remained on shore all night. Came off early this morning. Being the first Sunday in the month, of course the Rules and Regulations for the better government of the Navy were to be read, and general muster. The Captain's Clerk being on the Doctor's list, the former duty which devolves upon that gentleman, fell to my lot. It was my first time. I made no bones of it however, but read them off in a Demosthenes[-] like style, after which my accustomed duty of mustering the crew, which from long practice has become perfectly plain and easy. We then had Divine Service.

Early this morning the *Independence* shifted her berth ahead of the *Fredonia*.

Last evening made the acquaintance of the American Consul (Mr. Merwin) and family.

Tuesday, February 6. The English mail steamer arrived and brought us letters from home—Jany. 3rd—good news, all well.

Rear Admiral Bruce[16] arrived in the steamer. The Broad Pennant of the English was saluted by the *President* with 13 guns and then hauled down. Admiral Bruce then hoisted his flag on board the Eng Frigate *President* and she saluted him with 15 guns. The *St. Lawrence* and *Independence* both saluted with 13 guns, which the *President* returned with 13 guns each. Admiral Bruce then hoisted the Chilean Flag and saluted the town with 21 guns—which was returned.

Wednesday, February 7. The U.S. Frigate *St. Lawrence* got underway at 1 P.M. and stood out to sea, bound home. The *Independence, John Adams,* and this ship cheered, which was returned.

The English and French Consuls visited the *Independence*. She saluted them each with 9 guns with the different flags at the fore. Rear Admiral Bruce visited the *Independence*; she received him with a salute of 13, which the English flagship returned, with the same number.

As soon as the *St. Lawrence* was out of sight Commodore Mervine hauled down the Red Broad Pennant and hoisted the Blue, as Commander-in-Chief of the U.S. Naval Forces in the Pacific. The *John Adams,* this ship and the *President,* each saluted him with 13 guns, all of which she returned with 13 guns.

Friday, February 9. Finished coaling ship yesterday. Today at 11 the American Consul and Hawaiian Consul General[17] visited the ship, saluted them each with 9 guns.

At half past eleven Commodore Mervine visited the Frigate *President*; as he left she saluted him with 13 guns. He then visited this ship, and was received with a salute of 13 guns. A number of ladies and gentlemen have been on board during the day. We have had music and dancing and had a nice time.

At Sea, Saturday, February 10. Forenoon today hoisted in the "Ariel" and "Gig" & made preparations for getting underway. At 1 P.M. mustered the crew and found four men absent without permission. Struck their names off the ships Books as Deserters. At 1.20 started the fires. At half past four we got underway and stood out of the harbor of Valparaiso, Chile. The *Independence* and *John Adams* gave us three cheers which we returned. Sent down topgallant and made everything snug for sea.

Our stay in Valparaiso was quite pleasant; made the acquaintance of several families of American residents, by all of whom I was treated with a great deal of politeness. I had no opportunity of seeing much of the country about Valparaiso, as I did not once go out of the city limits, but enjoyed myself very much and shall always look back to our visit there with no small degree of pleasure.

Sunday, February 11. Sent down lower yards this morning, strong wind ahead.

At eleven called all hands to muster and read the sentence of a Court Martial in the case of three men for mutinous conduct, on board the *Independence* while in New York. Saw several sails during today.

Friday, February 16. Yesterday forenoon the wind came out fair and we made all sail and went along very nicely. During the night however it hauled ahead, and we are now again on our old snail's trot, six knots.[18]

I had forgotten to mention that a day or two before we got into Valparaiso, Master Sam Spooner, one of Commodore Perry's pet Japanese dogs took it into his head to kick the bucket, that is to die stone dead, and lo! and behold! this morning very early indeed, Madame Simoda was discovered to have departed this life, and gone to the land of Know Nothings. She was soon after however seen being tossed about upon the land of sea serpents.

Monsieur Yedo or Jeddo, the only one of the family left, has been running about all day with his rocky heart almost broken.[19]

Happy dogs to die,
  Upon the broad blue sea,
For there your bones will lie,
  Buried, and forever, be.

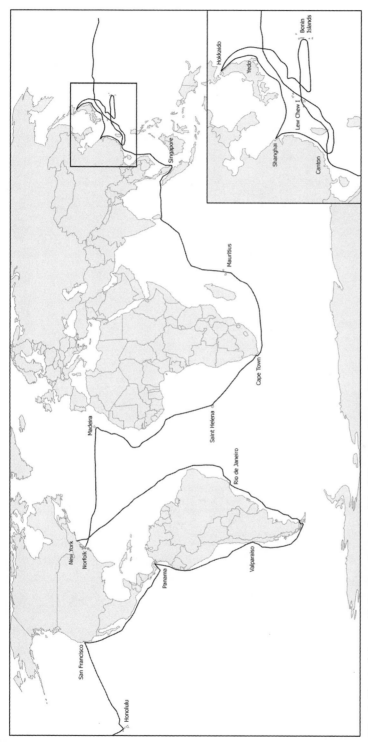

Map 5. Chart of the world showing the track of the U.S. steam frigates *Mississippi*, *Susquehanna*, and *Powhatan* as flagships of the Japan Squadron

Drawn by Alexander Paul Nohe, based on map held by the Library of Congress

APPENDIX A

General Orders

—∿∿—

No. 1
U.S. Steam Frigate *Mississippi*
At Sea December 21st 1852
General Order No 1

In promulgating the subjoined extract from the instructions addressed to me by the Hon'ble Secretary of the Navy, and bearing date the 13th Ultimo, I have to enjoin upon all Officers and other persons attached to the Vessels under my command, or in any other way connected with the Squadron, a most rigid adherence to all the requirements of said order.

Whatever notes, or drawings may be prepared by the Officers or other persons before mentioned, whether by special order or by their own volition, will be endorsed by the respective parties, and transmitted through the Capt. of the Fleet to the Commander-in-Chief, who will in due time lodge them at the Navy Department, from whence they may be reclaimed as it may suit the convenience of the Government.

All Arms, Curiosities and specemins [*sic*] of Natural History are also to become the property of the United States, unless voluntarily relinquished by the Commander-in-Chief.

M. C. Perry
Commander of the U.S. Naval Forces stationed in the East India, China & Japan Seas.

Extract

"A subject of great importance to the success of the Expedition, will present itself to your mind in relation to communication to the Prints & News Papers, touching the movements of your Squadron, as well as in relation to all matters connected with the discipline & internal regulations, of the Vessels composing it. You will therefore enjoin upon all under your command to abstain from writing to friends and others upon these subjects, the Journal and Private Notes of the Officers and other persons in the Expedition must be considered as belonging to the Government, until permission shall be received from the Navy Department to publish them."

To Commander S. S. Lee
U.S.S. *Mississippi*

No. 2
U.S. Steam Frigate *Mississippi*
At Sea December 23d 1852
General Order No 2

Entertaining the opinion that if the talents & acquirements of the Officers of the Squadron are properly developed and brought into action, they will be found equal to a plain & practical examination and elucidation of the various objects pertaining to the Arts and Sciences that may come under their observation during the present cruise & being aware of the limited accommodations of the vessels under my command, I have invariably objected to the employment of persons drawn from Civil Life to conduct those departments more immediately connected with science.

Therefore I have to request and to direct that each Officer of the respective Ships may employ such portions of his time as may be spared from his regular duties & proper hours of relaxation in contributing to the General mass of information which it is desirable to collect, and in order to simplify and methodize those researches, a paper is subjoined particularizing the various departments in reference to which information is more especially wanted, so that each Officer may select that or those departments which may seem most congenial to his tastes and inclinations.

All Captains & Commanders are required to render every facility consistant with the proper duties of their respective Vessels to those Officers, who may manifest a zealous cooperation in the persuits herein specified, and it is plainly to be understood that I do not officially require the Officers to perform any involuntary duty, I shall only exact that which may come legitimately within the sphere of my authority, leaving to the Officers themselves to engage as far as they may see fit in those investigations which may be considered in an official point of view, gratuitous.

And it will always give me the greatest pleasure to identify and bring to notice the labours of each and every individual who may contribute to the general work.

Signed M. C. Perry
Com'd'g East India Squadron

~ *Departments for Observations* ~
~ *referred to in General Order No 2* ~

1 Hydrography
2 Meterology, currents etc.
3 Naval Architecture, & its adaptations to war & commerce
4 Military Affairs
5 Geology & Geographical Observations
6 Terrestial Magnetism
7 Philology and Ethnology
8 Artistic Matters, Costumes etc.
9 Religeon [*sic*] of Nations
10 Diseases & Sanitary laws
11 Agricultural Observations
12 Statistics of Supplies
13 Mechanics as applied to Naval purposes
14 Infusorac and Marine Algae
15 Botany
16 Entomology
17 Ornithology
18 Zoology
19 Chonchology
20 Ichthiology
21 Magnetic Telegraph

No. 3

U.S. Steamer *Mississippi*
At Sea Jany 22d 1853
General Order No 3.

The regulation requiring that the Deck shall never be left, but in charge of a commissioned Officer is to be strictly enforced in the Squadron, so far as the contingencies of the service will allow; and when it becomes neccessary to put the Deck in charge of a Passed Midshipman, the authority can only be given by the Captain or Commander of the Vessel in which the contingency occurs, who is required to give such authority in writing, and the Officer so appointed is to be respected and obeyed as a commissioned Officer so long as he performed the duties appertaining to such grade.

> By order of the Commander-in-chief
> H. A. Adams
> Capt. of Fleet
> East India Squadron

No. 4

U.S.S. Frigate *Mississippi*
At Sea March 1st 1853
General Order No 4.

Reference is here made to the 20th Article of the laws for the better government of the Navy, approved April 23d 1850, in view of its being more rigidly observed,— For the better preservation of the health of the Petty Officers, Seamen & Marines belonging to the Ships & Vessels composing the East India Squadron, it is ordered that in no case are the Men to be allowed to sleep on deck, unless well protected by a good awning; & it is more especially forbidden that any person having the watch should be permitted to sleep during the period of such watch.

Commanders of Steamers may at their discretion and upon their own responsibility, put their respective crews into three watches, or may call a quarter watch at sea, when the men have been much fatigued.

Particular care should be observed in requiring the men to wear flannel next their skin, & at night either to wear a cloth jacket, or an additional blue flannel shirt with woollen trowsers.

As cleanliness of the body is essential to health, it is directed that every individual composing the respective crews shall bathe or was[h] their entire persons twice in each week, preparatory to their putting on clean flannel: say on the mornings of Sunday & Thursdays & the Officers of divisions, will report at the morning and evening musters at Quarters, any & every one, who be found without clean flannel.

The admission on board Ship of fruit or vegetables, whether for the use of the Officers or crew will, so far as regards their healthfulness or otherwise be under the supervision of the Medical Officers.

Experience has shown that the admissions of water in the Ship for purposes of purification of the hold, produces an effect contrary to that which has been expected—The better plan will be to remove as far as practicable the water that may find its way into the hold, first by the ordinary pumps, & then by those of smaller bore, made to reach the bottom plank or floor timbers; after which to send men into the pump wells (the passage to which should always be kept open) to bail & swab out that which will neaccessarily [*sic*] be left by the smaller pumps; & it is advisable to place in each pump well a quantity of Chloride of Lime.

For the better ventilation of the berth deck & orlops, the bags should be passed on deck whenever the weather will allow & the duties of the Ship will allow, & it is directed that each vessel shall have one or more stores placed on the berth deck, with safe stands lined with lead, & with paper leading up the hatches, to carry off the smoke. In the stoves, fires of coal are to be lighted every morning after the Decks are cleared for inspection, & to be kept burning until noon or 1 P.M. care being taken to have buckets of water at hand, in charge of one or more trust-worthy persons—other means of purification—such as the free use of the wind sail, fumigation &c, &c, will be constantly practised.

The Officers & Men are to be exposed as little to the sun & night air as the exigencies of the service will allow, & the practice of detaining boats on shore after dark, unless in cases of emergent duties of the service, is positively forbidden.

By order of the Commander-in-Chief
H. A. Adams
Capt. of the Fleet.

No. 5

U.S.S. Frigate *Mississippi*
At Sea March 5th 1853
General Order No 5.

As there is always great danger from fire in Steamers Cruising in warm latitudes, where all parts of the ship become dry & combustible, & the coal in the bunkers is the more liable to spontaneous combustion, it is ordered that in addition to the Deck fire buckets which are at all times to be kept filled, four fire tubs for the Deck of each Steamer & a tank for each fore & main top be provided, & be kept filled at sea & in port. And it is further ordered when Steamers are steaming against the wind at night, that additional buckets of water be placed on the Poop & Quarter Deck, & that all the fire apparatus be held in readiness for immediate use. It is also directed that the Sailing Ships of the East India Squadron, shall have fire tubs & tanks as above during their service on the station. The dimensions of the Deck fire tubs for Steamers must not be less than 3 ft. 6 in. long, 2 ft. wide & 1 ft. 8 in. deep.

By order of the Commander-in-Chief
H. A. Adams
Capt. of the Fleet

No. 6

U.S.S. Frigate *Mississippi*
At Sea March 5th 1853
General Order No 6.

The Commander of each Vessel in the East India Squadron is required to furnish to the Commander-in-Chief, in addition to the special Hydrographical report, a monthly report containing,—1st A tabular statement of the Barometer & Thermometer, taken every third hour, commencing at 3 A.M. The prevailing winds & the velocity direction of the current, when the Ship is cruising.—2nd An account of all Ports visited, direction for entering the Harbours, marks for the best anchorage, in what part wood & water can be most easily obtained & their quality. Notice of all Meteorological Phenomena, sketches of remarkable headlands and entrance to Port; & when the Latitude or Longitude of any place visited are ascertained to be given incorrectly in the Charts & Books, it must be specially mentioned. This report is to be prepared by the Sailing Master & after being examined and approved by the Commander of the Vessel is to be transmitted to the Commander-in-Chief through the Capt. of the Fleet.

By order of the Commander-in-Chief.
H. A. Adams.
Capt. of the Fleet

No. 7

Flag Ship *Mississippi*
Hong Kong April 11th 1853
General Order No 7.

As the East India Squadron is to be engaged in a special service of peculiar delicacy, it is ordered that no person be embarked on board any of the Vessels composing it, whether as passenger or otherwise, excepting persons holding Official stations under the Government of the United States, Pilots & recruited seamen. The order does not forbid the reception on board any vessel of the Squadron of persons of whatever sex or nation whose lives may be in danger or who may be found in distress at ports seldom frequented. In such cases when the Commander-in-Chief cannot be consulted, the Commanders of Vessels will exercise a proper discretion, never loosing [*sic*] sight of the claim of humanity, but guard'g against the importunity of those who apply to be taken on board for motives merely of convenience or pleasure.

By order of the Commander-in-Chief
H. A. Adams
Capt. of the Fleet

No. 8

Flag Ship *Mississippi*
April 14th 1853
General Order No 8.

The Boats of the Ships composing the East India Squadron when prepared for distant or active service are to be armed & provided in the following manner, & are always to be in readiness for a sudden call.

Anchor & Cable.

Spare Oars. (2)

Masts, Sails & Rigging.

Spun yarn & seizing stuff.

Battle Axes. (4)

1 Hand saw in each division

Screw driver, Nipple
   wrench, cleaning rags &
   oil for each boat.

1 Crow bar.

2 Blue lights, 2 Rockets, Candles
   (primed)

Boats colors and signals.

Oar Muffles—bandages &
   Laudanum for Wounded.

Flash Pan for each boat.

1 Wood axe. Spikes.

Bag, with hatchet, sheet iron, lead & nails.

Spy Glass for Com'd'g Off. of Division
   only.

Musket, Pistol & Cutlass for each man.

Board'g Pikes. one for every two men.

Musket & Pistol Cartridge box for each
   man (filled).

Lantern & materials for getting fire.

Match rope = to be kept in tin box.

Compass, Bread, Water & Provisions.

Awning completed

Lead line, small cooking apparatus
   for two largest boats.

By order of the Commander-in-Chief
H. A. Adams
Capt. of the Fleet

No. 9
Flag Ship *Mississippi*
Shanghai May 5th 1853
General Order No 9.

In obedience to the accompanying General Order of the Navy Department, dated August 16th 1852, you will be pleased to report to the Commander-in-Chief for the information of the Chief of the Bureau of Construction, Equipment & Repairs, whether the vessel under your command, has during her present cruise touched on a shoal or rock, or sustained any injury to her hull, lower masts or bowsprit, with all the circumstances attending the accident, & your opinion as to the probable injury sustained.

By order of the Com'd'g-in-Chief
H. A. Adams
Capt. of the Fleet

~ **General Order** ~

Instances having occurred of Vessels on their return from foreign service, being found to have sustained injury from having been ashore, or having struck on rocks, without any report of such circumstance being made either at the time of its occurrence or at the termination of the cruise, it is hereby ordered & directed that every Commander of a Vessel of the Navy, shall report to the Chief of the Bureau of Construction, Equipment & Repairs, immediately on its occurrence, every instance of the Vessel under his command touching on a Shoal or rock, or sustaining any injury to the hull, lower masts, or bowsprit, with all the circumstances attending the accident & his opinion as to the probable injury sustained, & at the termination of the cruise he will send duplicate of all such reports made during the cruise to the Bureau.

Navy Department
August 16th 1852
John P. Kennedy
Sec'y of the Navy

No. 10
Flag Ship *Mississippi*
Shanghai May 5th 1853
General Order No 10

In conformity with the enclosed Naval General Order, it will be the duty of the Commanders of all Vessels of the East India Squadron to state upon their requisitions for Articles for the use of their respective commands. Their reasons for making such requisitions, in order that the Commander-in-Chief may be able to comply with said Naval Order.

By order of the Commander-in-Chief
H. A. Adams
Capt. of Fleet

~ **General Order** ~

Wherever it shall become neccessary to purchase any Articles or Articles for the use of any Squadron or single ship on Foreign service, the Commander of the Squadron or single ship as the case may be, shall forward by the first opportunity a copy of the bill or bills for the Article so purchased, to the proper bureau accompanied by a statement of the reason making the purchase neccessary.

This is required that the several Bureau & may be kept fully advise[d] of the open purchases on Foreign as well as Home stations and of the state of their respective appropriations.

Navy Dept.
August 27th 1852
John P. Kennedy
Sec'y of the Navy

No. 11

General Order No 11.[1]
Flag Ship *Susquehanna*
May 23d 1853

The approach of the Squadron to parts of the ocean but rarely visited, & by consequence but little known, with fogs, winds, & current constantly interposing to perplex the navigator, make it proper to call the attention of Commanders of vessel in the Squadron to the strict necessity of adopting every possible precaution to guard against accident. To this end it is directed that when a ship is underway, and on soundings, deep sea, & hand leads, are to be constantly in use or the occasion requires, as well as the better to insure safety as to furnish the hydrographical information necessary to the accomplishment of the instruction of the Government as will be seen by reference to the enclosed papers. Within hand lead sounding when underway, leads men are to be stationed on both sides, and the soundings recorded with other remarks, describing the localities tides &c &c. And when ships are riding at single anchor, a man is to be stationed night & day at the drift lead.

The same lookouts are to be kept in port as at sea during the stay of the Squadron among the Japanese Islands, & every movement of vessels or collection of boats are to be reported to the authorities. Sentinels are the look outs both by night and day are to be provided with loaded arms with six rounds of ball cartridges; they are to be discharged and reloaded whenever the condition of the load may require it. General and division exercise of great guns & small arms, with Artillery and Infantry drills, are to be prosecuted with increased diligence, and it is expected that officers when they appear at General Quarter will have their arms properly attached to their persons.

All officers entitled to wear arms as pertaining to their uniform will appear at quarters armed accordingly.

In navigating these Seas attention is to be given more to precautionary measure to secure safety, than to accomplish quick passages, hence it is recommended not to run in thick stormy weather if there may be possibility of danger.

By order of the Commander-in-Chief
(signed) H. A. Adams
Captain of the Fleet.

Extract enclosed in the foregoing General Order.
(Copy)
Extract from Instruction to Commodore Perry
> "Your attention is particularly called to the Exploration of the Coast of Japan & of the adjacent continent & Islands. You will cause linear or perspective views to be made of remarkable places, sounding to be taken at the entrance of harbour rivers &c on and near shoals & collect all the hydrographical information necessary for the construction of Charts."

No. 12
(Copy)
General Order No 12.[2]
U.S. Steam Frigate *Susquehanna*
Off the river Yangtes Kiang, May 23d 1853.

The countries which the U.S. vessel Stationed in these seas are about to visit, are inhabited by a singular people, whose policy it has been during more than two centuries to decline all intercourse with strangers, to which end they have resorted to act, at [nescience], and irreconcilable with the practice of civilized nations.

One of the duties enjoined upon one is to endeavor to overcome these predjudice[s] by a course of friendly & conciliatory measure & to strive to convince the Japanese that we go amongst them as friends, not as enemies, though assuring them of our determination never to submit to insult or wrong, or desist from claiming & securing those rights of hospitality—justly due from one nation to another.

In pursuance of these objects it will be requisite that every individual under my command should exercise the greatest prudence, forbearance & discretion in their intercourse with all with whom they may come in contact.

That whilst distrustful of their apparent friendship and sincerity, and guarding—against treachery, they will extend toward these oppressed and misgoverned people every kindness & protection, and be careful not to molest, injure or maltreat them in any manner whatever.

It will be in time to resort to extreme measure when every friendly demonstration shall have been exhausted.

My instructions direct me to forbid in the most positive term, the acceptance of presents or supplies, unless those who proffer them are prepared to receive adequate return.

And I may remark in conclusion that trusting confidently in the prompt and zealous co-operation of all under my command in a work which will require the utmost vigilance & sound judgement, I need not advert to the painful necessity in which I should be placed of calling to my aid the whole force of the law, should these instructions be overlooked or in any manner disregarded.

(Signed) M. C. Perry
Commander-in-Chief U.S. Naval for East India, China & Japan Seas.
Commander S. S. Lee
Com'g U.S. Steam Frigate *Mississippi*.

No. 13
General Order No. 13.
[July 11, 1853]

In conformity with General Order No 1. All notes, Journals, Manuscripts, Drawings &c., &c. kept or collected by the Officers of the Squadron for the year 1853, must be sent in by the 15th of February 1854, to be safely deposited with the Store Keeper at Macao until they can be transmitted to the Navy Department.

By order of the Commander-in-Chief
H. A. Adams
Capt. of the Fleet

APPENDIX B

Correspondence

———◦◦◦———

No. 1

From the Japan Expedition Press, Simoda, Japan—May 1st 1854

Letter from the President of the United States.

Millard Fillmore

President of the United States of America

To his Imperial Majesty

The Emperor of Japan

Great and Good Friend!

I send you this public letter by Commodore Matthew C. Perry, an officer of highest rank in the Navy of the United States, and commander of the squadron now visiting your Imperial Majesty's dominions.

I have directed Commodore Perry to assure your Imperial Majesty that I entertain the kindest feelings towards your Majesty's person and government; and that I have no other object in sending him to Japan, but to propose to your Imperial Majesty that the United States and Japan should live in friendship, and have commercial intercourse with each other.

The constitution and laws of the United States forbid all interference with the religious or political concerns of other nations. I have particularly charged Commodore Perry to abstain from every act which could possibly disturb the tranquility of your Imperial Majesty's dominions.

The United States of America reach from ocean to ocean, and our territory of Oregon and state of California lie directly opposite to the dominions of your Imperial Majesty. Our steamships can go from California to Japan in eighteen days.

Our great state of California produces about sixty millions of dollars in gold, every year, besides silver, quicksilver, precious stones, and many other valuable articles. Japan is also a rich and fertile country, and produces many very valuable articles. Your Imperial Majesty's subjects are skilled in many of the arts. I am desirous that our two countries should trade with each other for the benefit both of Japan and the United States.

We know that the ancient laws of your Imperial Majesty's government do not allow of foreign trade except with the Dutch. But as the state of the world changes, and new governments are formed, it seems to be wise from time to time to make new law. There was a time when the ancient laws of your Imperial Majesty's government were first made.

About the same time, America, which is sometimes called the New World, was first discovered and settled by the Europeans. For a long time there were but a few people, and they were poor. They have now become quite numerous; their commerce is very extensive; and they think that if your Imperial Majesty were so far to change the ancient laws as to allow a free trade between the two countries, it would be extremely beneficial to both.

If your Imperial Majesty is not satisfied that it would be safe, altogether, to abrogate the ancient laws which forbid foreign trade, they might be suspended for five or ten years, so as to try the experiment. If it does not prove as beneficial as was hoped, the ancient laws can be restored. The United States often limit their treaties with foreign states to a few years, and then renew them or not, as they please.

I have directed Commodore Perry to mention another thing to your Imperial Majesty. Many of our Ships pass every year from California to China; and great numbers of our people pursue the whale fishery near the shores of Japan. It sometimes happens in stormy weather that one of our ships is wrecked on your Imperial Majesty's shores. In all such cases we ask and expect, that our unfortunate people should be treated with kindness, and that their property should be protected, till we can send a vessel and bring them away. We are very much in earnest in this.

Commodore Perry is also directed by me to represent to your Imperial Majesty that we understand there is great abundance of coal and provisions in the Empire of Japan. Our steamships, in crossing the great ocean, burn a great deal of coal, and it is not convenient to bring it all the way from America. We wish that our steam ships and other vessels should be allowed to stop in Japan and supply themselves with coal, provisions and water. They will pay for them, in money, or anything else your Imperial Majesty's subject may prefer; and we request your Imperial Majesty to appoint a convenient port in the southern part of the empire, where our vessels may stop for this purpose. We are very desirous of this.

These are the only objects for which I have sent Commodore Perry with a powerful squadron to pay a visit to your Imperial Majesty's renowned city of Yedo; friendship, commerce, a supply of coal, and provisions and protection for our shipwrecked people.

We have directed Commodore Perry to beg your Imperial Majesty's acceptance of a few presents. They are of no great value in themselves, but some of them may serve as specimens of the articles manufactured in the United States, and they are intended as tokens of our sincere and respectful friendship.

May the Almighty have your Imperial Majesty in his great and holy keeping!

In witness whereof I have caused the great seal of the United States to be hereunto affixed, and have subscribed the same with my name, at the city of Washington in America, the seat of my government, on the thirteenth day of the month of November, in the year one thousand eight hundred and fifty-two.

Your Good Friend
Millard Fillmore
By the President
Edward Everett
Secretary of State

No. 2

Lines found in a Japanese Tea box:

When the golden pipe send out its curling smoke,
    And the wind gently sighs through the thick fir grove,
Then choose some leaves from the fairy's blossom broke,
    And made the light yellow tea we so much love.

At the first sip, we feel the thrill
    And every vein & pore cries, Fill!
The teeth grow strong, the mouth grows sweet,
    The tongue prolongs the pleasant treat,
And spirits leap with gladd'ning beat.

Translated by the Rev. S. Wells Williams
Int. U.S. Japan Expedition

No. 3

Translation of some of the communications of the Japanese Authorities at Hakodade [Hakodate], Island of Yezo, during our stay there from the 17th of May to 3d of June 1854.

"To hear from the Commodore that since his arrival in Hakodadi he has been much pleased with his intercourse and communications with the local authorities, is truly a great gratification to us."

With regard to going through the streets and seeing shops and houses shut, with neither women or children in their ways, let it be here observed, that at Yo-ko-ha-ma this very matter was plainly spoken of by Morirgama the Interpreter, at that place.

The customs of our country are unlike yours, and the people have been unused to see persons from foreign lands; though the authorities did what they could to pacify them and teach them better, they still were disinclined to believe, and many absconded or hid themselves.

If the Commodore will recall to mind the day when he took a ramble at Yo-ko-ha-ma, in which some of us accompanied him, he will recollect that in the Villages and houses we hardly saw a woman during the whole walk. If he saw more of them at Shimoda as he went about, it was because there the people were gradually accustomed to the Americans, and their fears had been allayed, so that they felt no dread.

On these remote frontiers many hundred miles from Yedo, the usages of the people are so fixed that they are not easily influenced and altered; but pray how can the inhabitants here think of regarding the Americans with inimical feelings. Even when they see their officers, with the sight of whom they are not familiar, they also run aside, and as if from fear, they seek to escape us. It is the custom of our country that officers should accompany visitors about, a custom not to be so soon changed. Still the disposition of the men here is ingenuous, brave, upright and good; and that of the women, retiring and modest, not gazing at men as if without bashfulness. Such characteristics, and such usages, must be considered as estimable, and we think that you also will not dislike them. In the paper sent his Excellency this morning it was stated that we had received orders from Yedo to go to Karafto,[1] that on the road we heard that your ships were at Hakodadi, and as the consultations at Yo-ko-ha-ma were not fully known on these distant frontier places, there might some misunderstanding arise, and so we came here especially to see you. If there are any points connected with the Treaty, which need deliberation and settlement, we desire that you will let us know them.

{With regard to the conduct of Officers on Shore,}[2]

In general, when upright, cordial, propriety marks intercourse, then peace, good feeling, and harmony are real between the parties; but if harshness, violence and grasping, with collision, arise, and love will not be found to bring the hearts of the people together. This is a rule of heaven concerning which no one can have any doubt.

No. 4

Copy of a translated letter from two intelligent Japanese.

Superscription—"A secret communication to the American Man of War Ships; to go up higher."

Two scholars of Yedo in Japan, named Isagi Kooda & Kwano uchi Mangi, present this letter to the high Officers or others who manage affairs. That which we have received is meagre & trifling, as are our persons insignificant; so that we are ashamed to come before distinguished personages; we are ignorant of arms & their uses in battle, nor do we know the rules of strategy and discipline: we have in short, uselessed [*sic*] whiled away our months & years & know nothing. We heard a little of the customs & knowledge of the Europeans & Americans, & have desired to travel about in the five great continents, but the maritime prohibitions of our country are exceedingly strict, so that for foreigners to enter the "inner land," or for natives to go to other countries, are alike among the immutable regulations. Therefore our desire to travel has been checked, & could only go to & fro in our breasts, unable to find utterance, & our feet so hampered that they could not stir—This had been the case many years, when happily, the arrival of so many of your ships anchoring in our waters now for several days, & our careful & repeated observations of the kind & humane conduct of your officers & their love for others, has revived the cherished desire of years, which now struggles for its exit. We have decided on a plan, which is very privately to take us aboard of your ships & carry us to sea, that we may travel over the five continents, even if by so doing, we disregard our laws. We hope you will not regard our humble request with disdain, but rather enable us to carry it out: whatever we are able to do to serve will be considered as an order as soon as we hear it.

When a lame man sees another walking, or a pedestrian sees another riding, would he not be glad to be in his place? How much more, now, to us, who, for our whole lives, could not go beyond 30° E. to W., or 25° N. to S., when we behold you come riding on the high winds, and careering over the vast waves, with lightning speed coasting along the five continents, does it appear as if the lame had a way to walk, or the walker an opportunity to ride?

We hope you who manage affairs will condescend to regard & grant our request; for as the restrictions of our country are not yet removed, if this matter becomes known, we shall have no place to flee, & doubtless will suffer the extremest penalty, which result would greatly grieve your kind & benevolent hearts towards your fellowmen.

We trust to have our request granted, & also that you will secrete [sic] us until you sail, so as to avoid all risk of endangering life. When we return here at a future day, we are sure that what has passed will not be very closely investigated. Though rude & unpracticed in speach [sic], our desires are earnest, & we hope you will regard us in compassion, not doubt or oppose our request.

April 11

An inclosed [sic] note was, —"The inclosed letter contains the earnest request we have had for many days, & which we tried in many ways to get off to you at Yo-ko-ha-ma in a fishing boat by night; but the cruisers were too thick & none others were allowed to come alongside, so that we were in great uncertainty what to do. Learning that the ships were coming here, we have come to wait, intending to siege a [punt?] & come off, but have not succeeded.

Trusting that your honors will consent, after people are quiet tomorrow night, we will be at Ka-ki-za-ki in a punt at a place where there are no houses near the beach. There we greatly desire you to come & meet us, & thereby carry out our hopes to their fruition."—April 25th

Superscription on the Envelope, Copied from the original.

No. 5

From the Japan Expedition Press. Shimoda—Japan – May 1st 1854
Answer to the Presidents Letter to the Emperor of Japan, Through the Imperial Commissioners.

The return of your Excellency as Ambassador from the United States to this Empire, has been expected, according to the letter of his Majesty the President; which letter your Excellency delivered last year to his Majesty the Emperor of Japan. It is quite impossible to give satisfactory answers at once to all the proposals of your government, since those points are most positively forbidden by the laws of our Imperial house, but for us to continue bigotedly attached to the ancient laws, seems to misunderstand the spirit of the age, and we wish rather to conform to what necessity requires.

At the visit of your Excellency last year, his Majesty, the former Emperor, was sick, and is now dead. Since his Majesty, the present Emperor, has ascended the throne, the many occupations demanding his case in consequence thereof are not yet finished, and there is no time to settle other business thoroughly;

moreover, his Majesty the new Emperor at his accession to the throne promises to the Princes and high Officers of the Empire to observe the laws. It is therefore evident that he cannot now bring about any alteration in the ancient laws.

Last autumn at the departure of the Dutch ship, the superintendent of the Dutch trade in Japan, was requested to inform your government of this event, and a reply in writing has been received.

At Nagasaki, the Russian Ambassador recently arrived to communicate a wish of his government; he has since left that place, because no answer would be given to any nation that might communicate similar wishes.

However, we admit the urgency, and shall entirely comply with the proposals of your government, concerning coal, wood, water, provisions, and the saving of ships and their crews in distress. After being informed which harbor your Excellency has selected, that harbor shall be prepared, and this preparation, it is estimated, will take about five years. Meanwhile a commencement can be made with the coal at Nagasaki by the beginning of the next Japanese Year (10th February, 1855.).

Having no precedent with respect to coal, we request your Excellency to furnish us with an estimate, and upon due consideration this will be complied with, if not in opposition to our laws. What do you understand by provisions? and how much coal?

Finally, anything ships may be in want of, that can be furnished from the productions of this empire shall be supplied; the prices of merchandise and articles of barter to be fixed by Kurakawa Kakei and Moriyama Yenoske. After settling the point before mentioned, the treaty can be concluded, and signed at the next interview.

Seal attached by order of the Imperial Commissioners.

Imperial Commissioners
L. S.
Moriyama Yeno[s]ke
Kayei, 7th year, 1st moon, 26th day.
(February 23rd, 1854)

No. 6
Compact between the United States and the Kingdom of Lew Chew
Signed at Naha, Great Lew Chew, the 11th day of July 1854

Hereafter, whenever Citizens of the United States come to Lew Chew, they shall be treated with great courtesy and friendship. Whatever articles these persons ask for, whether from the Officers or people, which the country can furnish, shall be sold to them; nor shall the authorities interpose any prohibatory regulations to the people selling; and whatever either party may wish to buy, shall be exchanged at reasonable prices.

Whenever ships of the United States shall come into any harbor of Lew Chew, they shall be supplied with wood and water at reasonable prices; but if they wish to get other articles, they shall be purchasable only at Naha.

If ships of the United States are wrecked on Great Lew Chew, or on Islands under the jurisdiction of the Royal Government of Lew Chew, the local authorities shall despatch persons to assist in saving life and property, and preserve what can be brought ashore till the ship of that Nation, shall come to take away all that may have been saved; and the expenses incurred in rescuing these unfortunate persons, shall be refunded by the Nation they belong to.

At Tumai is a burial ground for the citizens of the United States, where their graves and tombs shall not be molested.

The Government of Lew Chew shall appoint skillful pilots, who shall be on the lookout for ships appearing off the Island, and if one is seen coming toward Naha, they shall go out in good boats beyond the reefs to conduct her in to a secure anchorage, for which service the Captain shall pay the pilot, Five dollars; and the same for going out of the harbor beyond the reef.

Whenever persons from ships of the United States come ashore in Lew Chew, they shall be at liberty to ramble where they please, without hindrance, or having Officials sent to follow them, or to spy what they do; but if they violently go into houses, or trifle with women, or force people to sell them things, or do other such like illegal acts; they shall be arrested by the local officers, but not maltreated, and shall be reported to the Captain of the ship to which they belong, for punishment by him.

Whenever ships anchor at Naha, the local authorities shall furnish them with wood at the rate of Three thousand six hundred copper cash per thousand catties; and with water at the rate of six hundred copper cash (43 cents) for one thousand catties, or six barrels full, each containing 30 American gallons.

Signed in the English and Chinese languages by Commodore Matthew C. Perry, Commander-in-chief of the U.S. Naval Forces in the East India, China and Japan Seas, and special envoy to Japan, for the United States; and by Sho Fu Fing, Superintendent of Affairs, (Tsu-li-kwan) in Lew Chew, and Ba Rio-si, Treasurer of Lew Chew at Shui, for the Government of Lew Chew, and copies exchanged this 11th day of July 1854, or the reign of Hien Fung, 4th year, 6th moon, 17th day, at the Town Hall of Naha.

APPENDIX C

Ship's Roster

—◦◦◦—

Officers attached to the USS *Mississippi*.

	Names	Rank	Remarks
1	Wm J. McCluney	Captain	Detached Nov 24 1852
2	Alfred Taylor	Lieutenant	
3	Thos A. Budd	"	Detached Nov 8 "
4	J. Hogan Brown	"	" Sept 30 "
5	William Speiden	Purser	
6	Danl S. Green	Surgeon	
7	L. J. Williams	Passd Asst Surgeon	Detached May 27 1853
8	Wm A. Webb	Master	" " "
9	Walter F. Jones	Passd Midsh'n	Detached April 22d
10	P. G. Watmough	"	Detached July 8 "
11	And. A. Randall	Gunner	" April 18 "
12	Amos Colson	Boatswain	
13	William Lee	Carpenter	Detached April 18 "
14	Jacob Stephens	Sail Maker	
15	Jesse Gay	Chief Engineer	
16	Robt Danby	1st Asst "	
17	Wm Holland	"	Detached Oct 5—1853
18	G. T. W. Logan	2nd Asst "	
19	Wm H. Rutherford	"	
20	Geo. W. Alexander	"	

	Names	Rank	Remarks
21	Ed. D. Robie	3rd Asst "	
22	J. Drumd Mercer	3d Asst Engineer	
23	Wm Speiden Jr	Purser's Clerk	
24	Wm E. Everett	1st Asst Engineer	Detached March 21 1852
25	Jas. W. Shirk	Midshipman	Detached Oct 1853
26	Wm McN. Armstrong	"	" October 10th "
27	A. M. Lynah	Asst Surgeon	" March 18—1854
28	J. Howard March	Passd Midsh'n	
29	And. F. Monroe	"	Detached Oct 13 "
30	C. St Geo. Noland	Lieutenant	" Sept 8 "
31	Matthew C. Perry	Commodore	Comr in Chief of E. I. Squadron Detached May 9th 1853
32	A. L. C. Portman	Commo'd's Clerk	" " "
33	J. Monroe Bibby	Captains Clerk	Detached Nov 24 "
34	Henry M. Lowry	Carpenter	
35	Henry A. Adams	Commander	Captain of Fleet Detached May 9 1853
36	N. B. Adams	Command's Clerk	" " "
37	E. C. Hine	Gunner	Detached July 29
38	Franklin Buchanan	Commander	Gone overland to E. I.
39	Jos. B. Smith	Passd Midsh'n	Detached July 28
40	Wash'g Sherman	Passd Asst Surgeon	"
41	K. R. Breese	Passd Midsh'n	
42	Eliph. Brown Jr	Act'g Mastr Mate	Detached May 9 1853
43	Henry Rolando	Lieutenant	Detached Sep 4 1852
44	John Contee	"	" May 9 1853
45	John C. Ritter	Gunner	Detached Sep 4 1852
46	Joshua D. Todd	Lieutenant	" Oct 1 "
47	Chas. E. Fleming	"	" " "
48	Wilhelm Heine	Act'g Mastr Mate	" May 9 1853
49	P. G. Watmough	Passd Midsh'n	Detached Oct 4 "
50	Ed. F. Gray		Gone overland to E. I. Detached May 1853
51	Simon C. Mish	Midshipman	" Oct "
52	Wm B. Draper	Act'g Mastr Mate	Detached May 9 1853
53	Ed. Lanier	Lieutenant	
54	Silas Bent	"	Detached April 5 1854

	Names	Rank	Remarks
55	Jno. M. B. Clitz	"	
56	Jno. R. Caulk	Gunner	
57	Geo. Jones	Chaplain	
58	Chas. M. Morris	Lieutenant	Left for home—Nov 30th "54
59	S. S. Lee	Commander	
60	J. W. Spalding	Command's Clerk	
	Jacob Zeilin	Capt & Bvt Major of Marines	Detached May 9 "52
	Geo. F. Lindsay	2d Lieut of Marines	Detached Nov 8th "
	Wm B. Slack	Lieut & Bvt Capt of Marines	" March 18 "54
	Jas H. Jones	" Marines	Detached—
	Robert Tansil	" "	
61	David Ochiltree	Acting Master	Detached July 1854
62	M. C. Perry	Commodore	Left for home Sept 11 "
63	O. H. Perry	" Sec'y	
64	A. L. C. Portman	" Clerk	
65	W. L. Maury	Lieutenant	
66	W. F. Jones	Passd Mid'n	
67	Leroy Arnold	3d Asst. Engineer	Detached July 8 1854
68	L. J. Williams	Passd Asst Surgeon	
69	Wm A. Webb	Act'g Lieutenant	

Notes

—◦◦—

Introduction

1. William S. Speiden Jr., journal, March 9, 1852 and March 21, 1852. William Speiden Papers, Manuscript Division, Library of Congress.

2. Samuel Eliot Morison, *"Old Bruin": Commodore Matthew C. Perry, 1794–1858* (Boston: Little, Brown and Company, 1967), ix–x.

3. The handwriting is identical to that of some muster rolls kept on the *Mississippi* that are known to have been indited by William Speiden Jr. Record Group 45, National Archives and Records Administration.

4. Speiden Journal, January 11, 1853.

5. Ibid., April 21, 1853.

6. Ibid., April 27, 1853, and May 23, 1853. Place names are as given by Speiden. Napa (Naha) is on the island of Okinawa, Ryukyu Islands.

7. Ibid., July 4, 1853.

8. Ibid., July 8, 1853. The town of Uraga is now included in Yokosuka.

9. Ibid., September 26, 1853.

10. Ibid., February 13, 1854.

11. This, at least, is the translated version provided in a copy of the letter of the Japanese Imperial Commissioner, dated February 23, 1854, and inserted in Speiden's journal under the date March 8, 1854.

12. Speiden Journal, March 8, 1854.

13. Ibid., March 17, 1854.

14. Ibid., March 27, 1854.

15. Ibid., April 10, 1854; Morison, *"Old Bruin,"* 381–82.

16. Speiden Journal, February 16, 1855.

17. William Speiden Jr., "How the United States Opened Japan to the World," *Japan and America* 2 (December 1902): 15.

18. United States Navy. Pension Application No. 53812. Record Group 15, National Archives and Records Administration. The file on Speiden includes some letters written by attorneys and others interceding on his behalf.

19. His burial site is Lot 10274 in Section 119, along with his wife.

Chapter 1. Volume One: 1852

1. The frigate *Mississippi*, a side-wheel steamer, was laid down by the Philadelphia Navy Yard in 1839 and was built under the personal supervision of Matthew C. Perry. Launched in 1842, she was 229 feet length overall (l.o.a.), and she had a beam of forty feet and a draft of nineteen feet. Two side-lever engines operated two paddlewheels twenty-eight feet in diameter, and her masts were rigged to spread nineteen thousand square feet of canvas. After service in the Mexican War and duty in the Mediterranean Squadron, the *Mississippi* returned to the United States to become Perry's flagship in the expedition to the China Seas and Japan in 1852–1854. Arriving back in the United States in 1855, she returned to the Far East again in 1857. When the Civil War broke out she was in New York and almost immediately saw action, but in March 1863, during the Port Hudson operation, she grounded in the Mississippi River and blew up and sank while under heavy fire. Morison, *"Old Bruin,"* 193; James L. Mooney, *Dictionary of American Naval Fighting Ships* (Washington, D.C.: Navy Department, Office of the Chief of Naval Operations, Naval History Division, 1959–1981), IV: 387–88; Roger Pineau, ed., *The Personal Journal of Commodore Matthew C. Perry* (Washington, D.C.: Smithsonian Institution Press, 1968), 225; Stephen Culver Craddock, "'To the Honor and Credit of the Country': A History of the Warships *Mississippi*," *Journal of the Mississippi History* 54 (May 1992): 129–34; Frank M. Bennett, *The Steam Navy of the United States, A History of the Growth of the Steam Vessel of War in the U.S. Navy, and of the Naval Engineer Corps* (Westport, CT: Greenwood Press, 1972), 126–36.

2. William Speiden Sr. (1805–1861) was a protégé of Timothy Winn, who appointed the eighteen-year-old Speiden to a position at the Washington

Navy Yard's purser's office. In 1836 Speiden was appointed U.S. Navy purser for Norfolk, Virginia. Speiden later served with Commodore Perry's expedition to Japan. Laurie Stahl, "Oregon to Antarctica to Japan: Navy Purser William Speiden," *Heritage Gazette* (Fall 2006): 4; Harold D. Langley, "A Naval Dependent in Washington, 1837–1842: Letters of Marian Coote Speiden," *Records of the Columbia Historical Society, Washington, D.C.* 50 (1980): 106, 122.

A purser is the shipboard officer who keeps the accounts and usually has charge of the provisions. Joseph Palmer, compiler, *Jane's Dictionary of Naval Terms* (London: MacDonald and Jane's, 1975), 188.

3. Louis Kossuth (1802–1894), leader of the Hungarian insurrection of 1848–1849, fled into exile following military defeats and the collapse of his republican government. He visited the United States in 1851–1852, where he appeared before both houses of Congress and was presented to President Millard Fillmore. William R. Denslow, *10,000 Famous Freemasons* (Whitefish, MT: Kessinger Publishing, 2004), II: 39.

4. Samuel Eliot Morison has called the ship-of-the-line *North Carolina* a "noble ship," and the "pride of the navy and the nation." Perry had served as her first lieutenant in 1824–1828. Because of her great size and draft there were only a few ports that could accommodate the *North Carolina*. She was not to take part in the Japan expedition. Mooney, *Dictionary of American Naval Fighting Ships*, V: 107.

5. William J. McCluney (ca. 1796–1864), who had served in the Mexican War, was to take command of the *Powhatan* in the Japan expedition. In 1858 he was placed in command of the Atlantic Squadron, and he was commissioned commodore in 1860 before retiring the following year. James Grant Wilson and John Fiske, eds., *Appleton's Cyclopaedia of American Biography* (New York: D. Appleton and Company, 1887), IV: 84.

6. The screw-steamer *Princeton*, the second naval vessel to bear that name, was laid down in 1851. Her machinery was installed at Baltimore in 1852 and she was scheduled to rendezvous with the *Mississippi* at Annapolis. While on her way there, she developed boiler trouble and was forced to drop out of the expedition. Mooney, *Dictionary of American Naval Fighting Ships*, V: 384.

7. Silas Horton Stringham (1797–1876) served in the War of 1812 and the Mexican War, took command of the Mediterranean Squadron in 1852, and

in May 1861 was given command of the Atlantic Blockading Squadron. He became a close confidant of Secretary of the Navy Aidean Welles.

The frigate *Cumberland* was launched at the Boston Navy Yard in 1842. She saw service in the Mexican War and was flagship of the Mediterranean Squadron in 1852–1855. During the Civil War, she was in the North Atlantic Blockading Squadron. In March 1862, in an encounter with the Confederate ironclad *Virginia* (formerly the USS *Merrimack*), she was rammed and sunk. Allen Johnson and Dumas Malone, eds., *Dictionary of American Biography* (New York: Charles Scribner's Sons, 1958), IX: 139–40; John A. Garraty and Mark C. Carnes, eds., *American National Biography* (New York: Oxford University Press, 1999), XXI: 30–31; Mooney, *Dictionary of American Naval Fighting Ships*, II: 214.

8. Jamaica Plain was a former village in Suffolk County, Massachusetts, now a part of Boston. *Merriam-Webster's Geographical Dictionary*, 3rd ed. (Springfield, MA.: Merriam-Webster, 2007), 548.

9. McKean Buchanan (1798–1871) received a commission as a purser in 1826. He sailed in nine vessels, served eight times at shore stations (one being at Boston Navy Yard in 1852), made four cruises to the Pacific, and took part in two wars (Mexican War and Civil War). He was placed on the retired list in 1861, and before he died he acquired the title of pay-director with the rank of commodore. Roberdeau Buchanan, *Genealogy of the Roberdeau family: including a biography of General Daniel Roberdeau, of the Revolutionary Army, and the Continental Congress; and Signer of the Articles of Confederation* (Washington: Joseph L. Pearson, 1876), 133–36.

10. Established in 1831, Mount Auburn Cemetery in Cambridge, Massachusetts, is the burial place of many Massachusetts notables, including Henry Wadsworth Longfellow, Edward Everett, and Charles Sumner. Visitors to the Boston area frequently included it in their itineraries, and guides were published to accommodate them.

11. Cape Henry is a Virginia promontory at the south side of the entrance to the Chesapeake Bay. Saul B. Cohen, *The Columbia Gazetteer of the World* (New York: Columbia University Press, 1998), 1268.

12. The *Mississippi* was equipped with two side-lever engines with a 75-inch by 7-foot stroke cylinder. Included were 28-foot by 11-foot wheels and 3 copper boilers. Erik Heyl, *Early American Steamers*, Vol. V (Buffalo, NY: Erik Heyl, 1967), 181.

13. The Speiden family lived on Missouri Avenue in what is now the Federal Triangle area in the first ward in Washington, D.C. 1850 U.S. Census, Washington, District of Columbia, pop. sch., Washington Ward 1, 87 (penned), William Speiden. Ancestry.com. http://www.ancestry.com/ : 2011; Langley, "A Naval Dependent in Washington," 115.

14. Chagres (Nuevo Chagres) was a minor port on the Caribbean Sea at the mouth of the Chagres River. The river now is largely utilized by the Panama Canal. The remains of the old town lie approximately 14 miles southwest of Colon. Cohen, *Columbia Gazetteer*, 2240.

15. The East India Squadron was established in 1835, acquiring responsibilities in this region formerly assumed by the Pacific Squadron. Secretary of the Navy Abel P. Usher formally recognized the Squadron in 1842. It was abolished in 1862 but re-established as the Asiatic Squadron in 1865. Curtis T. Henson Jr., *Commissioners and Commodores: The East India Squadron and American Diplomacy in China* (Tuscaloosa, AL: University of Alabama Press, 1982), iv, 179.

16. Henry Clay (1777–1852) of Kentucky died on June 29, 1852, after a long congressional career and service as secretary of state. *The National Cyclopaedia of American Biography* (New York: J.T. White, 1892), V: 77.

17. After the War of 1812, the British began to restrict the fishing banks southeast of Newfoundland Island, Canada, to American fishermen. In 1818 the two nations negotiated a new convention that prohibited the United States from fishing within three miles of the British provinces' shores. Tensions occurred when questions were raised as to how this three miles was to be reckoned. The Americans considered the three-mile line to be one following the coast, but the British drew a line between the most prominent points on the coast, which would in some cases be six miles from the coast. In the 1850s the British threatened again to close the inshore fisheries. In 1854 the two nations struck the Marcy-Elgin Reciprocity Treaty, which removed duties on numerous goods and allowed Americans to fish in areas closed by the Convention of 1818. In return, Canadians secured fishing rights along the Atlantic coast of the United States above the thirty-sixth parallel. The United States received free navigation of the St. Lawrence River and its canals in exchange for giving the British reciprocal rights to Lake Michigan. Alexander DeConde, Richard Dean Burns, and Fredrik Logevall, eds., *Encyclopedia of American Foreign Policy*, Second Edition (New York: Charles Scribner's Sons, 2002), II: 50;

Howard Jones, *Crucible of Power: A History of American Foreign Relations to 1913* (Lanham, MD: Rowman & Littlefield Publishers, Inc., 2009), 186; *Proceedings in the North Atlantic Coast Fisheries Arbitration before the Permanent County of Arbitration at the Hague Under the Provisions of the General Treaty of Arbitration of April 4, 1908, and the Special Agreement of January 27, 1909, between the United States of America and Great Britain* (Washington, D.C.: Government Printing Office, 1912), IV: 632.

18. William A. Webb began his naval career as a midshipman in 1838. He was promoted to master in 1853 and lieutenant in 1854. He resigned his commission in 1861 to accept a commission in the navy of the Confederate States of America. During the Civil War, he served as commander of the CSS *Teaser* and the CSS *Richmond* in the James River Squadron and the CSS *Atlanta* in the southern region. Pineau, *The Personal Journal of Commodore Matthew C. Perry*, 232; United States, Office of Naval Records and Library, United States Navy Department, *Register of Officers of the Confederate States Navy, 1861–1865* (Mattituck, NY: J. M. Carrol & Company, 1983), 207.

19. Machias Seal Island is an island located in the Gulf of Maine, approximately ten miles southeast from Cutler, Maine, and approximately twelve miles southwest of Southwest Head, New Brunswick, on Grand Manan Island. Cohen, *Columbia Gazetteer*, 1822.

20. Logbooks of the *U.S.S. Mississippi* identifies the pilot as Obadiah Clark.

21. Grand Manan Island, New Brunswick, is an island (sixteen miles by seven miles) in the Bay of Fundy, fifteen miles southeast of Eastport. *Geographical Dictionary*, 443.

22. Charles D. Sherwood (b. ca. 1817) was the British vice consul residing in Eastport, Maine. *The Maine Register and State Reference Book, 1852* (Hallowell: Masters, Smith & Company, 1852), 28; 1860 U.S. Census, Washington County, Maine, pop. sch., Eastport, 79 (penned), Charles D. Sherwood. http://www.ancestry.com/ : 2011.

23. Cdr. Henry A. Adams, Perry's trusted chief of staff, was given the title of captain of the fleet. He was to be given much responsibility in conducting conferences and making decisions preliminary to the final treaty negotiations with Japan. He was also placed in charge of carrying the treaty to the United States for ratification, and in September 1854 he sailed for Japan with the ratified treaty. Adams, it appears, was second in importance only to Perry himself in the conduct of the entire diplomatic affair. He

became a commodore in 1862 and died in 1869. Edward W. Callahan, *List of Officers of the Navy of the United States and of the Marine Corps from 1775 to 1900, comprising a complete register of all present and former commissioned, warranted, and appointed officers of the United States Navy, and of the Marine Corps, regular and volunteer* (New York: L. R. Hamersly & Co., 1901), 17.

24. St. John, New Brunswick, at the mouth of the St. John River, is the province's largest town and a major port on the Bay of Fundy. *Geographical Dictionary*, 1023.

25. Campobello Island, New Brunswick, is in the Bay of Fundy at the entrance to Passamaquoddy Bay. It is the site of the Franklin D. Roosevelt Campobello International Park. *Geographical Dictionary*, 205.

26. William Fitzwilliam Owen (1774–1857) had a full career in the British Navy serving all over the world. An eminent hydrographic surveyor and explorer, he became a vice-admiral in 1854. He went on the reserved list in 1855 and died at St. John, New Brunswick, on November 3, 1857. *Dictionary of Canadian Biography*, s.v. "William Fitzwilliam Owen," VIII: 668–72.

27. Speiden likely meant Carleton. When St. John's was first settled, Carleton was laid out on the west side of Saint John Harbour. It was named after Sir Guy Carleton. Cohen, *Columbia Gazetteer*, 541.

28. Fredericton, the capital of New Brunswick, is on the St. John River, fifty-five miles northwest of St. John. *Geographical Dictionary*, 405.

29. Lieutenant Colonel F. Murray was then replaced by Sir Edmund Walker Head, Baronet as governor. Alexander Monro, *New Brunswick; with a brief outline of Nova Scotia and Prince Edward Island* (Halifax, Nova Scotia, Canada: Richard Nugent, 1855), 22.

30. Cornet is a short, swallow-tailed pendant indicating a commodore's ship in a squadron; a signal for all hands to report on board a naval vessel at once, or for every ship to prepare to receive a message. Dean King, John B. Hattendorf, and J. Worth Estes, *A Sea of Words: A Lexicon and Companion for Patrick O'Brian's Seafaring Tales* (New York: Henry Holt, 1995), 334; Gershom Bradford, *A Glossary of Sea Terms* (New York: Yachting, Inc., 1927), 42.

31. Halifax, the capital and largest city of the province of Nova Scotia, is a major seaport, and at the time it served as the base of Britain's North American naval squadron. *Geographical Dictionary*, 467–68.

32. British admiral Sir George Frances Seymour (1787–1870) had served under Horatio Nelson as a young man. During the years 1851–1853 he was commander in chief of the North American and West Indies Station and had the responsibility of keeping the American fishing fleet under observation. The *Cumberland* was his flagship. Sidney Lee, Leslie Stephen, and George Smith, eds., *The Dictionary of National Biography* (London: Oxford University Press, 1938), XVII: 1259; Morison, *"Old Bruin,"* 281.

33. William Walsh (1804–1858) was appointed archbishop of Nova Scotia in 1852. Before that, he became bishop of Halifax in 1845. *Dictionary of Canadian Biography*, s.v. "William Walsh," VIII: 919–20.

    John Joseph Hughes (1797–1864) was appointed the first archbishop of the Archdiocese of New York in 1850. Robert C. Broderick, ed., *The Catholic Encyclopedia* (Nashville, TN: T. Nelson, 1976), s.v. "John Joseph Hughes," VII: 516–18.

34. Speiden likely intended to indicate Fairhaven, Massachusetts, across the Acushnet River from New Bedford.

35. The Island of St. Paul is approximately twenty miles off the northern tip of mainland Nova Scotia in the Cabot Strait between the Atlantic and the Gulf of St. Lawrence. *Geographical Dictionary*, 1028.

36. Cape Breton Island (110 miles by 80 miles) forms the northeast section of Nova Scotia. *Geographical Dictionary*, 213.

37. The Magdalen Islands (Iles de la Madeleine) are a group of islands and islets in the Gulf of St. Lawrence, fifty miles north of Prince Edward Island and one hundred miles west of Newfoundland. *Geographical Dictionary*, 689.

38. John K. Contee served Perry as flag lieutenant and aide. He was to be utilized frequently in conferences and preliminary negotiations with the Japanese. Perry's *Narrative of the Expedition* alludes to making use of a journal kept by Contee but does not identify it specifically. He began his naval career as a midshipman in 1832 and promoted to lieutenant in 1843. He resigned his commission in 1854. Callahan, *List of Officers of the Navy*, 127.

39. Owned by George Friend & Co., the schooner *Ocean Star* was lost at Souris in the Bay of St. Lawrence on October 15, 1852. George H. Procter, *The Fishermen's Memorial and Record Book, containing a list of vessels and their crews, lost from the port of Gloucester from the year 1830 to October 1, 1873* (Gloucester, MA: Procter Brothers, 1873), 16.

40. Miscou Island is at the mouth of Chaleur Bay, Gulf of St. Lawrence. *Geographical Dictionary*, 749.

41. Lying directly north of Nova Scotia, in the Gulf of St. Lawrence, Prince Edward Island is Canada's smallest province. French explorer Jacques Cartier discovered the island in 1534. *Geographical Dictionary*, 957.

42. Launched in 1841 at Woolwich, the HMS *Devastation* was a 130-foot-l.o.a., 36-foot-beam, wood-paddle sloop that weighed 1,058 tons. Commanded by Cdr. Colin Yorke Campbell, she was in active service until 1866. J. J. Colledge, *Ships of the Royal Navy: The Complete Record of all Fighting Ships of the Royal Navy* (Mechanicsburg, PA: Stackpole Books, 2003), 98.

43. "Landsman" is a term for an inexperienced seaman, rated below an ordinary seaman. John V. Noel Jr. and Edward L. Brach, *Naval Terms Dictionary* (Annapolis, MD: Naval Institute Press, 1988), 164.

44. Henry Rolando (1820–1869) entered the naval service as a midshipman in 1836. He was promoted to master in 1849 and to lieutenant a year later. In 1853 he participated in the Bering Straits expedition under Admiral Ringgold to exterminate the Chinese pirates in China waters. During the Civil War he was given the rank of commander in charge of the Philadelphia Navy Yard. He also was placed in command of the *Keystone State*, which participated in the bombardment of Fort Fisher. After the war he was transferred to the *Florida* and assigned to the West Indies. He retired his commission in 1867. "Death of a Navy Officer in Baltimore," *The New York Times*, March 24, 1869, 2; Callahan, *List of Officers of the Navy*, 472.

     John C. Ritter (1815–1902) received a commission as a gunner in 1845 and served until his retirement in 1877. Callahan, *List of Officers of the Navy*, 464; *Official Army Register for 1907* (Washington, D.C.: Government Printing Office, 1907), 179; "Obituary Notes," *The New York Times*, September 29, 1902, 9.

45. The *Powhatan* was launched in February 1850 at the Norfolk Navy Yard and commissioned in September 1852. First assigned to the Home Squadron, she joined Perry's East India Squadron in Chinese waters and became his flagship when the treaty with Japan was signed. She was on continuous active service throughout the Civil War. She was decommissioned in 1886 and was broken up the following year. Mooney, *Dictionary of American Naval Fighting Ships*, V: 365; Lincoln P. Paine, *Ships of the World* (New York: Houghton Mifflin Company, 1997), 401–2.

46. John Pendleton Kennedy (1745–1870), secretary of the Navy, 1852–1853. He had served early on as a Whig congressman from Maryland in 1838 and in 1841–1845. He was also a well-known author. *National Cyclopaedia of American Biography*, VI: 181.

47. William B. Shubrick (1790–1874) had served on board the *Constellation* and the *Constitution*, and he led a naval expedition to Paraguay in 1858–1859. John Howard Brown, ed., *Lamb's Biographical Dictionary of the United States* (Boston: James H. Lamb Co., 1900), VII: 73.

   John T. Newton (1893–1857) commanded the Home Squadron from 1852 to 1855. Brown, *Lamb's Biographical Dictionary*, VI: 1.

   Cadwalader Ringgold (1802–1867) had taken part in the United States exploring expedition of 1838–1842 under Charles Wilkes, and in 1853–1854 he commanded a surveying expedition in the North Pacific. Brown, *Lamb's Biographical Dictionary*, VI: 484.

48. The sloop-of-war *Vandalia* was launched in 1828. After service in the Brazil, West Indies, Home, and Pacific Squadrons, she joined Perry's East India Squadron in 1853 and was commanded by John Pope (1798–1876). During the Civil War the *Vandalia* was in the South Atlantic Blockading Squadron. She was broken up in the 1870s. Mooney, *Dictionary of American Naval Fighting Ships,* VII: 461; Callahan, *List of Officers of the Navy,* 440.

49. The sloop-of-war *Cyane* was launched in 1837. She had seen much service in the Mexican War and was part of the Home Squadron, cruising the Atlantic, in 1851–1852. In 1819 Perry, as a young officer, had served in an earlier *Cyane,* searching for slaves off the coast of Africa. Mooney, *Dictionary of American Naval Fighting Ships,* II: 225–26; Morison, *"Old Bruin,"* 63.

50. George Jones (1800–1870) was an Episcopal clergyman and chaplain of the *Mississippi*. He also acted as an astronomer and geologist on the expedition. His study of zodiacal lights comprises volume three of the *Narrative of the Expedition*. He twice served as chaplain of the United States Naval Academy. Johnson and Malone, *Dictionary of American Biography,* V: 170–71; Pineau, *The Personal Journal of Commodore Matthew C. Perry,* xvii, 52; Morison, *"Old Bruin,"* 279, 424, 434.

51. The *Rainbow* was built of iron by John Laird at Birkenhead in 1837. The paddle steamer was 185 feet l.o.a. with a 25-foot beam, weighed 600 tons, and was fitted with a 180-horsepower engine. Alfred Pugsley, *The Works of Isambard Kingdom Brunel: An Engineering Appreciation* (London: Institution of Civil Engineers, 1976), 138, 148.

52. Millard Fillmore (1800–1874) was the thirteenth president of the United States. He succeeded to the office in 1850 as vice president upon the death of Zachary Taylor and served until 1853. His sending Perry to open relations

with Japan is considered his "most notable accomplishment." In 1856 he was the presidential candidate of the American, or Know-Nothing, party and was overwhelmingly defeated. Garraty and Carnes, *American National Biography*, VII: 911.

53. Enock Louis Low (1820–1892) of Frederick, Maryland, served as governor in 1851–1854. He declined an appointment as minister to China in 1857. During the Civil War he supported the Confederacy and moved to the South. John W. Raimer, ed., *Directory of the Governors of the United States* (Westport, CT: Mechler Publishing, 1978), II: 665–66; *National American Biography* (New York: James T. White & Co., 1907), IX: 305–6.

54. Sidney Smith Lee (1802–1869), who became commanding officer of the *Mississippi*, was a close friend of Perry's from the Mexican War. A brother of Robert E. Lee, he supported the South in the Civil War and commanded the naval defenses of the James River. Douglas Southall Freeman in his biography of Robert E. Lee described him as "almost as handsome as Robert and of fine cordial manners." Pineau, *The Personal Journal of Commodore Matthew C. Perry*, 229; Morison, *"Old Bruin,"* 219, 433, 275; Edmund Jennings Lee, ed., *Lee of Virginia, 1642–1892: Biographical and Genealogical Sketches of the Descendants of Colonel Richard Lee* (Philadelphia: Edmund Jennings Lee, 1895), 408–10; Douglas S. Freeman, *R. E. Lee: A Biography* (New York, London: Charles Scribner's Sons, 1935), I: 105; Henry P. Beers, *Guide to the Archives of the Government of the Confederate States of America* (Washington, D.C.: Government Printing Office, 1968), 364.

55. Boatswain is a multipurpose petty officer who was in charge of all deck activities, including inspecting the sails and rigging every morning. King et al., *A Sea of Words*, 113.

56. Madeira is the largest of the Madeira Islands, a Portuguese archipelago some four hundred miles west of the African coast. Ships could acquire ample supplies here and take advantage of the northeast trade winds as well. *Geographical Dictionary*, 687.

57. An Englishman by birth, Robert Bayman was the American vice-consul in Funchal Madeira. United States. Naval War Records Office, *Official Records of the Union and Confederate navies in the War of the Rebellion*, Series I, Volume 2 (Washington, D.C.: Government Printing Office, 1895), 614.

58. John Howard March was the U.S. consul in Funchal Madeira from 1816 to 1861. John M. Johnson, compiler, *Congressional Directory for the First Session of the Thirty-Second Congress of the United States of America*

(Washington, D.C.: Gideon and Co., 1852), 21; John M. Johnson, compiler, *Congressional Directory for the Second Session of the Thirty-Second Congress of the United States of America* (Washington, D.C.: Gideon and Co., 1853), 50; John M. Johnson, compiler, *Congressional Directory for the Second Session of the Thirty-Third Congress of the United States of America* (Washington, D.C.: Gideon and Co., 1855), 42; Robert Morris, compiler, *Congressional Directory for the Third Session of the Thirty-Fourth Congress of the United States of America* (Washington, D.C.: Gideon and Co., 1856), 42.

59. Probably Januária Maria de Braganza (1822–1901), daughter of Pedro I of Brazil and IV of Portugal and Maria Leopoldina, Archduchess of Austria. Roderick J. Barman, *Citizen Emperor: Pedro II and the Making of Brazil, 1825–91* (Stanford, CA: Stanford University Press, 1999), 507; Daniel P. Kidder and James C. Fletcher, *Brazil and the Brazilians, Portrayed in Historical and Descriptive Sketches* (Philadelphia: Childs & Peterson, 1857), 592.

60. Teneriffe, or Tenerife, is the largest of the Canary Islands. The volcanic Pico de Teide is more than 12,000 feet high. *Geographical Dictionary*, 1169.

61. The Rev. George Jones states that "what is called the Zodiacal Light, is a brightness which appears in the western sky after sunset, and before sunrise in the east, following nearly or quite the line of the ecliptic in the heavens, and stretching upwards to various elevations, according to the seasons of the year." Francis L. Hawks, *Commodore Perry and the Opening of Japan: Narrative of the Expedition of an American Squadron to the China Seas and Japan, 1852–1854: The Official Report of the Expedition to Japan* (Stroud, England: Nonsuch, 2005), III: iii.

62. Jacob Zeilin (1806–1880) entered the Marine Corps as a second lieutenant in 1831 after several years of study at the United States Military Academy. He was promoted to first lieutenant in 1836. He served on board the USS *Columbus* and the USS *Congress* from 1842 to 1848. In 1847 he was promoted to captain and appointed military commandant of San Diego. In 1852 he was appointed as a fleet marine officer attached to *Mississippi*. He was the second man to set foot on shore at the formal landing at Yokohama in 1853. Although he received a rank of brevet major in 1847, he was appointed in 1861 to the regular rank of major and given a command of a company of Marines. In 1864 Zeilin was appointed colonel commandant of the Marine Corps and assumed command of the Marine Barracks at Portsmouth, New Hampshire. In 1867 he became the

Marine Corps' first general officer when he was promoted to brigadier general. After the war, Zeilin officially approved the design of the "Eagle, Globe, and Anchor" as the emblem for the Marine Corps. He retired in 1876. Pineau, *The Personal Journal of Commodore Matthew C. Perry*, 232; Callahan, *List of Officers of the Navy*, 679; Alan Reed Millett and Jack Shulimson, *Commandants of the Marine Corps* (Annapolis, MD: Naval Institute Press, 2004), 85–96.

63. See Appendix A.

64. A hermaphrodite brig is a two-masted sailing ship with square sails on the foremast like a brigantine and fore-and-aft rigged sails on the mainmast like a schooner. Erik Abranson, *Ships of the High Seas* (New York: Crescent Books, 1976), 14–17.

Chapter 2. Volume One: 1853

1. Kidder Randolph Breese (1831–1881), born in Philadelphia, began his naval career as a midshipman in 1846. During the Mexican War he served with Commander Farragut on the USS *Saratoga* and later on the USS *St. Mary's*, *Brandywine*, and *St. Lawrence*. In 1855 he was promoted to master and lieutenant. During the Civil War he was appointed fleet captain of the third division of Porter's Mortar Flotilla and participated in the attack on New Orleans and Vicksburg. In 1862 he was promoted to lieutenant commander, and after the war he was ordered to the Naval Academy and served until 1866 as assistant to the superintendent. In 1866 he was appointed commander; in 1870 he was ordered to the command of USS *Plymouth*, and he was commissioned as captain in 1874 in charge of the Torpedo Station. Callahan, *List of Officers of the Navy*, 75; Wilson and Fiske, *Appletons' Cyclopaedia of American Biography*, I: 366–67.

2. Probably Isabella Bolton Perry, the commodore's only living, unmarried daughter at this time. Perry had five daughters. Morison, *"Old Bruin,"* 447.

3. Saint Helena, discovered in 1502 by Joao da Nova Costella, a Spanish navigator in the service of Portugal, lies in the South Atlantic 1,200 miles off the coast of Africa. Taken over by the Dutch in 1645, Saint Helena was later occupied by the English and came under their full control in 1661. Jamestown is its capital and port. *Geographical Dictionary*, 1022.

4. Passed midshipman was a midshipman who had passed his examination and was awaiting promotion to the rank of lowest commissioned officer, usually lieutenant. *A naval encyclopedia: comprising a dictionary of nautical words and phrases; biographical notices, and records of naval officers; special*

articles on naval art and science, written expressly for this work by officers and others of recognized authority in the branches treated by them. Together with descriptions of the principal naval stations and seaports of the world (Philadelphia: L. R. Hamersly & Co., 1881), 496.

J. Howard March (d. 1858) began his career as a midshipman in 1841 and was promoted to lieutenant in 1855. He served on the USS *Mississippi*. Pineau, *The Personal Journal of Commodore Matthew C. Perry*, 229; Callahan, *List of Officers of the Navy*, 350.

5. Napoleon had five physicians at St. Helena: Irish surgeon Barry O'Meara (1786–1836), British surgeon to the *Conqueror* John Stokoe (1775–1852), British surgeon to the Royal Artillery James Verling (1787–1858), Corsican surgeon Francesco Antommarchi (1789–1838), and British surgeon to the 20th Foot Regiment Archibald Arnott (1771–1855). Arnold Chaplin, *A St. Helena Who's Who or A Dictionary of the Island During the Captivity of Napoleon* (London: Arnold Chaplin, 1914), 43, 44, 93, 106, 108.

6. Saldana Bay is an inlet of the Atlantic Ocean about sixty miles north-northwest of Cape Town. Cohen, *Columbia Gazetteer*, II: 2721.

7. Table Mountain, approximately 3,500 feet high, overlooks Cape Town and Table Bay. The summit is flat and covered by a white mist. Cohen, *Columbia Gazetteer*, III: 3079.

8. The British steamer *Mauritius* was built by C. J. Mare and Company at Leamouth, London, in 1852. In 1855 she was damaged by fire, and in 1892 she wrecked at Cardiff. The Ships List, "The Fleets: General Screw Steam Shipping Company 1848–1857," http://www.theshipslist.com/ships/lines/generalscrewssc.htm.

9. Port Phillip Bay is a large bay in southern Victoria, Australia (31 miles by 20 miles). First settled by the English in 1803, the harbor of Melbourne is situated on the north side of the bay. *Geographical Dictionary*, 949.

10. Wynberg began as a farm called De Oude Wjinbergh, situated near the Liesbeek River, in 1658. In 1795 the area developed into a garrison town and became a halfway point between Table Bay and False Bay. George McCall Theal, *History of South Africa Under the Administration of the Dutch East India Company (1652 to 1795)* (London: Swan Sonnenschein & Co., Ltd, 1897), II: 461.

11. "Kaffir" is a now-offensive term formerly used by Europeans to refer to black Africans of the Xhosa tribe. *Webster's Third New International Dictionary of the English Language Unabridged* (Springfield, MA: Merriam-Webster, 1986), 1230.

12. Siyolo (ca. 1813–1878) was a chief of the Ndlambe Xhosa. In May 1855 he was sent to Robben Island. George McCall Theal, *History of South Africa from 1873 to 1884: Twelve Eventful Years* (London: George Allen & Unwin, Ltd., 1919), I: 132; Harriet Deacon, *The Island: A History of Robben Island, 1488–1990* (Cape Town, South Africa: Mayibuye Books, University of the Western Cape, 1996), 49; John Maclean, *A Compendium of Kafir Laws & Customs, including Genealogical Tables of Kafir Chiefs and Various Tribal Census Returns* (Grahamstown, South Africa: J. Slater, 1906), 134.

13. Constantia is a town in western Cape Province in the Republic of South Africa, located near False Bay and eight miles south-southeast of Cape Town. Cohen, *Columbia Gazetteer*, 717.

14. Sandile (ca. 1823–1878) was a chief of the Gaikas and king of the Kharhabe tribe during the Kaffir Wars. Charles Brownlee, *Reminiscences of Kaffir Life and History and Other Papers* (Lovedale, South Africa: Lovedale Mission Press, 1896), 306–21; Maclean, *A Compendium of Kafir Laws & Customs*, 135; Eric Rosenthal, *Southern African Dictionary of National Biography* (London and New York: Frederick Warne & Co., 1966), 328.

15. Maqoma (1798–1873) was the most renowned Xhosa chief in South Africa's nineteenth-century frontier wars. He died as a prisoner on Robben Island. Maclean, *A Compendium of Kafir Laws & Customs*, 136; Mark R. Lipschutz and R. Kent Rasmussen, *Dictionary of African Historical Biography*, Second Edition (Berkeley and Los Angeles: University of California Press, 1986), 136; Barbara Hutton, *Robben Island: Symbol of Resistance* (Johannesburg, South Africa: SACHED Books, 1997), 27.

16. Natal is a province of the East Republic of South Africa. *Geographical Dictionary*, 619.

17. Kaffraria was the descriptive name given to the southeast part of what is today the Eastern Cape of South Africa. *Geographical Dictionary*, 564.

18. See Appendix A.

19. Commanded by Commander William King Hall, the 1,057-ton paddle steamer *Styx* was launched in 1841. Measuring 180 feet l.o.a. with a 36-foot beam, she broke down in 1866. Colledge, *Ships of the Royal Navy*, 311.

20. Founded by the French in 1736, Port Louis is the commercial center of the island's sugar exportation. *Geographical Dictionary*, 948.

21. Le Morne Brabant is an imposing rock approximately 1,800 feet above sea level on a peninsula at the extreme southwestern tip of Mauritius. Tom Masters, Jan Dodd, and Jean-Bernard Carillet, *Mauritius, Réunion & Seychelles* (Footscray, Victoria, Australia: Lonely Planet, 2007), 110.

22. Daniel S. Green (1812–1864) was the fleet surgeon during Commodore Perry's expedition (1852–1854). At the outbreak of the Civil War, he received an appointment in the Confederate States Navy and established hospitals in Culpeper and Lynchburg. In 1862 he was assigned to the CSS *Patrick Henry* of the James River Squadron. Daniel D. Hartzler, *Medical Doctors of Maryland in the C.S.A.* (Westminster, MD: Heritage Books, Inc., 2007), 40–41.

23. Inspired by the shipwreck of the *Saint-Geran* (1744) off the coast at Poudre d'or, Bernardin de St. Pierre wrote the romantic novel *Paul & Virginie* in 1788. The tombs of the fictitious lovers are situated in the village of Pamplemousses. "Mauritius," *Appletons' Journal of Literature, Science and Art* VII no. 145 (January 6, 1872), 14; Alain Proust and Alan Mountain, *This Is Mauritius* (London: New Holland, 1995), 32–33.

24. The Champ de Mars is a large public green space in Paris, France, located in the seventh arrondissement, between the Seine River to the northwest and the École Militaire to the southeast. The Eiffel Tower was erected there. The park is named after the Campus Martius (Mars Field) in Rome, a tribute to the Roman god of war. Cohen, *Columbia Gazetteer*, 592.

25. See Appendix A.

26. See Appendix A.

27. The light was from an eighty-foot-high, white iron lighthouse situated on the south bastion of a Dutch fort on Point de Galle, Sri Lanka. It projected a beam one hundred feet above sea level and was visible for twelve miles. The light showed two flashes every sixty seconds by flashing for two seconds, then waiting for three seconds, flashing for two seconds, and waiting for twenty-three seconds. Great Britain. Hydrographic Department, *The Bay of Bengal Pilot, including South-west Coast of Ceylon, North Coast of Sumatra, Nicobar and Andaman Islands* (London: The Hydrographic Office, 1887), 44–45; A. D. Taylor, compiler, *The West Coast of Hundustan Pilot including the Gulf of Manar, the Maldive and Laccadive Islands* (London: The Hydrographic Office, 1898), 82.

28. In 1850 John Black, an American merchant residing in Colombo, was appointed the first American commercial agent in Ceylon. Samuel Brownback (KS), "Senate Resolution 172—Relative to the Democratic Socialist Republic of Sri Lanka," *Congressional Record: Proceedings and Debates of the 105th Congress, Second Session* (February 3, 1998): 503;

Johnson, *Congressional Directory (1853)*, 21; Johnson, *Congressional Directory (1855)*, 40; Morris, *Congressional Directory (1856)*, 39.

29. The Nicobar Islands lie east of the Bay of Bengal. The largest is Great Nicobar. *Geographical Dictionary*, 827.

30. The island of Sumatra is located in the Indian Ocean along the equator, south and west of the Malay Peninsula and northwest of Java. The first European to visit the island was Marco Polo around 1292. The Portuguese came in 1509, the Dutch in 1596, and the British controlled the island shortly in the late eighteenth century and early nineteenth century. Cohen, *Columbia Gazetteer*, 3048–49.

31. Amos Colson (d. 1858) entered the U.S. Navy in 1842 as a boatswain and resigned his commission a year later. In 1847 he reenlisted as a boatswain serving on the *Mississippi*. Pineau, *The Personal Journal of Commodore Matthew C. Perry*, 227; Callahan, *List of Officers of the Navy*, 124.

32. Penang, or Prince of Wales's Island, is situated two and a half miles off the west coast of the Malay Peninsula. *Geographical Dictionary*, 916.

33. The Strait of Malacca links the Indian Ocean with the South China Sea, dividing Sumatra and the Malay Peninsula. Perry in his journal wrote that "navigation of the straits is not so dangerous as might be supposed from an examination of the chart, yet it is somewhat intricate and not free from danger." Pineau, *The Personal Journal of Commodore Matthew C. Perry*, 45; *Geographical Dictionary*, 694.

34. W. W. Shaw was a British subject residing in Singapore and the senior partner of the house of Bonstead and Company. Owing to his knowledge of American business, ailing U.S. consul Joseph Balestier nominated Shaw to serve in his stead in March 1851 until a replacement could be made. Charles William Bradley (1807–1865), former U.S. consul of Amoy (1847–1851), replaced Joseph Balestier as the U.S. consul of Singapore. Johnson, *Congressional Directory (1852)*, 53; Johnson, *Congressional Directory (1853)*, 25; Johnson, *Congressional Directory (1855)*, 40; Morris, *Congressional Directory (1856)*, 39; 116–17, 120; "Oriental Literary Intelligence," *Trubner's American Oriental Literary Record* 7 (September 21, 1865):131; *Message from the President of the United States in answer to a resolution of the Senate, calling for information in relation to the mission of Mr. Balestier, late United States consul at Singapore to Eastern Asia*, Thirty-second Congress First Session, Senate Executive Document 38 (1851), 117, 120; Eldon Griffin, *Clippers and Consuls: American Consular*

and Commercial Relations with Eastern Asia, 1845–1860 (Ann Arbor, MI: Edwards Brothers, Inc., 1938), 358.

35. Ho Ah Kay (1816–1880), better known as Mr. Whampoa, was a wealthy Chinese merchant who resided in Singapore. He was a member of the legislative council and the admiralty contractor for stores. In 1853 he became the first Chinese consul at Singapore and was later appointed consul for Russia and Japan. R. H. Vetch, ed., *Life of Lieut.-General The Hon. Sir Andrew Clarke G.C.M.G., C.B., C.I.E.* (New York: E. P. Dutton and Company, 1905), 180; Wilfred L. Blythe, *The Impact of Chinese Secret Societies in Malaya: A Historical Study* (London: Oxford University Press, 1969), 67.

36. Joseph Balestier was the first U.S. consul at Singapore, serving from 1837 to 1852. Johnson, *Congressional Directory (1852)*, 48.

37. Ladrone Islands is an island group in the China Sea, opposite the entrance to the Zhu or Pearl River, which forms part of the delta of the Xi. *Geographical Dictionary*, 623.

38. Located on the northwest side of Hong Kong Island at the foot of Victoria Peak, Victoria, or Hong Kong, was formerly a British Crown colony. It is now called Xiang-Gang. Cohen, *Columbia Gazetteer*, 1304; *Geographical Dictionary*, 495.

39. Silas Bent (1820–1887), the flag lieutenant on the *Mississippi*, was appointed midshipman at age sixteen and served in the Navy for the next twenty-five years, during which he became well versed in the science of oceanography. In 1849 he was promoted to lieutenant. During the expedition to Japan, he made hydrographic surveys of Japanese waters and published his findings in 1857 in *Sailing Directions and Nautical Remarks: by Officers of the Late U.S. Naval Expedition to Japan*. In 1860 he was detailed to the hydrographic division of the Coast Survey, but he resigned from the Navy a year later at the outbreak of the Civil War. Mooney, *Dictionary of American Naval Fighting Ships*, VI: 505; Callahan, *List of Officers of the Navy*, 53; Edward L. Towle, "Lieutenant Silas Bent's Device to Eliminate Variation Correction in the Magnetic Compass, 1849," *The American Neptune* XXV (1965): 93–98.

40. The U.S. naval storekeeper was Robert P. DeSilver, who also served as U.S. consul at Macao from 1849–1855. Pineau, *The Personal Journal of Commodore Matthew C. Perry*, 130; Johnson, *Congressional Directory (1852)*, 50; Johnson, *Congressional Directory (1853)*, 21; George Henry Preble, *The Opening of Japan: A Diary of Discovery in the Far East, 1853–1856*, ed.

Boleslaw Szczesniak (Norman: University of Oklahoma Press, 1962), 54; Griffin, *Clippers and Consuls*, 352.

41. Louis Francois Auguste Marie Gaston Roquemaurel (1804–1878) was appointed commander of *La Capricieuse* in 1850 and sailed for the Pacific Ocean via Cape Horn with a mission to survey the coasts of Korea, Siberia, and Japan. Pineau, *The Personal Journal of Commodore Matthew C. Perry*, 52.

42. In 1848 J. N. A. Griswold began serving as the U.S. consul of Shanghai, but he was absent from December 1851. This left Edward Cunningham to perform the consular duties until March 1854, when Robert C. Murphy became the first official U.S. consul in Shanghai. Johnson, *Congressional Directory (1852)*, 53; Johnson, *Congressional Directory (1853)*, 25; Johnson, *Congressional Directory (1855)*, 45; Griffin, *Clippers and Consuls*, 363–64.

43. See Appendix A.

44. See Appendix A.

45. Whampoa (Huangpu) is a city on an island in the Pearl River, lying southeast of Canton, for which it served as an outpost. *Geographical Dictionary*, 500.

46. A picul is a Chinese and Southeast Asian unit of weight, approximately 10 kilograms. *Webster's International Dictionary*, 1712.

47. Founded by William Shephard Wetmore and Joseph Archer in 1833, Wetmore and Company was an American firm with branches at Shanghai, Fuzhou, and New York. Preble, *The Opening of Japan*, 255.

48. Zhoushan is an archipelago in the East China Sea off the northeast coast of Zhejiang Province, at the entrance to Hangzhou Bay, consisting of about one thousand islands. *Geographical Dictionary*, 1340.

49. Chang Jiang or Yangzi River is the longest river of China and Asia (approximately 3,450 miles). It flows from the Tibetan plateau generally east through central China into the East China Sea at Shanghai. Cohen, *Columbia Gazetteer*, 594.

50. Chusan or Zhoushan is the largest island of the Zhoushan Archipelago in the East China Sea, about fifty miles east of Ningbo. *Geographical Dictionary*, 1320.

51. Wusong or Woosung was a port town located fourteen miles downriver from Shanghai. *Geographical Dictionary*, 1320.

52. Edward R. Cunningham (1823–1889) was vice-consul of Shanghai from 1850 to 1854. Arriving in China in 1845, he started as a clerk with Russell and Company and retired in 1877 as the managing partner of the firm.

He also served as president of the Shanghai Steam Navigation Company in 1862–1863 and 1868–1869. In 1856, with British businessman Charles Wills, Cunningham constructed the Wills' Bridge over the Suzhou Creek. Zhaojin Ji, *A History of Modern Shanghai Banking: The Rise and Decline of China's Finance Capitalism* (New York: M. E. Sharpe, Inc., 2003), 61; David Shavit, *The United States in Asia: A Historical Dictionary* (New York: Greenwood Press, 1990), 116.

53. Suzhou Creek, also known as Wusong River, is a river in China that passes through the Shanghai city center. One of the principal outlets of Lake Tai, Suzhou Creek has a length of seventy-eight miles and flows into the Huangpu River at the northern end of the Bund in Huangpu District. Cohen, *Columbia Gazetteer*, 3063.

54. Nanking is the commercial city of Jiangsu Province in East China on the south bank of the Chang, 150 miles northwest of Shanghai. Founded in 1368 during the Ming Dynasty, Nanking was taken by the British in 1842 and then largely destroyed by Taiping rebels, who held it from 1853 to 1864. *Geographical Dictionary*, 790–91.

55. See Appendix A.

56. A coach whip is a long, narrow pennant at the masthead of a war vessel that is in commission. Charles Kendall Adams, ed., *The Universal Cyclopedia* (New York: D. Appleton and Company, 1900), IV: 380.

57. Probably Eliphalet M. Brown Jr. (1816–1886), "a pioneer photographer who gave up a lucrative business in New York to accompany Perry. He brought a daguerrotype [*sic*] camera and an abundance of plates with which he took many 'stills' of scenery and people and some of our illistrations [*sic*] initialed W T Peters or H Patterson were undoubtedly redrawn by these rather obscure New York artists from Brown's daguerreotypes of which most of the originals have been lost." Before the expedition, he spent thirteen years working for various establishments, including Currier and Ives, producing portraits and historical and marine lithographs. He learned daguerreotype from his younger brother, James Sydney Brown, and made approximately four hundred daguerreotypes during the expedition. He spent twenty years in the U.S. Navy as a master and ensign, beginning in the Civil War, and later was in the Mediterranean as an admiral's secretary. He retired in 1875 and never was active in any area of art or photography. Morison, *"Old Bruin,"* 278, 393, 419, 434; Pineau, *The Personal Journal of Commodore Matthew C. Perry*, xvii; Callahan, *List of Officers of the Navy*, 80; Bruce T. Erickson, *Encyclopedia of Nineteenth-*

Century Photography, ed. John Hannavy (New York: Routledge, 2008), I: 222–24.

William B. Draper set up the first telegraph system in Japan. In 1862, in the Civil War, he held the rank of mate and resigned his commission a year later. Pineau, *The Personal Journal of Commodore Matthew C. Perry*, 228.

German-born Peter Bernard Wilhelm Heine (1827–1885) immigrated to New York City in 1849. He served with the Perry expedition to Japan from 1852 to 1854. In 1859 he returned to Europe. During the Civil War, he served as a colonel in the 103rd Regiment of New York Volunteers. In 1869 he was appointed consular clerk at the U.S. Embassy in Paris and served until 1871. William Cullen Bryant II and Thomas G. Voss, eds., *The Letters of William Cullen Bryant* (New York: Fordham University Press, 1992), V: 93–94; Wilhelm Heine, *With Perry to Japan: A Memoir*, trans. Frederic Trautmann (Honolulu: University of Hawaii Press, 1990), 178–84.

58. The HMS *Lily* was a 432-ton brig that was launched in 1837 at Pembroke Dock. She measured 101 feet l.o.a. with a 32-foot beam. In 1851 she was commanded by John Sanderson. She was sold in 1908. Colledge, *Ships of the Royal Navy*, 191.

59. "Lighting up" means to assist in hauling or to get a better haul on a rope, as in taking turns around a ballard. *Naval Encyclopedia*, 439.

60. Saddle Island, or Nanyushan, is the southernmost and largest of the Hieshan Islands, located within the entrance of the Ninghau River. United States Hydrographic Office, *Asiatic Pilot: Volume III—Coast of China, Yalu river to Hong Kong entrance* (Washington, D.C.: Government Printing Office, 1920), 323.

61. See Appendix A.

62. Naha is a seaport on the west coast of Okinawa Island and commercial center of the Ryukyu Islands. *Geographical Dictionary*, 787.

63. David Ochiltree received a commission as a midshipman in 1839. He was promoted to the rank of master on March 1855 and dropped from active service six months later. Pineau, *The Personal Journal of Commodore Matthew C. Perry*, 230; Callahan, *List of Officers of the Navy*, 412.

64. Lewis J. Williams (1819–1888) was appointed assistant surgeon, USN, in 1842 and promoted to surgeon in 1853. During the Civil War he was assigned to Admiral Farragut's West Gulf Squadron (1864–1865). In 1871 he was made medical director at the Naval Hospital and the Naval Laboratory in Brooklyn, New York. He retired in 1881. Pineau, *The*

Personal Journal of Commodore Matthew C. Perry, 232; "Archer-Mitchell-Stump-Williams Family Papers, 18th-20th century (MS. 1948)," Maryland Historical Society, http://www.mdhs.org/library/Mss/ms001948.html.

65. William B. Slack (d. 1895) started his career in the U.S. Marine Corps in 1839 with a rank of second lieutenant. In 1847 he was promoted to first lieutenant, and then quickly was appointed brevet captain. In 1860 he became a quartermaster with the rank of major and held that position until his retirement in 1885. Pineau, *The Personal Journal of Commodore Matthew C. Perry*, 231; Callahan, *List of Officers of the Navy*, 501.

66. Sho Taimu, the regent of Okinawa, was a member of the royal family and the hereditary lord of Mabuni Village, eight miles south of Naha. As king of Ryukyu, Sho Tai (1843–1901) was only ten years old when Perry visited. Bruce D. Clayton, *Shotokan's Secret: The Hidden Truth Behind Karate's Fighting Origins* (Valencia, CA: Black Belt Books, 2004), 76; *Encyclopedia of People of Okinawan History* (Naha: Okinawa Bunka-sha, 1996), 42.

67. Also known as Ogasawara Islands, Bonin Islands are a group of twenty-seven volcanic islands in the western Pacific Ocean, six hundred miles south of Tokyo, Japan, that were first colonized in 1830 by a small group of Europeans and Hawaiians. *Geographical Dictionary*, 159.

68. The Rev. Dr. Bernard J. Bettelheim (1811–1870) served for eight years (April 1846–February 1854) as the first Church of England representative of the Lew Chew mission at Naha. Born in Pressburg to a Hungarian Jewish family, he earned a medical degree at Padua in 1836 and served as a cholera specialist in Naples and Trieste and a surgeon in the Egyptian and Turkish navies. In 1853 he sent a Japanese translation of the New Testament to London. On his journey back to England after serving in Lew Chew, his ship was damaged near Bermuda, and he eventually settled in the United States. During the Civil War he served as a surgeon of the 106th Regiment Illinois Volunteer Infantry from August 16 to December 28, 1863. His later years were spent in Brookfield, Missouri. B. R. Burg, ed., *An American Seafarer in the Age of Sail: The Erotic Diaries of Philip C. Van Buskirk 1851–1870* (New Haven and London: Yale University Press, 1994), 103–4; William Leonard Schwartz, ed., "Commodore Perry at Okinawa from the Unpublished Diary of a British Missionary," *American Historical Review* 51 (January 1946): 276; Edmond Papinot, *Historical and Geographical Dictionary of Japan* (New York: Frederick Ungar Publishing Co., 1910, republished 1964, second printing 1968), 768.

69. Named after the First Lord of the Admiralty, Port Melville, or Oonting, is a harbor on the northwest side of Lew Chew and distant about thirty-five miles from Naha. J. Willet Spalding, *The Japan Expedition. Japan and Around the World; an Account of Three Visits to the Japanese Empire, with Sketches of Madeira, St. Helena, Cape of Good Hope, Mauritius, Ceylon, Singapore, China, and Loo-Choo* (New York: Redfield, 1855), 365; Basil Hall Chamberlain, "The Luchu Islands and Their Inhabitants: I. Introductory Remarks," *The Geographical Journal* 5 no. 4 (April 1895): 294; Aaron Haight Palmer, *Letter to the Hon. John M. Clayton, Secretary of State, Enclosing A Paper, Geographical, Political, and Commercial, on the Independent Oriental Nations; and Submitting a Plan for Opening, Extending, and Protecting American Commerce in the East, &c: Respectfully Submitted to the President and Cabinet, By Aaron Haight Palmer, Counsellor of the Supreme Court of the U.S.—Published by Direction of the Department of State in the National Intelligencer of the 6th September, 1849. Revised, and Now Republished with an Appendix* (Washington, D.C.: Gideon & Co., 1849), 15.

70. The schooner *Brenda* was built in 1852 at Portsmouth, New Hampshire, and was used by Russell & Co. in the opium trade between India and Canton. John Robinson and George Francis Dow, *The Sailing Ships of New England 1607–1907* (Salem, MA: Marine Research Society, 1922), 107.

71. George Washington Alexander (ca. 1829–1895), born in Francesville, Pennsylvania, was appointed third assistant engineer in 1848, promoted to second assistant engineer in 1852, and promoted to first assistant engineer in 1855. He resigned his commission in 1861 and offered his service to the Confederacy. He was part of the expedition to capture the *St. Nicholas* in 1862, was appointed assistant provost-marshal of Richmond, and served as the commandant at Castle Thunder Prison and Salisbury (North Carolina) Prison. After the Civil War he was a wanted man and escaped to Canada, spending several years teaching French to children. After the amnesty of 1872 he returned to the United States and worked as an editor of the *Sunday Gazette* in Washington, D.C. Callahan, *List of Officers of the Navy*, 19; "Old Castle Thunder: Death of Colonel Alexander, Who Was Superintendent of This Prison," *Richmond Times-Dispatch*, March 3, 1895, 1; Frances Harding Casstevens, *George W Alexander and Castle Thunder: A Confederate Prison and Its Commandant* (Jefferson, NC: McFarland & Co., 2004), 1–3.

72. Horse block is a grating platform for the convenience of the officer in charge of the deck. *Naval encyclopedia*, 348.

73. Oragawa, or Uraga, is about twenty-five miles from Edo and has a harbor that is capable of accommodating 1,200 junks. In 1846 the first U.S. emissaries, under Commo. James Biddle, landed at the port to establish relations with Japan but were repulsed. S. B. Kemish, *The Japanese Empire. Its Physical, Political and Social Condition and History. Japan in English* (London: Ganesha Publishing, 2003), 233; *Geographical Dictionary*, 1244.

74. John Kelly (d. 1863) entered service as a midshipman on February 1, 1814. He was promoted to lieutenant on January 13,1825; commander on September 8, 1841; and captain on September 14, 1855. He was given the rank of commodore on the retired list in 1862. Callahan, *List of Officers of the Navy*, 309.

   William S. Walker's naval career mirrored that of Captain Kelly, as they both entered the Navy as midshipmen on November 30, 1814. He was promoted on the same days as Captain Kelly and rose through the ranks to reach captain on September 14, 1855. He was given the rank of commodore on the retired list in 1862 and died nine months before Captain Kelly in 1863. Callahan, *List of Officers of the Navy*, 566.

75. Among them were two *yoriki*, or police magistrates, Nakajima Saburosuke and Kayama Eizaemon. Kato Yuzo, "The Opening of Japan and the Meiji Restoration, 1837–72," in *The History of Anglo-Japanese Relations. Vol. 1, The Political-Diplomatic Dimension, 1600–1930*, ed. by Ian Nish and Yoichi Kibata (Basingstoke, England: Macmillan, 2000), 68; Peter Booth Wiley and Korogi Ichiro, *Yankees in the Land of the Gods: Commodore Perry and the Opening of Japan* (New York: N.Y. Viking, 1990), 286–90; Pineau, *The Personal Journal of Commodore Matthew C. Perry*, 93–94.

76. Actually, Nakajima Saburosuke, with his Dutch interpreter Hori Tatsunosuke, returned to the *Susquehanna*. Wiley and Ichiro, *Yankee in the Land of the Gods*, 292.

77. "Trip an anchor" is to break out the flukes of a ship's anchor from an obstruction on the bottom. This is done by hauling up the anchor by its buoy-rope or tripping line, which is always made fast to its crown. *Naval Encyclopedia*, 820.

78. Mount Fuji is an active stratovolcano just west of Tokyo that last erupted in 1707–1708. Cohen, *Columbia Gazetteer*, 1055; *Geographical Dictionary*, 409.

79. The last sentence is not in Speiden's hand.

80. Written by Joseph Hopkinson in 1798, "Hail Columbia" was the unofficial national anthem of the United States of America until it was replaced with

"The Star Spangled Banner" by official mandate in 1931. Martin J. Manning and Clarence R. Wyatt, *Encyclopedia of Media and Propaganda in Wartime America* (Santa Barbara, CA: ABC-CLIO, LLC, 2011), I: 143–44.

81. "Rigamarole," or rigmarole, is a complex and sometimes ritualistic procedure. *Webster's International Dictionary*, 1957.

82. "Low Back'd Car" was a song composed by singer, songwriter, novelist, and painter Samuel Lover (1797–1868). The tune is a variant of the English folksong, "The Jolly Ploughboy." Annemarie Bean, James V. Hatch, and Brooks McNamara, eds., *Inside the Minstrel Mask: Readings in Nineteenth-Century Blackface Minstrelsy* (Hanover, NH: Wesleyan University Press, 1996), 215.

83. John Mellen Brady Clitz (1821–1897), son of Capt. John Clitz, entered the Navy as a midshipman in 1837, and then promoted to the rank of master in 1850, lieutenant in 1851, and commander in 1862. During the Civil War he commanded at different times the blockading steamers *Penobscot*, *Juniata*, and *Osceola*. After the war he was commissioned captain in 1866, performing ordnance duty at the Brooklyn Navy Yard in 1870. He reached the rank of rear admiral in 1880 and commanded the Asiatic Station, retiring his commission three years later. Pineau, *The Personal Journal of Commodore Matthew C. Perry*, 227; Callahan, *List of Officers of the Navy*, 119; Brown, *Lamb's Biographical Dictionary*, II: 78.

84. At this point in the journal, there is inserted a copy in Speiden's hand of the "Letter from the President of the United States." See Appendix B.

85. Perry's name for Kurihama, a town on the southwestern shore of Kurihama Bay, a few miles northwest of Uraga. United States Hydrographic Office, *Asiatic Pilot: Volume II—The Japan Islands* (Washington, D.C.: Government Printing Office, 1920), II: 183; J. A. Guthrie, *Seeing the World Through a Porthole* (Lynchburg, VA: J. P. Bell Company, 1916), 42.

86. The sounding spar was a pole that could be deployed off the side of the ship to act as a fishing pole for sounding the depth of the water as the ship entered and left port. Palmer, *Jane's Dictionary of Naval Terms*, 235.

87. Born in approximately 1835, Hugh Ellis of Syracuse, New York, was a cigar maker's apprentice before he enlisted in the Marine Corps. Assigned to the *Mississippi*, he sustained a fall while the vessel was en route to Japan. He developed a brain fever (possibly encephalitis or meningitis) and died. He was interred at the International Cemetery in Tomari, Naha City, Okinawa, Japan. "Syracuse Woman Finds Grave of Gallant Syracuse Marine Thousands of Miles Away," *Syracuse (NY) Post-Standard*, January 7, 1905,

6; "Sailor Boy is not Forgotten," *Syracuse (NY) Post-Standard*, February 3, 1905, 7; Paul E. Truesdell, Jr., "Interment.net Cemetery Records Online," International Cemetery—Tomari, Naha City, Okinawa, Japan. May 28, 2006, http://www.interment.net/data/japan/international_cemetery.htm.

88. Lei Yue Mun, or Lyemun, Pass is a quarter-mile strait between northeast Hong Kong Island and the mainland. *Geographical Dictionary*, 642.

89. Capsing Moon Passage is the northern entrance of the bay of Hong Kong into the China Sea. Spalding, *The Japan Expedition*, 86.

90. Blenheim Reach is ten miles south of Canton. It was named after the HMS *Blenheim*, which turned the Chinese flank during the Anglo-Chinese War in 1841. Spalding, *The Japan Expedition*, 178.

91. The Bogue, or Boca Tigris, is part of the large estuary of the Canton, or Pearl, River between Hong Kong and Macao. Several Qing Dynasty forts, including the Weiyuan and Shajiao Forts, were built at Humen Town. Cohen, *Columbia Gazetteer*, 2388.

92. Commanded by Captain Willis, the *Star of the Union* was built at Medford, Massachusetts, in 1852 by James O. Curtis. Her length from the knight heads to the taffrail was about 200 feet; her beam was 35 feet, and she weighed 1,057 tons. Owned by Reed, Wade & Co., the clipper had the bust of Daniel Webster for her head. McLean, "The New Clipper Ship *Star of the Union*, of Boston" *The Boston Daily Atlas*, December 21, 1852; Octavius T. Howe and Frederick C. Matthews, *American Clipper Ships, 1833–1858* (New York: Argosy Antiquarian Ltd., 1967), 630–33.

93. Edmund Lanier (1814–1872) began his naval career as a midshipman in 1831, and then promoted to lieutenant in 1841 and commander in 1861. He retired in 1864 and was promoted to captain in 1867 while on the retired list. Callahan, *List of Officers of the Navy*, 322.

94. The Taiping Rebellion was a widespread civil war in China from 1850 to 1864, led by Hong Xiuquan against the ruling Qing Dynasty, in which twenty million people died. Morison, *"Old Bruin,"* 297; Pineau, *The Personal Journal of Commodore Matthew C. Perry*, 116–17.

95. The copy of a general order on the increase of pay was not annexed as Speiden indicated.

96. Launched in 1850, the clipper *Sea Serpent* was built by George Raynes at Portsmouth, New Hampshire, and was owned by Grinnell, Minturn & Company of New York. Captained by William Howland, the 1,402-ton clipper was 196 feet l.o.a. with a 39-foot beam and a 21-foot depth of

hold. In 1851 she raced the *Stag Hound* and the *John Bertram* from New York to San Francisco. The *Stag Hound* won by completing the voyage in 107 days. Hugh McCulloch Gregory, *The Sea Serpent journal: Hugh McCulloch Gregory's Voyage around the World in a Clipper Ship, 1854–55,* ed. Robert H. Burgess (Charlottesville: University Press of Virginia, 1975), xiv; Walton Advertising and Printing Company, compiler, *Some Ships of the Clipper Ship Era, Their Builders, Owners, and Captains: A Glance at an Interesting Phase of the American Merchant Marine so Far as It Relates to Boston* (Boston: State Street Trust Company, 1913), 16; Carl C. Cutler, *Greyhounds of the Sea: The Story of the American Clipper Ship* (Annapolis, MD: Naval Institute Press, 1960), 414.

97. Theodore Speiden (1845–1917) was the seventh child of William and Marian (Coote) Speiden. Thomas Hamm Jr., "Speiden Family Tree," December 2008, http://worldconnect.rootsweb.ancestry.com.

98. Bayard Taylor (1825–1878) was a *New York Tribune* correspondent whom Perry described as a "landscape painter in words." In 1853 he received an appointment as master's mate in the U.S. Navy in order to journey to Japan with Perry on the *Mississippi*. He wrote about his Asian voyage in *A Visit to India, China and Japan, in the Year 1853*. Marie Hansen-Taylor and Horace E. Scudder, eds., *Life and Letters of Bayard Taylor* (Boston: Houghton, Mifflin and Co., 1885), I: 250; Bennett, *The Steam Navy of the United States,* 131.

99. Built in 1852 by Thomas Collyer at Sing Sing, New York, the steamer *Confucius,* commanded by Captain T. D. Dearbourn, had orders to tow vessels up and down the Yangtze-Kiang River. "Once Famous for Shipbuilding," *The New York Times,* April 5, 1896, 12; *Shanghae Almanac for the Bissextile or Leap Year 1856 and Miscellany* (Shanghai: The "N.C. Herald" Office, 1856), 9; *The Straits Times and Singapore Journal of Commerce,* August 30, 1853, 5.

100. Sir Fleetwood Broughton Reynolds Pellew (1789–1861) was the son of Sir Edward Pellew, First Viscount Exmouth (1757–1833). Lee, et al., *Dictionary of National Biography,* XV: 715–16.

101. Cumsing Moon or Chin-hsing-Men is an anchorage north of Macao. Pineau, *The Personal Journal of Commodore Matthew C. Perry,* 120.

102. The first USS *Southampton* was a storeship in the U.S. Navy during the Mexican War. The *Southampton* was laid down at Norfolk, Virginia, as a side-wheel steamer in October 1841, but her machinery proved to

be unsatisfactory and was removed. Apparently purchased by the U.S. government in 1845, the ship was commissioned on May 27, 1845, with Lt. Henry W. Morris in command. Mooney, *Dictionary of American Naval Fighting Ships*, VI: 564.

103. Joseph Harrod Adams (1817–1853), grandson of President John Adams and nephew of President John Quincy Adams, entered the Navy as a midshipman in 1831 and was promoted to lieutenant in 1843. He was buried in the Old Protestant Cemetery in Macao. Callahan, *List of Officers of the Navy*, 17; Pineau, *The Personal Journal of Commodore Matthew C. Perry*, 121, 226; Shyama Peebles, "Old Protestant Cemetery in Macau" (Gwulo: Old Hong Kong, October 2010), http://gwulo.com/sites/gwulo .com/files/Gwulo-Macau-Old-Protestant-Cemetery.pdf.

104. A *lorcha* is a Chinese junk-rigged coaster with a European-model hull. *Naval Encyclopedia*, 450.

105. The 30-gun *Constantine* was a 1,142-ton, 144-foot l.o.a., 37-foot beam, sail spardeck corvette. Designed by Forquenot in 1846 at Rochefort Naval Yard and commanded by Admiral Guerin, she launched in 1851 and was commissioned in 1852. John D. Grainger, *The First Pacific War: Britain and Russia, 1854–1856* (Woodbridge, Suffolk, UK, and Rochester, NY: The Boydell Press, 2008), 91; Stephen S. Roberts, "French Navy Ships, 1816–1859," 2010, http://www.shipscribe.com/marvap/311c.html.

106. William McN. Armstrong was a midshipman from 1848 until he resigned in 1854. Callahan, *List of Officers of the Navy*, 28; Pineau, *The Personal Journal of Commodore Matthew C. Perry*, 236.

107. Commanded by Capt. David S. Babcock, the *Swordfish* was a 1,036-ton, 169-foot l.o.a., 36-foot beam, three-masted wooden extreme clipper ship built in 1851 by William H. Webb for Barclay & Livingston of New York. She was sold to Crocker & Warren of New York in 1854. Howe and Matthews, *American Clipper Ships*, 649–50.

108. Luis de Camoens (1524–1580) was a Portuguese poet whose epic "The Lusiads" celebrated Vasco de Gama's voyage to India. Illustrations of his cave, or tomb, in Macao are reproduced in Roger Pineau's edition of *The Personal Journal of Commodore Matthew C. Perry*, 129. Magnus Magnusson, ed., *Cambridge Biographical Dictionary* (Cambridge: Cambridge University Press, 1990), 252.

109. Joseph C. Eldredge (d. 1881) served as a purser from 1847 until he was promoted to pay director in 1871. He retired in 1880. Callahan, *List of*

Officers of the Navy, 180; Pineau, *The Personal Journal of Commodore Matthew C. Perry*, 212–13.

110. Mrs. Hunter was the wife of William C. Hunter (1812–1891), a partner in Russell & Co., who authored *Bits of Old China* and *The "Fan Kwae" of Canton before Treaty Days, 1825–1844*. Preble, *The Opening of Japan*, 244.

111. Possibly Mary E. Nye, wife of Gideon Nye, who operated one of the important early American firms in Canton and Shanghai. They traded in tea, opium, camphor, and shipping. Preble, *The Opening of Japan*, 247.

112. The *Jamestown* was launched in 1844 at the Gosport, Virginia, Navy Yard. She operated off the western coast of Africa to suppress the slave trade, carried food to the starving poor of Ireland, protected American citizens during the epidemic of revolutions in 1848, and was assigned to the Brazil Squadron from 1851 to 1854. In 1861 she was assigned to the Atlantic Blockading Squadron. She was destroyed by fire in 1913. Her measurements were 1,150 tons, 163 feet l.o.a., with a 32-foot beam. Mooney, *Dictionary of American Naval Fighting Ships*, III: 501–2.

113. The *Colbert*, named in honor of Jean Baptiste Colbert, was a 1,294-ton French paddle corvette, which launched in 1848. Her length was 189 feet, her beam was 56 feet, and she was fitted with a 320-horsepower engine. Roberts, "French Navy Ships, 1816–1859," http://www.shipscribe.com/marvap/321b.html.

114. A founding member of Thomas Hunt & Co., well-known ships' chandlers, James Bridges Endicott (1815–1870) controlled the river route between Macao and Hong Kong. Arriving in China in 1833, he was employed by the firm of Russell & Co. and was put in charge of their receiving ship, *Ruparell*, which was anchored at Cumsing Moon, an opium transfer point in the mouth of the Pearl River. In 1851 he moved to Macao and began a steamer service with the little steamer *Spark*. Patricia Lim, *Forgotten Souls: A Social History of the Hong Kong Cemetery* (Hong Kong: Hong Kong University Press, 2011), 169–70.

115. Perhaps Mrs. William D. Lewis of William D. Lewis & Co., an American merchant in Canton. *Correspondence Relative to the Naval Expedition to Japan*, U.S. Senate, 33rd Congress, 2nd Session, Senate Executive Document 34, 79.

116. *Campo* is Portuguese for an open space or field. *Webster's International Dictionary*, 323.

117. Charles Manigault Morris (1820–1895) of South Carolina entered the U.S. Navy as a midshipman in December 1837. He was promoted to the rank of master and lieutenant in 1851 and resigned his commission in January 1861. In March of that year he was appointed a first lieutenant in the Confederate States Navy. Morris served on the Savannah, Georgia, Station in 1861–1863 and commanded CSS *Florida* from January 1864 until her capture the following October. During the remainder of the Civil War, he served abroad as an agent of the Confederacy. Pineau, *The Personal Journal of Commodore Matthew C. Perry*, 230; Society of the Cincinnati of Maryland, *Register of the Society of the Cincinnati of Maryland Brought Down to February 22nd, 1897* (Baltimore: Society of the Cincinnati of Maryland, 1897), 79–80; *National Cyclopaedia of American Biography*, IX: 118.

Probably Oliver Hazard Perry II (1825–1870), fourth child of Matthew C. Perry, who served as his father's flagship secretary after joining the expedition in China. He remained in China after the expedition and was made U.S. consul at Canton in 1855 and served for many years. Morison, *"Old Bruin,"* 447; Preble, *The Opening of Japan*, 395.

118. Possibly the clipper *Atalanta* that was built at Baltimore in 1852 by Gardner & Palmer for Montell & Co. Commanded by Captain Wallace, she had a 200-foot l.o.a., a 37-foot beam and weighed 1,289 tons. In 1856 she was sold to a Spanish merchant, H. A. Coit, who renamed her the *Marguerita*. Howe and Matthews, *American Clipper Ships*, 28.

119. A comprador is a Chinese agent of a foreign business. *Webster's International Dictionary*, 467.

120. Manned by twenty sailors and ten Chinese, the jolly-boat English steamer *Queen* weighed 150 tons and carried an armament of 4 guns of 4-pound caliber each. Spalding, *The Japan Expedition*, 346, 351.

121. Located in a group of islands of the Asiatic Archipelago between the Philippine and Molucca Islands, Salibabu (18 miles in length from northwest to southeast) lies to the south of Tulour and is separated by a channel about one mile in breadth. "Salibaboo" is discussed by Morison, *"Old Bruin,"* on page 353: "Her [*Southampton's*] passage had been eventful. Off Cape Engano Luzon, she picked up some interesting castaways—six men and boys in a twelve-foot boat. Blown out to sea by a typhoon fifteen days earlier, they had drifted the entire length of the Philippine Archipelago and were in bad shape—[Perry] figured they were from an island of that name in the Talaud group between Mindonao and

Morotai—now hence the 'Sally Babbooans.'" Royal Geographical Society, *A Gazetter of the world, or Dictionary of Geographical Knowledge, compiled from the most recent authorities, and forming a complete body of modern geography, physical, political, statistical, historical, and ethnographical* (London and Dublin: A. Fullarton & Co., 1856), VI: 406.

122. Located on the lower end of Lapa Island, west of Macao, Ringing Rocks was a pile of granite boulders that created a bell-like sound when struck. They were known to the Chinese as the Silver Gorge. William Fred. Mayers, N. B. Dennys, and Charles King, *The treaty ports of China and Japan: A complete guide to the open ports of those countries, together with Peking, Yedo, Hongkong and Macao*, ed. N B Dennys (London: Trubner and Co., 1867), 219–20.

123. Humphrey Marshall (1812–1872) was a Whig congressman from Kentucky in 1849–1852, and U.S. commissioner and consul to China in 1852–1854. He later served as a Know-Nothing congressman (1853–1854) and was a Confederate brigadier general in 1861–1863. Johnson and Malone, *Dictionary of American Biography*, VI: 310–11; *National Cyclopaedia of American Biography*, II: 368; Preble, *The Opening of Japan*, 73.

124. HMS *Rattler* was an 888-ton sloop fitted with an engine and screw propeller, rather than paddlewheels. The 176-foot-l.o.a., 32-foot-beam ship was launched in 1843 at Sheerness Dockyard. Colledge, *Ships of the Royal Navy*, 268; Pineau, *The Personal Journal of Commodore Matthew C. Perry*, 140.

125. Commanded by Lt. John J. Glasser, the *Lexington*, a 691-ton, 127-foot-l.o.a., 33-foot-beam converted storeship, was bringing a printing press and other bulky presents for the emperor of Japan. She was built by the New York Navy Yard in 1825 and was commissioned in 1826. She was decommissioned in 1855 and sold in 1860. Pineau, *The Personal Journal of Commodore Matthew C. Perry*, 136; Morison, "Old Bruin," 316, 353, 356; Mooney, *Dictionary of American Naval Fighting Ships*, IV: 101–2.

126. William Rufus de Vane King (1786–1853) was a congressman from North Carolina in 1811–1816, a senator from Alabama in 1819–1844 and 1844–1846, and vice president for six weeks in 1853. *National Cyclopaedia of American Biography*, IV: 147.

Chapte 3. Volume One: 1854

1. Sir Samuel George Bonham (1803–1863) served as the third governor of Hong Kong and chief superintendent of British trade in China (1849–

1854). G. B. Endacott, *A Biographical Sketch-Book of Early Hong Kong* (Hong Kong: Hong Kong University Press, 2005), 30–35.

2. Jonathan Goble (1827–1896) enlisted in the U.S. Marines in 1851 and served on the *Mississippi* during the Perry's expedition. Ordained in 1859, he returned to Japan a year later as the first missionary of the American Baptist Free Mission Society. In 1871 he translated the Gospel of Mark into Japanese, the first portion of the New Testament to be printed in Japan. Also in the same year, he invented the *jinrikisha*, or rickshaw, to transport his invalid wife. He returned to the United States in 1883. His journal is in the Navy Department Library in Washington, D.C. Helen Barrett Montgomery, *Following the Sunrise: A Century of Baptist Missions, 1813–1913* (Philadelphia: American Baptist Publication Society, 1913), 181–82; William Elliot Griffis, "American Makers of the New Japan," *The Century Illustrated* LXXXVI no. 1 (May 1913): 697; Shavit, *The United States in Asia*, 191.

3. Built in 1846 by William Fairbairn for the Peninsular and Oriental Steam Navigation Company, the *Pottinger*, weighing 1,250 tons, was fitted with 450-horsepower engines. She was scrapped in 1867. Charles F. T. Young, *The Fouling and Corrosion of Iron Ships: Their Causes and Means of Prevention with the Mode of Application to the Existing Iron-clads* (London: The London Drawing Association, 1867), 29, 57.

4. The flagship of Rear Adm. Fleetwood Broughton Reynolds Pellew, the 173-foot-long, 44-foot-beam HMS *Winchester* was commanded by Capt. Granville Gower Loch. The 52-gun, 1,487-ton, fourth-rate ship was launched in 1822 at Woolwich Dockyard. She became a training ship in 1861. Colledge, *Ships of the Royal Navy*, 358.

5. Taiwan, also known as Formosa, is an island situated in the Western Pacific Ocean and located off the southeastern coast of mainland China. Some Dutch settlements were established in the seventeenth century but were driven out by the Chinese. It was not available to Europeans again until the Treaty of Tientsui opened a few ports in 1858. *Geographical Dictionary*, 1154–55; Cohen, *Columbia Gazetteer*, 3087.

6. The island of Great Botel Tobago, or Lan Yu Island, lies southeast of Taiwan and forty-five miles east of Cape Oluanpi. Cohen, *Columbia Gazetteer*, 1678.

7. Elizabeth M. Bettelheim (b. 1815). 1870 U.S. Census, Linn Co., MO, pop. sch., Brookfield, 41 (penned), Elizabeth Bettelheim, http://www.ancestry.com/: 2011.

8. Probably James Willett Spalding (b. 1827), who was the captain's clerk.

9. Shuri is a port on Okinawa Island. It was formerly a separate city unto itself, and the royal capital of the Ryukyu Kingdom. Papinot, *Historical and Geographical Dictionary of Japan*, 595.

10. Eli Crosby (d. 1854) began his career in 1849 as a third assistant engineer and was promoted to second assistant engineer in 1851. Callahan, *List of Officers of the Navy*, 140.

11. Arthur Sinclair Jr. was the captain's clerk of the *Supply*, and son of the *Supply*'s commanding officer. He began his career as a midshipman in 1823. He was promoted to lieutenant in 1835 and commander in 1855. He was dismissed from his duties in 1861. Callahan, *List of Officers of the Navy*, 499.

12. Breese was attached to the USS *Macedonian* in search of coal on the north end of the island of Formosa, and in investigation of the captivity of Americans by the inhabitants of that island. Wilson and Friske, *Appletons' Cyclopaedia of American Biography*, I: 366–67.

13. Samuel Wells Williams (1812–1884) began his career in China as a printer to the American Board of Foreign Missions in 1832. Ten years later he was appointed corresponding secretary of the Morrison Education Society. After returning to the United States in 1845, he published "The Middle Kingdom" three years later. He accepted a position as editor of the *Chinese Repository*, a leading western journal, from 1848 to 1851. He accompanied Perry to Japan, serving as an official interpreter. In 1860 he was appointed charge d'affaires in Peking and served in this capacity until 1876. In 1881 he was elected president of the American Bible Society. Frederick Wells Williams, *The Life and Letters of Samuel Wells Williams, LL.D.: Missionary Diplomatist, Sinologue* (New York and London: G. P. Putnam's Sons, 1889), 11, 168, 447, 461; "Obituary—Prof. S. Wells Williams," *The Publishers' Weekly* XXV (1884): 243; *Memorials of Protestant Missionaries to the Chinese: Giving a List of their Publications, and Obituary Notices of the Deceased* (Shanghai: American Presbyterian Mission Press, 1867), 76–78.

14. Edward Dunham Robie (1831–1911) began his naval career as the third assistant engineer of the *Mississippi* in 1852. He was promoted to second assistant engineer in 1855, first assistant engineer in 1858, and chief engineer in 1861. He erected and operated the first line of telegraph ever seen in Japan and instructed the Japanese in building and operating the first steam railways. He was chief engineer of the Norfolk Navy Yard from 1874 to 1877 and from 1887 to 1891. He was placed on the retired

list in 1893 with the rank of commodore. Callahan, *List of Officers of the Navy*, 466; Erik S. Hinckley and Tom Ledoux, eds., *They Went to War: A Biographical Register of the Green Mountain State in the Civil War* (Victoria, BC, Canada: Trafford Publishing, 2010), 193.

15. Amami-O-Shima is the largest island in the Amami-Gunto island group in the Ryukyu Archipelago. It lies roughly halfway between the islands of Okinawa and Kyushu. During the Perry expedition, it was apparently named Preble Island. Cohen, *Columbia Gazetteer*, 89; *Geographical Dictionary*, 40; Preble, *The Opening of Japan*, 202.

16. Perry had named this Anchorage in his journal entry of July 15–16, 1853, during his first visit to Japan. It is off present day Yokosuka Ko. Morison, *"Old Bruin,"* 322.

17. Junius J. Boyle (ca. 1807–1870), commander of the *Southampton*, started his naval career as a midshipman in 1823. He was promoted to lieutenant in 1832. He prepared the "Report of an Examination of Volcano Bay," which appears in Vol. II of Perry's *Narrative*. Callahan, *List of Officers of the Navy*, 71.

18. William L. Maury (1813–1878) began his naval career as a midshipman in 1829. He was promoted to lieutenant in 1841 and resigned his commission in 1861. Maury Island was named after him during the 1841 Wilkes expedition. Callahan, *List of Officers of the Navy*, 357; Pineau, *The Personal Journal of Commodore Matthew C. Perry*, 229; Morison, *"Old Bruin,"* 316, 360, 419.

19. "They brought with them." Speiden repeated these four words in his journal.

20. Known also as Natsu Shima, Webster Island is a partly wooded island about one and a half miles south of Koshiba Zaki, or Fillmore Point, in the "American Anchorage." United States Hydrographic Office, *Asiatic Pilot*, II: 164; Pineau, *The Personal Journal of Commodore Matthew C. Perry*, 165; Morison, *"Old Bruin,"* 322.

21. Point Hope was situated near Graham Bluff, or Konosu Bana, north of Koshiba Zaki. Morison, *"Old Bruin,"* 322.

22. Kawasaki is a southern suburb of Tokyo on the west coast of Japan. Kanagawa is a subdivision of Yokohama, where the United States and Japan signed a treaty on March 31, 1854, that opened the port for trade. *Geographical Dictionary*, 579; Cohen, *Columbia Gazetteer*, 1521.

23. Shinagawa is a ward south of Tokyo on Honshu Island in Tokyo Bay. It is bordered north by Minato Ward, south by Ota Ward, and west by Meguro Ward. Cohen, *Columbia Gazetteer*, 2901.

24. Contee has described Eizaemon Kayama, who was an aid to the governor of Uraga, as "a gentleman, clever, polished, well-informed, a fine large man, about thirty-four, of most excellent countenance, taking his wine freely, and a boon companion." Frederick Hadland Davis, *Japan, from the age of the gods to the fall of Tsingtau* (New York: Frederick A. Stokes Co., 1916), 234.

25. Hayashi, Daigaku no Kami, served as the prince counselor. The lord rector of the University at Edo, he was "about fifty-five years old, well formed, of middle size, of grave and reserved deportment. He might be likened in appearance to Maryland Congressman Reverdy Johnson." Pineau, *The Personal Journal of Commodore Matthew C. Perry*, 162, 184.

26. Founded by the Portuguese in the sixteenth century, Nagasaki is the capital and the largest city of Nagasaki Prefecture on the island of Kyushu in Japan. *Geographical Dictionary*, 787; Cohen, *Columbia Gazetteer*, 2104.

27. During this period, a Russian mission under Admiral Yevfimy Vasilyevich Putyatin was in Nagasaki to negotiate a treaty. In 1855 the two countries concluded negotiations and signed the Shimoda treaty. Marius B. Jansen, *The Making of Modern Japan* (Cambridge, MA: Belknap Press of Harvard University Press, 2000), 270, 283.

28. Yokohama was a fishing village in 1854, eighteen miles southeast of Edo on the west shore of Tokyo Bay. *Geographical Dictionary*, 1331.

29. Franklin Buchanan (1800–1874) entered the Navy as a midshipman in 1815. He was promoted to lieutenant in 1825, commander in 1841, and captain in 1855. He was dismissed of his duties in 1861 and became an admiral in the Confederate Navy during the Civil War, during which he participated in the battles of Hampton Roads and Mobile Bay. Callahan, *List of Officers of the Navy*, 86; *Webster's New Biographical Dictionary*, 208.

30. Robert Williams (ca. 1830–1854) was buried in the cemetery of Gyokusenji Temple in Shimoda. Oliver Statler, *The Black Ship Scroll. An account of the Perry expedition at Shimoda in 1854 and the lively beginnings of people-to-people relations between Japan & America, based on contemporary records, with translations by Richard Lane, Ph.D. and scroll paintings in full color by an anonymous Japanese eyewitness* (Rutland, VT: Charles E. Tuttle Company, 1964), 73.

31. Presumably this is the chaplain's report, but it is written in Speiden's hand.

32. At this point in the journal, there is inserted a copy in Speiden's hand of "Answer to the Presidents [*sic*] letter to the Emperor of Japan through the Imperial Commissioners." See Appendix B.

33. The Shimabara Peninsula is located on the west coast of Kyushu, east of Nagasaki, between Tachibana and Shimabara Bays. The peninsula was the site of an early Christian establishment, and individuals from this area and nearby Amakusa Island rebelled in 1637–1638. About 37,000 Christians perished in the siege and fall of a castle stronghold ordered by Japanese emperor Cemitsu. After the insurrection was quelled, Christianity was outlawed. Cohen, *Columbia Gazetteer*, 2900; *Geographical Dictionary*, 1082–83.

34. Dr. Arthur Middleton Lynah (1825–1890) graduated from the Medical College of the State of South Carolina in 1847. He continued his studies in Philadelphia in 1850. After the Perry expedition, he assisted in laying the Atlantic Cable and served in the cholera hospital in Philadelphia. During the Civil War he entered the Confederate naval service under Commodore Ingraham, attached to the iron-clad gunboats *Chicora* and *Palmetto State* in the Charleston harbor. After the war, he was associated with Dr. Raoul in the drug business and practiced on Sullivan's Island. Joseph Ioor Waring, *A History of Medicine in South Carolina 1825–1900* (Columbia: South Carolina Medical Association, 1967), 260–61.

35. Morison, in his account of the burial at Yokohama of Robert W. Williams, the marine private who died on board the *Mississippi*, states that Williams' body was later disinterred and buried at Shimoda, where it is still marked by a gravestone. Morison, *"Old Bruin,"* 369–70.

36. Increase Carpenter Smith (1838–1905) of New York was only fourteen years old when he served as a first class boy on the *Mississippi*. During the Civil War he served as an acting third assistant engineer in 1863 and acting second assistant engineer in 1864. He was honorably discharged in 1865. A year later he was recommissioned as an acting second assistant engineer and served one year until he was mustered out. In 1902 he was the chief engineer of the SS *City of Savannah* of the O. S. S. Company. In 1905 he was the chief engineer of the steamer *City of Atlanta*. Callahan, *List of Officers of the Navy*, 504; "Obituary," *The Brooklyn Daily Eagle*, January 2, 1906, 22; "Obituary," *The New York Sun*, January 2, 1906, 2.

37. Edmund C. Bittinger (d. 1889) served as a chaplain in the U.S. Navy from 1850 to 1881. Morison, *"Old Bruin,"* 372–73; Callahan, *List of Officers of the Navy*, 59.

38. The telegraphists were William B. Draper and John P. Williams (ca. 1826–1857), the brother of S. Wells Williams. On Williams' tombstone in

Morrison Chapel and Protestant Cemetery at Macao, the transcription states "he assisted in setting up the first magnetic telegraph in Japan in 1854." After the expedition, he remained in Asia and took command of the river steamer *Spark*, which was owned by J. B. Endicott. Lindsay Ride and May Ride, *An East India Company Cemetery: Protestant Burials in Macao*, ed. Bernard Mellor (Hong Kong: Hong Kong University Press, 1996), 101.

39. The daguerreotypist was Eliphalet M. Brown Jr.

40. Dr. James Morrow (1820–1865), the expedition's agriculturalist/botanist, had his journal published, *A Scientist with Perry in Japan: The Journal of Dr. James Morrow*, ed. Allan B. Cole (Chapel Hill: University of North Carolina Press, 1947). Morison, *"Old Bruin,"* 279, 353, 386, 420, 433, 411, 421–23; Pineau, *The Personal Journal of Commodore Matthew C. Perry*, xvi, xvii, 177, 230.

41. Jesse Gay began his naval career as a first assistant engineer in 1847. He was promoted to chief engineer in 1848 and resigned his commission in 1859. Pineau, *The Personal Journal of Commodore Matthew C. Perry*, 228; Callahan, *List of Officers of the Navy*, 213.

42. Shimoda is a port southeast of Izu Peninsula. Papinot, *Historical and Geographical Dictionary of Japan*, 572.

43. The Ethiopian Minstrels were played partly by Negroes in Perry's squadron but mostly by white sailors in blackface. The folk-cultural show sprang up in 1843. A line of banjo players was drawn up with the two men at either end, "Mistah Bones" and "Mistah Tambo," exchanging jokes and insults. A man called the Interlocutor umpired the two men. The banjo orchestra accompanied popular songs and dances, and the entertainment concluded with a burlesque on some popular play or opera, in Negro dialect, such as Bulwer Lytton's romantic play, "The Lady of Lyons." Samuel Eliot Morison, "Commodore Perry's Japan Expedition Press and Shipboard Theatre," *Proceedings of the American Antiquarian Society* 77 no. 1 (1967): 39.

44. No card is present in the journal.

45. The town of Matsumae is located on the extreme southwest peninsula of Hokkaido on the Tsugaru Strait, which separates Honshu to the south and Hokkaido to the north and provides passage between the northwest Pacific Ocean and the Sea of Japan. Cohen, *Columbia Gazetteer*, II: 199.

46. Ido, the prince of Tsushima and one of the Uraga *bugyo*, was "about fifty years old, tall and rather corpulent with a pleasant expression, resembling the Minister of London James Buchanan." Pineau, *The Personal Journal of*

Commodore Matthew C. Perry, 184; Wiley and Ichiro, *Yankees in the Land of the Gods*, 391.

47. Izawa, the prince of Mimasaka and the Nagasaki *bugyo*, was "forty-one years old, best looking, quite gay, fond of fun and frolic and had the reputation of being a Lothario, had the most liberal view with respect to foreign intercourse. He resembled Secretary of the Treasury Thomas Corwin." Pineau, *The Personal Journal of Commodore Matthew C. Perry*, 184; Wiley and Ichiro, *Yankees in the Land of the Gods,* 391.

48. Nagatoshi Udono was a "member of the Board of Revenue and metsuke or censor, about fifty-five years old, tall, having prominent features, resembling Postmaster General Cave Johnson." Pineau, *The Personal Journal of Commodore Matthew C. Perry*, 184; Wiley and Ichiro, *Yankees in the Land of the Gods*, 391.

49. Michitaro Matsuzaki, the official scribe, was "sixty years old, tall and lank and very nearsighted." Pineau, *The Personal Journal of Commodore Matthew C. Perry*, 184.

50. Perhaps Speiden's sister, Marian Eliza Speiden (1829–1903). Hamm, "Speiden Family Tree," http://worldconnect.rootsweb.ancestry.com; Langley, "A Naval Dependent in Washington," 106.

51. John Rodgers Goldsborough (1809–1877) served for a year on board the USS *John Adams* before being appointed midshipman in 1824. He was promoted to lieutenant in 1837. From 1844 to 1850 he was on coast survey duty, and from 1850 to 1854 he commanded the U.S. sloop *Saratoga* in the East Indies. In 1855 he was promoted to commander and ordered to command the naval rendezvous at Philadelphia. During the Civil War he commanded the U.S. steamer *Union* in the Atlantic Blockading Squadron, the Potomac Flotilla, and the South Atlantic Blockading Squadron. In 1862 he was promoted to captain, and to commodore in 1867. Pineau, *The Personal Journal of Commodore Matthew C. Perry*, 228; John Rodger Goldsborough, "Commodore Perry's Landing in Japan, 1853," *The American Neptune* VII (1947): 18–20.

52. James H. Jones (d. 1880) entered the U.S. Marine Corps as a second lieutenant in 1847. He was promoted to first lieutenant in 1853, captain in 1861, lieutenant colonel in 1864, and colonel in 1879. Callahan, *List of Officers of the Navy*, 689; Pineau, *The Personal Journal of Commodore Matthew C. Perry*, 229.

53. Anton L. C. Portman traveled to Japan with Perry as an interpreter from the Dutch. In 1861 he returned to Japan to assist the American government

until 1866, when he accepted a position as secretary of the American delegation. Just prior to the fall of the shogunate, he successfully negotiated the establishment of a railroad line from Yokohama to Edo (Tokyo). Louis-Frédéric, *Japan Encyclopedia*, trans. Kathe Roth (Cambridge, MA: Belknap Press of Harvard University Press, 2002), 776–77.

54. G. W. Parish (ca. 1830–1854) from Hebron, Connecticut, was buried in the cemetery of Gyokusenji Temple in Shimoda. Statler, *The Black Ship Scroll*, 73; Grant Romer, "Near the Temple at Yokushen. . . ." *Image: Journal of Photography and Motion Pictures of the International Museum of Photography at George Eastman House* 29 no. 2 (August 1986): 6.

55. Hakodate is a city and port located on Hokkaido, Japan. It is the capital city of Oshima Subprefecture. *Geographical Dict*ionary, 467.

56. After this point in the journal, there is a four-page copy of "a translated letter from two Intelligent Japanese." See Appendix B.

57. Hori Tatsunosuke (1823–1892) was an official interpreter and translator of Dutch. He learned English and founded a school for teaching English, and he published an important manual for learning English entitled "A Pocket Dictionary of the English-Japanese Language." Donald Keene, *Emperor of Japan: Meiji and his World, 1852–1912* (New York: Columbia University Press, 2002), 729; James Stanlaw, *Japanese English: Language and Culture Contact* (Hong Kong: Hong Kong University Press, 2004), 50.

58. Tsugaru Strait, also known as the Straits of Sangar or Matsmai, is a channel between Honshu and Hokkaido in northern Japan connecting the Sea of Japan with the Pacific Ocean. Julia H. Macleod, "Three Letters Relating to the Perry Expedition to Japan," *The Huntington Library Quarterly*, Vol. 6, No. 2 (February 1943): 234.

59. In 1811, Captain Vasilii Mikhailovich Golovnin (1776–1831), commander of the *Diana*, was assigned to survey the Japanese-controlled southern Kurile Islands. At that time, Japanese only allowed foreign ships to enter the port at Nagasaki. As he approached the southernmost island of Kunashir, the Japanese tricked Golovnin into coming ashore. Although he proclaimed his peaceful intentions, Golovnin and seven other sailors were taken prisoner by the Japanese and held until 1813, when his second-in-command, Pyotr Ivanovich Rikord (1776–1855), negotiated his release. In 1816 he published his account of captivity, entitled *Narrative of my captivity in Japan, during the years 1811, 1812 & 1813 . . . to which is added an account of voyages to the coasts of Japan, and of negotiations with the Japanese, for the release of the author and his companions, by Captain*

Rikord. It was the first description of the Japanese to appear in Russian and only the second European account since German naturalist and physician Kaempfer's *History of Japan* in 1727. Vasilii Golovnin, *Around the World on the Kamchatka, 1817–1819*, trans. Ella Lury Wiswell (Honolulu: The Hawaiian Historical Society and The University Press of Hawaii, 1979), xix, xxiii, xxvi; *Geographical Dictionary*, 615.

60. A mace is a Chinese monetary unit and a measurement of weight, equal to one tenth of a tael (weight of silver). *Webster's International Dictionary*, 1352, 2327.

61. Volcano, or Uchiura, Bay is a crescent-shaped inlet on the east coast of the southern extension of Hokkaido, Japan. *Geographical Dictionary*, 1215; Cohen, *Columbia Gazetteer*, 3255.

62. At this point in the journal, there is inserted a translation of some Japanese communication received at Hakodate. See Appendix B.

63. Per treaty, Shimoda and Hakodate became open ports to the United States on March 31, 1854. Morison, *"Old Bruin,"* 279–80.

64. At this point in the journal, Speiden inserted "Lines found in a Japanese Tea box." See Appendix B.

65. Catty is an Asian unit of weight, equivalent to approximately one and one-third pounds. *Webster's International Dictionary*, 355.

66. Succeeding Bettelheim, Rev. G. H. Moreton arrived with his wife and his son, Philip, on Okinawa in February 1854. Moreton's health failed and he left Okinawa in October of 1855. Hawks, *Commodore Perry and the Opening of Japan*, 498.

Chapter 4. Volume Two: 1854

1. William Board, apparently while intoxicated, allegedly entered a house and raped an Okinawan woman. The villagers chased him down, beat and stoned him, and drowned him. His body was interred in a small, private Naha cemetery that commemorated Perry's voyages. Chuck Overby, "Six Letters from Japan," 2007, http://www.article9society.org/pp-17.pdf; Wiley and Ichiro, *Yankees in the Land of the Gods*, 456–57; Hawks, *Commodore Perry and the Opening of Japan*, 492.

2. LeRoy Arnold received his commission as a third assistant engineer in 1852 and served on the USS *Powhatan*. He resigned his commission in 1856. Pineau, *The Personal Journal of Commodore Matthew C. Perry*, 226; Callahan, *List of Officers of the Navy*, 28.

3. Robert Tansill (1812–1890) enlisted in the U.S. Marine Corps in 1833 and was promoted to second lieutenant in 1840, first lieutenant in 1847, and captain in 1858. He relinquished his commission in 1861 and accepted a position in the Confederate Marine Corps in 1862 with the rank of captain. During the Civil War he was taken prisoner while near Fort Fisher and was exchanged in 1865. After the war he served as mayor of Manassas. Pineau, *The Personal Journal of Commodore Matthew C. Perry*, 231; Callahan, *List of Officers of the Navy*, 698; Bruce S. Allardice, *Confederate Colonels: A Biographical Register* (Columbia: University of Missouri Press, 2008), 364.

4. See Appendix B.

5. There is no program or playbill of the Ethiopic Concert present in the journal.

6. Located in Zhejiang Province, Ningbo is one of China's oldest seaports. Known to the Portuguese as Liampo and lying on the south side of Hangzhou Bay and facing the East China Sea to the east, it served as a trade city two thousand years ago and a major port in the Tang and Song Dynasties. Xiamen, or Amoy, is a coastal city in southeastern China in the Fujian Province, and it lies near the Taiwan Strait at the mouth of the Jiulong, or Amoy, River. Thomas Allom, "The City of Ning Po," 2010, http://www.chinese-outpost.com/history/thomas-allom-china-illustrated/the-city-of-ning-po.asp; *Geographical Dictionary*, 832; Cohen, *Columbia Gazetteer*, 2189.

7. James Keenan (1823–1862) was appointed U.S. consul of Hong Kong in May 1853, but he did not arrive to his post until February 1854. He held the position until 1862. Griffin, *Clippers and Consuls*, 361.

8. Formerly the New York pilot boat *Skiddy*, the USS *Fenimore Cooper*, weighing ninety-five tons, was purchased by the Navy in 1853. She was commissioned the same year to be used as a tender for the North Pacific exploring and surveying expedition with Master H. K. Stevens in command of her. In 1859 she was lost in a typhoon near Yokohama. Mooney, *Dictionary of American Naval Fighting Ships*, II: 401.

9. The USS *Vincennes*, a 703-ton, *Boston*-class sloop-of-war, was launched in 1826. During her service, *Vincennes* patrolled the Pacific, explored the Antarctic, and blockaded the Confederate Gulf Coast in the Civil War. Named for the Revolutionary War Battle of Vincennes, she was the first U.S. warship to circumnavigate the globe. Mooney, *Dictionary of American Naval Fighting Ships*, VII: 525–27.

10. American Reach is the eastern end of Elliot Passage, an immediate branch of the Canton River leading to Whampoa from Canton. United States Hydrographic Office, *Asiatic Pilot: Volume IV—The Shores of the China Sea From Singapore Strait to and including Hongkong* (Washington, D.C.: Government Printing Office, 1915), IV: 444.

11. Launched by the Boston Navy Yard in 1850 for service as a steam tug, the *John Hancock* was damaged by a storm in 1851 near Havana, Cuba. She was rebuilt almost entirely and relaunched in 1853, measuring 382 tons, 165 feet l.o.a., with a 22-foot beam and a 10-foot draft, and Lt. John Rodgers in command. As part of Ringgold's Northern Pacific survey expedition, she surveyed the waters surrounding the large islands off the coast of Southeast Asia. The *John Hancock* was decommissioned at Mare Island Navy Yard in 1856 and sold at auction in 1865. Mooney, *Dictionary of American Naval Fighting Ships*, III: 531–32.

12. The breed of the dogs was the Japanese Chin or Spaniel. James Watson, *The Dog Book: A Popular History of the Dog, with Practical Information as to Care and Management of House, Kennel, and Exhibition Dogs; and Descriptions of All the Important Breeds* (New York: Doubleday, Page & Co., 1906), II: 733.

13. Green Island Passage is off the northwest coast of Kennedy Town on Hong Kong Island, separated by the Sulphur Channel. Spalding, *The Japan Expedition*, 86.

14. The *Jeanne d'Arc* started off as a second-class, 58-gun sail frigate. Built in Brest, the 2,275-ton, 170-foot l.o.a. ship was launched and commissioned in 1821. She participated in the Crimean War. In Lorient she was converted into a third-class sail frigate, weighing 1,675 tons and 157 feet l.o.a. She was launched in 1847 and commissioned in 1852. In 1865 she became the hospital hulk *Prudence*, subsequently serving at St. Nazaire. She was decommissioned in 1898. Roberts, "French Navy Ships, 1816–1859," http://www.shipscribe.com/marvap/212a.html and http://www.shipscribe .com/marvap/213b.html.

15. Bamboo Town is located on the northern side of Danes Island, or Chang chau. James B. Lawrence, *China and Japan, and a voyage thither: an account of a cruise in the waters of the East Indies, China, and Japan* (Hartford, CT: Press of Case, Lockwood and Brainard, 1870), 166.

16. The storeship *J. P. Kennedy* was transferred from Ringgold's U.S. North Pacific surveying expedition to Perry's squadron to protect the American interest in China during the Taiping Rebellion. John H. Schroeder,

Shaping a Maritime Empire: The Commercial and Diplomatic Role of the American Navy, 1829–1861 (Westport, CT, and London: Greenwood Press, 1985), 160.

17. Robert Milligan McLane (1815–1898) was appointed by President Franklin Pierce as commissioner to China in 1853 with the powers of a minister plenipotentiary. During his political career, he served as ambassador to Mexico, France, and China; as a member of the Maryland House of Representatives; and as the thirty-ninth governor of Maryland. Garraty and Carnes, *American National Biography*, XV: 134–36.

18. Leonard Moses (ca. 1816–1857) was a carpenter in the USS *Saratoga*. Pineau, *The Personal Journal of Commodore Matthew C. Perry*, 230; 1850 U.S. Census, Rockingham Co., NH, pop. sch., Portsmouth, 185 (penned), Leonard Moses, Ancestry.com. http://www.ancestry.com/ : 2011.

19. Monsiuer Alphonse de Bourboulon (1809–1877) served as the French minister to Canton from 1851 to 1857. James D. Johnston, *China and Japan: Being a Narrative of the Cruise of the U.S. Steam-Frigate Powhatan in the Years 1857, '58, '59, and '60 including an Account of the Japanese Embassy to the United States, Illustrated with Life Portraits of the Embassadors and their Principal Officials* (Philadelphia: Charles DeSilver, 1860), 225; W. F. Vande Walle and Noel Golvers, eds., *The History of the Relations Between the Low Countries and China in the Qing Era (1644–1911)* (Leuven, Belgium: Leuven University Press, 2003), 385; Preble, *The Opening of Japan*, 379.

20. The *Shooting Star* was designed, modeled and draughted by Capt. John Wade and built by James O. Curtis, one of the best shipbuilders in Medford, Massachusetts, in 1851. She was owned by Reed, Wade & Co. and W. & F. H. Whittemore & Co. Commanded by Capt. Judah P. Baker, she was a 903-ton, 171-foot-l.o.a., 35-foot-beam clipper with a full female figure ornamenting the bow. McLean, "The New Clipper Ship *Shooting Star*, of Boston" *The Boston Daily Atlas*, March 6, 1851; Howe and Matthews, *American Clipper Ships*, 571–73.

21. Sir John Bowring (1792–1872) was an English political economist, traveler, miscellaneous writer, polyglot, and the fourth governor of Hong Kong (1854–1859). Endacott, *A Biographical Sketch-Book of Early Hong Kong*, 36–44.

22. Many sources have Perry and Bent leaving on the Peninsular & Oriental mail steamer *Hindostan* and traveling via the Isthmus of Suez to Trieste, Vienna, Dresden, Berlin, and Holland. Interestingly, on April 23, 1855, from 3:15 p.m. to 3:50 p.m., Perry visited the *Mississippi* one last time

two days before she was decommissioned at the Brooklyn Navy Yard. Wiley and Ichiro, *Yankees in the Land of the Gods*, 454; Morison, *"Old Bruin,"* 409; John H. Schroeder, *Matthew Calbraith Perry: Antebellum Sailor and Diplomat* (Annapolis, MD: Naval Institute Press, 2001), 249; Bennett, *The Steam Navy of the United States*, 135; *Logbooks of the U.S.S. Mississippi*.

23. The USS *Porpoise*, a 230-ton square-rigged foremast and schooner-rigged mainmast brig, was authorized by Congress in 1834, built in 1835, and launched from Boston, Massachusetts, in 1836, with Lt. William Ramsay in command. After conducting coastal surveying operations in the summer of 1837, she hunted pirates along the southern coast before resuming her survey work in December 1837. With Lt. Cadwalader Ringgold in command, she was assigned to the Wilkes U.S. Exploring Expedition Squadron and confirmed the existence of the Antarctic, charted vast areas of the South Pacific, and circumnavigated the globe. In 1842–1843 she patrolled for slavers off the west coast of Africa. Between February 1845 and July 1847, *Porpoise* cruised in the Gulf of Mexico, participating in the naval operations against Tampico, Pánuco, and Veracruz during the Mexican War. During the next three and a half years she again hunted slavers along the west coast of Africa. In May 1853 she was assigned to the North Pacific exploring and surveying expedition to chart many of the Pacific islands. While on this expedition, she parted from the other vessel on September 21, 1854, between Formosa and China and was never heard from again. Mooney, *Dictionary of American Naval Fighting Ships*, V: 353.

24. Isa Sintshiro, or Shinjiro Isa, the second lieutenant governor of Shimoda, was a minor official of the Tokugawa shogun. Pineau, *The Personal Journal of Commodore Matthew C. Perry*, 211; Spalding, *The Japan Expedition*, 319; Herbert Henry Gowen, *Five Foreigners in Japan* (Freeport, NY: Books for Libraries Press, 1967), 259; James A. B. Scherer, *Japan—Whither?: A Discussion of Japanese Problems* (Tokyo: The Hokuseido Press, 1933), 102.

25. Honolulu is a city on the south coast of Oahu Island. It became the permanent capital of the Kingdom of Hawaii in 1845. Cohen, *Columbia Gazetteer*, 1305.

26. The USS *Portsmouth*, designed by Josiah Barker and built in Portsmouth, New Hampshire, was a wooden sloop-of-war. She launched in 1843 and was commissioned in 1844, with Cdr. John Berrien Montgomery in command. Mooney, *Dictionary of American Naval Fighting Ships*, V: 361.

Sloop-of-war *St. Mary's* was built in 1843–1844 at the Washington Navy Yard, Washington, D.C., and was commissioned in the fall of 1844 with Cdr.

Theodorus Bailey in command. She was assigned to the Pacific Squadron. Mooney, *Dictionary of American Naval Fighting Ships*, VI: 250–51.

27. According to *Logbooks of the U.S.S. Mississippi*, Lt. John Clitz recorded from noon to 3 p.m. that there was "Considerable damage to the Ship in different places about her woodwork and rigging—Ship under Storm Mizzen and behaving beautifully—The Sea very heavy and in my opinion, the wind in puffs it at its Maximum—The Weather Cloudy and Squally— the Scud passing very low and with great rapidity—The Starboard bow Gun Capsized—secured it on deck—The Gun was Capsized [owing] to Sh[r]oud being placed against Carriage to support the bulwark." Lt. Charles Morris, from 3 to 6 p.m., reported: "Discovered the Sixth Shroud of the Starboard Main Rigging to have parted a Link of the Chain in wake of Smoke Stack [Grip] up hooked and Set up a pennant Tackle—Bent and Set Single reefed, the Main Storm Try Sail—The Wind until 4 blowing with the force of a Hurricane in puffs, flattening the Sea, and filling the Air with 'Spoon drift' resembling heavy rain Squalls—11 to 4 a general appearance for the better, the Wind having Subsided into a heavy gall. The Clouds Consisting principally of heavy masses of Scuds, were very low & travelled with great velocity—Shackled the lower Shroud that parted and Set it up[.]"

28. Lt. William A. Webb (see *Logbooks of the U.S.S. Mississippi*) reported that "At 2 [p.m.] Squally[,] took in Fore Top Mast Steering Sail—At 2.30 [p.m.] Carried away the Fore Top Gallant Mast[,] took in the Main Top Gallant Sail—Clewed down the Top Sails double reefed them and furled the fore.— At 2.45 [p.m.] the Main Top Gallant Sail blew from the Yard—hauled down the Jib & Stowed it—Cleared the wreck of the Top Gallant Mast & made every thing Secure[.]"

29. King Kamehameha III (1813–1854) was the first Christian king of Hawaii (1824–1854). Merriam-Webster, Inc., *Webster's New Biographical Dictionary* (Springfield, MA: Merriam-Webster, 1988), 803.

30. During the reign of Kamehameha the Great, a battery of two cannons was mounted at the rim of the crater, known as Punchbowl Crater (Puowaina in Hawaiian), an extinct volcanic tuff cone located in Honolulu, Hawaii, one mile from downtown. Cohen, *Columbia Gazetteer*, 2532; Charles W. Baldwin, *Geography of the Hawaiian Islands* (New York, Cincinnati, and Chicago: American Book Company, 1908), 41.

31. Mataio Kekuanao'a (1794–1868) was the governor of Oahu from 1839 to 1864. Pauline King, *The Diaries of David Lawrence Gregg: An American*

Diplomat in Hawaii 1853–1858 (Honolulu, Hawaii: Hawaiian Historical Society, 1982), 57; Mark Twain, *Roughing It*, eds. Harriet Elinor Smith et. al. (Berkeley: University of California Press, 1993), 715.

32. French consul Lewis Emile Perrin; Peruvian consul Robert Grimes Davis; Bremen consul Stephen Reynolds; Danish consul Ludwig Holberg Anthon; U.S. consul Benjamin Franklin Angel. King, *The Diaries of David Lawrence Gregg*, 14, 514, 517, 564; Elizabeth Douglas Van Denburgh, *My Voyage in the United States Frigate "Congress"* (New York: Desmond FitzGerald, Inc., 1913), 332.

33. Robert Crichton Wyllie (1798–1865) served as minister of foreign affairs for Hawaii (1845–1865). Elisha Hunt Allen (1804–1883) was the U.S. consul in Hawaii (1850–1853), minister of finance for King Kamehameha III and King Kamehameha IV (1854–1857), and chief justice of the Kingdom of Hawaii Supreme Court (1857–1877). Johnson and Malone, *Dictionary of American Biography*, I: 187; Johnson, *Congressional Directory (1852)*, 54; Johnson, *Congressional Directory (1853)*, 25.

34. Elisha Hunt Allen.

35. Golden Gate is a two-mile-wide strait uniting the San Francisco Bay with the Pacific Ocean. In the spring of 1846 John C. Frémont chose the name "Chrysopylae (golden gate), on the same principle that the harbour of Byzantium (Constantinople) was called Chrysoceras (golden horn)." Erwin G. Gudde, *California Place Names: The Origin and Etymology of Current Geographical Names* (Berkeley and Los Angeles, CA: University of California Press, 1998), 147; Donald Jackson and Mary Lee Spence, eds., *The Expeditions of John Charles Frémont* (Urbana: University of Illinois Press, 1970), II: 45–46.

36. Captained by James Madison Alden, the U.S. Coast Survey *Active* was a side-wheel steamer. Her tasks included taking soundings and transporting surveyors. She discovered a deep submarine valley, or "gulch," in the center of the Monterey Bay, as well as the first known sea-floor canyon, now called Monterey Canyon. Mooney, *Dictionary of American Naval Fighting Ships*, I: 43.

37. The crank pin is a cylindrical piece of metal fitted to or wrought upon the end of a crank, forming a journal for the connecting rod. *Naval Encyclopedia*, 181.

38. Thomas Oliver Larkin (1802–1858) served as the U.S. consul to the California Republic (1844–1848). He actively promoted the Bear Flag

Revolt in California, and was a signer of the original California constitution. Garraty and Carnes, *American National Biography*, XIII: 197–98.

39. Bacchus Minstrels could have been the first Negro troupe who performed in Australia. John H. Heaton, *Australian Dictionary of Dates and Men of the Time: Containing the History of Australasia from 1542 to May, 1879* (Sydney: George Robertson, 1879), 167.

40. Located along the north bank of the Carquinez Strait, Benicia is a waterside city in Solano County, California. Founded in 1847 by Dr. Robert Semple, Thomas O. Larkin, and Comandante General Mariano Guadalupe Vallejo, it was named for the general's wife, Francisca Benicia Carillo de Vallejo. It served as the state capital for nearly thirteen months from 1853 to 1854. *Geographical Dictionary*, 134; Cohen, *Columbia Gazetteer*, 319; Hubert Howe Bancroft, *West American History* (New York: The Bancroft Co., 1902), 670–71; J. M. Hutchings, *Scenes of Wonder and Curiosity in California* (New York and San Francisco: A. Roman and Company, 1875), 24.

41. Samuel Purdy was the third lieutenant governor of California in 1852–1856. He ran for office as a Democrat and also became the first mayor of Stockton, California, in 1851. Theodore Henry Hittell, *History of California* (San Francisco: N.J. Stone & Company, 1898), IV: 81–82, 135; Hutchings, *Scenes of Wonder and Curiosity in California*, 34.

42. Draining into the San Francisco Bay, the eight-mile-long Carquinez Strait connects the San Pueblo Bay to Suisun Bay. Cohen, *Columbia Gazetteer*, 546; *Geographical Dictionary*, 219.

43. The Pacific Mail Steamship Company was founded in 1848 by William H. Aspinwall, Gardiner G. Howland, and Henry Chauncey of the firm of Howland and Aspinwall to execute a contract to carry mail from the Isthmus of Panama to the newly annexed territory of California. Pacific Mail Steamship Company, *Charter of the Pacific Mail Steamship Company, with its amendments; also, the by-laws, as recently adopted* (New York: Slate & Janes, 1863), 3; American Society of Civil Engineers, *Transactions of the American Society of Civil Engineers, Volume 36, December 1896* (New York: American Society of Civil Engineers, 1897), 598.

44. Later in the American Civil War, the *Queen City* was purchased by the U.S. Navy from Samuel Wiggins in 1863 and then commissioned with acting master Jason Goudy in command. She was a 212-ton, wooden, side-wheel steamer. Mooney, *Dictionary of American Naval Fighting Ships*, V: 411–12.

45. Brother of Marian Coote Speiden, Clement W. Coote (ca. 1820–1855) married Sarah R. Beaky (b. ca. 1821) in 1844 in St. Louis, Missouri. Employed as a civil engineer, Clement died on January 25 in Sacramento, California. He was the city surveyor of Sacramento in 1848. "Obituary," *California Farmer and Journal of Useful Sciences*, February 1, 1855, 38.

46. Wilson's Exchange was a hotel in San Francisco on Sansome Street. The building was damaged during the earthquake of 1856, and the front wall near the south end cracked from the foundation to the roof. Elisha Smith Capron, *History of California, from its discovery to the present time: comprising also a full description of its climate, surface, soil, rivers, towns, beasts, birds, fishes, state of its society, agriculture, commerce, mines, mining, &c.* (Boston: John P. Jewett & Co., 1854), 164; "Two Weeks Later from California," *The New York Times*, March 14, 1856, 1.

47. Approximately thirty miles long, American River runs from the Sierra Nevada mountains through the Sacramento metropolitan area, where it enters into the Sacramento River on its way to the San Francisco Bay. The discovery of gold along the river at Sutter's Mill, near Coloma, led to the Gold Rush of 1849. Cohen, *Columbia Gazetteer*, 96.

48. Perhaps William H. Thomas (1816–1880), who resided on J Street. Cutter (D. S.) & Co., *Sacramento city directory for the year A. D. 1860: being a complete general and business directory of the entire city* (Sacramento: D. S. Cutter & Co., 1859), 114; 1850 U.S. Census, Sacramento Co., CA, pop. sch., Sacramento, 138 (stamped), William H. Thomas, http://www.ancestry. com/ : 2011.; 1860 U.S. Census, Sacramento Co., CA, pop. sch., Sacramento Ward 1, 18 (penned), William H. Thomas, http://www.ancestry.com/ : 2011; 1870 U.S. Census, Sacramento Co., CA, pop. sch., Sacramento Ward 1, 7 (penned), William H. Thomas, http://www.ancestry.com/ : 2011.

49. Located twelve miles north-northeast of Oakland, Martinez is located on the south side of the Carquinez Strait in the San Francisco Bay area, directly facing the city of Benicia. Cohen, *Columbia Gazetteer*, 1902; *Geographical Dictionary*, 714.

50. John Ellis Wool (1784–1869) was an officer in the U.S. Army during three consecutive U.S. wars: the War of 1812, the Mexican-American War, and the Civil War. By the time of the Mexican-American War, he was widely considered one of the most capable officers in the Army and a superb organizer. He was one of the four general officers of the U.S. Army in 1861 and was the one who saw the most Civil War service. When the war began, Wool, at age seventy-seven, a brigadier general for twenty years,

commanded the Department of the East. Garraty and Carnes, *American National Biography*, XXIII: 842–44.

51. Mare Island is a peninsula alongside the city of Vallejo, California, about twenty-three miles northeast of San Francisco. The Napa River forms its eastern side as it enters the Carquinez Strait juncture with the east side of San Pablo Bay. *Geographical Dictionary*, 709; Cohen, *Columbia Gazetteer*, 3310.

52. John McIntosh Kell (1823–1900) entered the U.S. Navy in 1841 as a midshipman. He was promoted to master and lieutenant in 1855. He resigned his commission in 1861. During the Civil War he received a commission of commander in the Confederate States Navy in Alabama during the fight with the *Kearsarge*. Pineau, *The Personal Journal of Commodore Matthew C. Perry*, 229; Callahan, *List of Officers of the Navy*, 308.

Chapter 5. Volume Two: 1855

1. Discovered by Europeans in 1515, Taboga Island is a volcanic island in the Gulf of Panama ten miles south of Panama City. Spanish explorer Vasco Núñez de Balboa originally named the island Isla San Pedro. *Geographical Dictionary*, 1152; Cohen, *Columbia Gazetteer*, 3079.

2. Chama is situated seven miles south of Taboga Island. James Imray, *Sailing Directions for the West Coast of North America; Embracing the coasts of Central America, California, Oregon, Fuca Strait, Puget Sound, Vancouver Island, and the islands and rocks off the coasts of Central America and California* (London: James Imray, 1853), 11–12.

3. The Gulf of Tehuantepec is a large body of water on the Pacific coast of Oaxaca and Chiapas, South Mexico. The Isthmus of Tehuantepec is an isthmus in south Mexico between the Bay of Campeche and the Gulf of Tehuantepec. Cohen, *Columbia Gazetteer*, 3124.

4. Tomás José Ramón del Carmen de Herrera y Pérez Dávila (1804–1854) became the first head of state of the Free State of the Isthmus (Panama) in 1840 and president of the Republic of the New Granada in 1854. Robert H. Davis, *Historical Dictionary of Colombia* (Metuchen, NJ: The Scarecrow Press, Inc., 1977), 123; Basil C. Hedrick and Anne K. Hedrick, *Historical Dictionary of Panama* (Metuchen, NJ: The Scarecrow Press, Inc., 1970), 53.

5. SS *Panama* was a 1,087-ton, 200-foot-l.o.a., 34-foot-beam, wooden hull, side paddle-wheeled, three-masted steamer. She was launched by William H. Webb in 1848 for the Pacific Mail Steamship Company and sailed regularly between San Francisco and Panama until 1857. From 1858 to

1861 she was used on the San Francisco–Columbia River service. In 1868 she was presented to the Mexican government as a revenue and transport steamer. D. Blethen Adams Levy, "The Maritime Heritage Project," 2009, http://www.maritimeheritage.org/ships/ss.html#SSPacific.

6. Nicholas Pike was U.S. consul in Lisbon from 1852 to 1861. Johnson, *Congressional Directory (1853)*, 21; Johnson, *Congressional Directory (1855)*, 42; Morris, *Congressional Directory (1856)*, 42.

7. SS *Columbus* was a 460-ton, 148-foot-l.o.a., 25-foot-beam, wooden hull, single-screw, three-masted steamer. Built by Reeves & Brothers from Allowaytown, New Jersey, in 1848, *Columbus* was sold to the Pacific Mail Steamship Company in 1851 and operated the San Francisco–Panama route until 1854. Chartered to the U.S. Navy for a while in 1854, she was then sold to the Panama Railroad Company and operated on the west coast of Central America. In 1861 she was lost at Punta Remedios, Central America. Levy, "The Maritime Heritage Project," http://www .maritimeheritage.org/ships/ss.html.

8. The U.S. frigate *St. Lawrence* was built at the Norfolk Navy Yard and commissioned in 1848. Based on the same plans as USS *Brandywine*, she was 175 feet l.o.a. with a 45-foot beam and weighed 1,726 tons. In 1853, with Commo. Bladen Dulany as captain, she relieved *Raritan* as flagship of the Pacific Squadron and continued this duty until she relinquished her role to *Independence* in 1855. Mooney, *Dictionary of American Naval Fighting Ships*, VI: 242–43.

9. Bladen Dulany (1792–1856) was appointed commander of the Pacific Squadron from 1853 to 1855. He began his career in 1809 as a midshipman. He was promoted to lieutenant in 1814 and served at the Lake Erie Station. In 1831 he was promoted to master commandant, and to captain in 1841. In 1851 he was ordered to command the frigate *St. Lawrence*. Callahan, *List of Officers of the Navy*, 172; J. I. McLallen, "Family Members Personal Histories and Links," August 2008, http://www.mclallens.com/Dulany/ commodore_dulany.htm.

10. *John Adams* was originally built as a corvette under contract to Paul Pritchard and launched from Charleston, South Carolina, in 1799. In 1830 she was converted to a frigate and served the U.S. Navy until her decommission in 1867. She was 139 feet in length, had a beam of 32 feet, and weighed 544 tons. Mooney, *Dictionary of American Naval Fighting Ships*, III: 521–23.

11. The *Fredonia* was built in 1845 at Newburyport, Massachusetts, and was storeship for the Pacific Squadron. Stationed at Valparaiso, she served in this capacity until 1862. Mooney, *Dictionary of American Naval Fighting Ships*, II: 448.

12. Captained by Richard Burridge, the HMS *President* served as the flagship of the Pacific Station from 1853–1857. Launched in 1829 at the Portsmouth Dockyard, the 52-gun, 173-foot-l.o.a., 45-foot-beam, 1,537-ton frigate was converted to a drillship in 1862. Colledge, *Ships of the Royal Navy*, 256.

13. Former Ohio governor Reuben Wood (ca. 1792–1864) served as U.S. consul to Valparaiso from 1853 to 1855. George B. Merwin replaced him and served from 1855 to 1857. Johnson, *Congressional Directory (1855)*, 48; Morris, *Congressional Directory (1856)*, 47.

14. A razee is a wooden sailing ship that has been cut down to reduce the number of decks. King et al., *A Sea of Words*, 367.

15. William Mervine (1791–1868) was a rear admiral in the U.S. Navy, whose career included service in the War of 1812, the Mexican-American War, and the Civil War. He started his career as a midshipman in 1809. He rose to the rank of captain in 1841. During the Civil War he commanded the Gulf Blockading Squadron until he retired his commission in late 1861. However, one year later he was recommissioned as a commodore. Callahan, *List of Officers of the Navy*, 378; Johnson and Malone, *Dictionary of American Biography*, VI: 575–76.

16. In 1854 Sir Henry William Bruce (1792–1863) was appointed commander in chief of the ships of the Pacific Station and was instrumental in starting the first on-shore establishment in Esquimalt at the southern tip of Vancouver Island. Kenneth Bourne, *Britain and the Balance of Power in North America 1815–1908* (Berkeley and Los Angeles: University of California Press, 1967), 193, 209, 416.

17. David L. Gregg (d. 1868) was the U.S. diplomatic commissioner to the Hawaiian Islands from 1853 to 1858. He also was U.S. attorney for Illinois (1845–1849) and the secretary of state of Illinois (1850–1853). Johnson, *Congressional Directory (1855)*, 48; Morris, *Congressional Directory (1856)*, 47.

18. After leaving Valparaiso, the *Mississippi* sailed through the Straits of Magellan to Rio de Janeiro, and arrived at Brooklyn Navy Yard on Sunday, May 25, 1855. Speiden, "How the United States Opened Japan to the World," 29; *Logbooks of the U.S.S. Mississippi*.

19. Speiden recollected that Master Sam Spooner died in January 1855, while Madame Jeddo died in the month of February. Speiden's pet, Madame Simoda, named after the town in which he received the dog, died a month later. They were put in shotted canvas bags and buried at sea in sailor fashion. Watson, *The Dog Book*, II: 734.

Appendix A: General Orders

1. General Order 11 was not found in the journal but transcribed from *Logbooks of the U.S.S. Mississippi*.
2. General Order 12 was not found in the journal but transcribed from *Logbooks of the U.S.S. Mississippi*.

Appendix B: Correspondence

1. This is the Japanese name of Sakhalin Island.
2. The braced insertion was made by Speiden.

Bibliography

Books

A naval encyclopedia: comprising a dictionary of nautical words and phrases; biographical notices, and records of naval officers; special articles on naval art and science, written expressly for this work by officers and others of recognized authority in the branches treated by them. Together with descriptions of the principal naval stations and seaports of the world. Philadelphia: L. R. Hamersly & Co., 1881.

Abranson, Erik. *Ships of the High Seas.* New York: Crescent Books, 1976.

Allardice, Bruce S. *Confederate Colonels: A Biographical Register.* Columbia: University of Missouri Press, 2008.

American Society of Civil Engineers. *Transactions of the American Society of Civil Engineers, Volume 36, December 1896.* New York: American Society of Civil Engineers, 1897.

Baldwin, Charles W. *Geography of the Hawaiian Islands.* New York, Cincinnati, and Chicago: American Book Company, 1908.

Bancroft, Hubert Howe. *West American History.* New York: The Bancroft Co., 1902.

Barman, Roderick J. *Citizen Emperor: Pedro II and the Making of Brazil, 1825–91.* Stanford, CA: Stanford University Press, 1999.

Bean, Annemarie, James V. Hatch, and Brooks McNamara, eds. *Inside the Minstrel Mask: Readings in Nineteenth-Century Blackface Minstrelsy.* Hanover, NH: Wesleyan University Press, 1996.

Beasley, W. G., ed. *Select Documents on Japanese Foreign Policy 1853–1868*. New York, Toronto, London: Oxford University Press, 1955.

Beers, Henry P. *Guide to the Archives of the Government of the Confederate States of America*. Washington, D.C.: U.S. Government Printing Office, 1968.

Bennett, Frank M. *The Steam Navy of the United States, A History of the Growth of the Steam Vessel of War in the U.S. Navy, and of the Naval Engineer Corps*. Westport, CT: Greenwood Press, 1972.

Blumberg, Rhoda. *Commodore Perry in the Land of the Shogun*. New York: Lothrop, Lee & Shepard Books, 1985.

Blythe, Wilfred L. *The Impact of Chinese Secret Societies in Malaya: A Historical Study*. London: Oxford University Press, 1969.

Bourne, Kenneth. *Britain and the Balance of Power in North America 1815–1908*. Berkeley and Los Angeles: University of California Press, 1967.

Bradford, Gershom. *A Glossary of Sea Terms*. New York: Yachting, Inc., 1927.

Broderick, Robert C. *The Catholic Encyclopedia*. Nashville, TN: T. Nelson, 1976.

Brown, John Howard, ed. *Lamb's Biographical Dictionary of the United States*. Boston: James H. Lamb Co., 1900.

Brownlee, Charles. *Reminiscences of Kaffir Life and History and Other Papers*. Lovedale, South Africa: Lovedale Mission Press, 1896.

Bryant, William Cullen II and Thomas G. Voss, eds. *The Letters of William Cullen Bryant*. New York: Fordham University Press, 1992.

Buchanan, Roberdeau. *Genealogy of the Roberdeau family: including a biography of General Daniel Roberdeau, of the Revolutionary Army, and the Continental Congress; and Signer of the Articles of Confederation*. Washington, D.C.: Joseph L. Pearson, 1876.

Burg, B. R., ed. *An American Seafarer in the Age of Sail: The Erotic Diaries of Philip C. Van Buskirk 1851–1870*. New Haven and London: Yale University Press, 1994.

Callahan, Edward W., ed. *List of Officers of the Navy of the United States and of the Marine Corps from 1775 to 1900, comprising a complete register of all present and former commissioned, warranted, and appointed officers of the United States Navy, and of the Marine Corps, regular and volunteer*. New York: L. R. Hamersly & Co., 1901.

Capron, Elisha Smith. *History of California, from its discovery to the present time: comprising also a full description of its climate, surface, soil, rivers, towns, beasts, birds, fishes, state of its society, agriculture, commerce, mines, mining, &c.* Boston: John P. Jewett & Co., 1854.

Casstevens, Frances Harding. *George W Alexander and Castle Thunder: A Confederate Prison and Its Commandant*. Jefferson, NC: McFarland & Co., 2004.

Chaplin, Arnold. *A St. Helena Who's Who or A Dictionary of the Island During the Captivity of Napoleon*. London: Arnold Chaplin, 1914.

Clayton, Bruce D. *Shotokan's Secret: The Hidden Truth Behind Karate's Fighting Origins*. Valencia, CA: Black Belt Books, 2004.

Clunas, Craig. *Chinese Export Watercolours*. London: Victoria and Albert Museum—Far Eastern Series, 1984.

Cole, Allan B. *With Perry in Japan: The Diary of Edward Yorke McCauley*. Princeton, NJ: Princeton University Press, 1942.

Colledge, J. J. *Ships of the Royal Navy: The Complete Record of all Fighting Ships of the Royal Navy*. Mechanicsburg, PA: Stackpole Books, 2003.

Correspondence Relative to the Naval Expedition to Japan. U.S. Senate, 33rd Congress, 2nd Session, Senate Executive Document 34.

Cortazzi, Hugh. *Isles of Gold: Antique Maps of Japan*. New York and Tokyo: Weatherhill, 1983.

Crossman, Carl L. *The China Trade: Export Paintings, Furniture Silver & Other Objects*. Princeton, NJ: The Pyne Press, 1972.

Cutler, Carl C. *Greyhounds of the Sea: The Story of the American Clipper Ship*. Annapolis, MD: Naval Institute Press, 1960.

Cutter (D. S.) & Co. *Sacramento city directory for the year A. D. 1860: being a complete general and business directory of the entire city*. Sacramento, CA: D. S. Cutter & Co., 1859.

Davis, Frederick Hadland. *Japan, from the age of the gods to the fall of Tsingtau*. New York: Frederick A. Stokes Co., 1916.

Davis, Robert H. *Historical Dictionary of Colombia*. Metuchen, NJ: The Scarecrow Press, Inc., 1977.

Deacon, Harriet. *The Island: A History of Robben Island, 1488–1990*. Cape Town, South Africa: Mayibuye Books, University of the Western Cape, 1996.

DeConde, Alexander, Richard Dean Burns, and Fredrik Logevall, eds. *Encyclopedia of American Foreign Policy*. Second Edition. New York: Charles Scribner's Sons, 2002.

Denslow, William R. *10,000 Famous Freemasons*. Whitefish, MT: Kessinger Publishing, 2004.

Eiichi, Kato. "Aspects of Early Anglo-Japanese Relations," in *The History of Anglo-Japanese Relations, Vol. 1, The Political-Diplomatic Dimension, 1600–1930*. Edited by Ian Nish and Yoichi Kibata. Basingstoke, England: Macmillan, 2000.

Endacott, G. B. *A Biographical Sketch-Book of Early Hong Kong*. Hong Kong: Hong Kong University Press, 2005.

Erickson, Bruce T. *Encyclopedia of Nineteenth-Century Photography*. Edited by John Hannavy. New York: Routledge, 2008.

Freeman, Douglas S. *R. E. Lee: A Biography*. New York and London: Charles Scribner's Sons, 1935.

Golovnin, Vasilii M. *Around the World on the Kamchatka, 1817–1819*. Translated by Ella Lury Wiswell. Honolulu: The Hawaiian Historical Society and The University Press of Hawaii, 1979.

Gowen, Herbert Henry. *Five Foreigners in Japan*. Freeport, NY: Books for Libraries Press, 1967.

Graff, Henry F., ed. *Bluejackets with Perry in Japan: A Day-by-Day Account Kept by Master's Mate John R. C. Lewis and Cabin Boy William B. Allen*. New York: The New York Public Library, 1952.

Grainger, John D. *The First Pacific War: Britain and Russia, 1854–1856*. Woodbridge, Suffolk, UK and Rochester, NY: The Boydell Press, 2008.

Great Britain. Hydrographic Department. *The Bay of Bengal Pilot, including South-west Coast of Ceylon, North Coast of Sumatra, Nicobar and Andaman Islands*. London: The Hydrographic Office, 1887.

Gregory, Hugh McCulloch. *The Sea Serpent Journal: Hugh McCulloch Gregory's Voyage Around the World in a Clipper Ship, 1854–55*. Edited by Robert H. Burgess. Charlottesville: University Press of Virginia, 1975.

Griffin, Eldon. *Clippers and Consuls: American Consular and Commercial Relations with Eastern Asia, 1845–1860*. Ann Arbor, MI: Edwards Brothers, Inc., 1938.

Gudde, Erwin G. *California Place Names: The Origin and Etymology of Current Geographical Names*. Berkeley and Los Angeles, CA: University of California Press, 1998.

Guthrie, J. A. *Seeing the World Through a Porthole*. Lynchburg, VA: J. P. Bell Company, 1916.

Hamersly, Thomas H. S. *General Register of the United States Navy and the Marine Corps, Arranged in Alphabetical Order, For One Hundred Years, (1782 to 1882)*. Washington, D.C.: T. H. S. Hamersly, 1882.

Hansen-Taylor, Marie and Horace E. Scudder, eds. *Life and Letters of Bayard Taylor*. Boston: Houghton, Mifflin and Co., 1885.

Hartzler, Daniel D. *Medical Doctors of Maryland in the C.S.A.* Westminster, MD: Heritage Books, Inc., 2007.

Hawks, Francis L. *Commodore Perry and the Opening of Japan: Narrative of the Expedition of an American Squadron to the China Seas and Japan, 1852–1854: the Official Report of the Expedition to Japan*. Stroud, England: Nonsuch, 2005.

Heaton, John H. *Australian Dictionary of Dates and Men of the Time: Containing the History of Australasia from 1542 to May, 1879*. Sydney: George Robertson, 1879.

Hedrick, Basil C. and Anne K. Hedrick. *Historical Dictionary of Panama.* Metuchen, NJ: The Scarecrow Press, Inc., 1970.

Heine, Wilhelm. *With Perry to Japan: A Memoir.* Translated by Frederic Trautmann. Honolulu: University of Hawaii Press, 1990.

Henson, Curtis T. Jr. *Commissioners and Commodores: The East India Squadron and American Diplomacy in China.* Tuscaloosa, AL: University of Alabama Press, 1982.

Heyl, Erik. *Early American Steamers.* Vol. V. Buffalo, NY: Erik Heyl, 1967.

Hinckley, Erik S. and Tom Ledoux, eds. *They Went to War: A Biographical Register of the Green Mountain State in the Civil War.* Victoria, BC, Canada: Trafford Publishing, 2010.

Hittell, Theodore Henry. *History of California.* San Francisco: N.J. Stone & Company, 1898.

Howe, Octavius T. and Frederick C. Matthews. *American Clipper Ships, 1833–1858.* New York: Argosy Antiquarian Ltd., 1967.

Hutchings, J. M. *Scenes of Wonder and Curiosity in California.* New York and San Francisco: A. Roman and Company, 1875.

Hutton, Barbara. *Robben Island: Symbol of Resistance.* Johannesburg, South Africa: SACHED Books, 1997.

Imray, James. *Sailing Directions for the West Coast of North America; Embracing the coasts of Central America, California, Oregon, Fuca Strait, Puget Sound, Vancouver Island, and the islands and rocks off the coasts of Central America and California.* London: James Imray, 1853.

Jackson, Donald and Mary Lee Spence, eds. *The Expeditions of John Charles Frémont.* Urbana: University of Illinois Press, 1970.

Jansen, Marius B. *The Making of Modern Japan.* Cambridge, MA: Belknap Press of Harvard University Press, 2000.

Ji, Zhaojin. *A History of Modern Shanghai Banking: The Rise and Decline of China's Finance Capitalism.* New York: M. E. Sharpe, Inc., 2003.

Johnson, John M., compiler. *Congressional Directory for the First Session of the Thirty-Second Congress of the United States of America.* Washington, D.C.: Gideon and Co., 1852.

——. *Congressional Directory for the Second Session of the Thirty-Second Congress of the United States of America and Guide Book through the Public Offices.* Washington, D.C.: Alfred Hunter, 1853.

——. compiler. *Congressional Directory for the Second Session of the Thirty-Third Congress of the United States of America.* Washington, D.C.: Gideon and Co., 1855.

Johnson, Robert Erwin. *Far China Station: The U.S. Navy in Asian Waters, 1800–1898.* Annapolis, MD: Naval Institute Press, 1979.

Johnston, James D. *China and Japan: Being a Narrative of the Cruise of the U.S. Steam-Frigate Powhatan in the Years 1857, '58, '59, and '60 including an Account of the Japanese Embassy to the United States, Illustrated with Life Portraits of the Embassadors and their Principal Officials.* Philadelphia: Charles DeSilver, 1860.

Jones, Howard. *Crucible of Power: A History of American Foreign Relations to 1913.* Lanham, MD: Rowman & Littlefield Publishers, Inc., 2009.

Keene, Donald. *Emperor of Japan: Meiji and His World, 1852–1912.* New York: Columbia University Press, 2002.

Kemish, S. B. *The Japanese Empire. Its Physical, Political and Social Condition and History. Japan in English.* London: Ganesha Publishing, 2003.

Kerr, George H. *Okinawa, the History of an Island People.* Rutland, VT: C.E. Tuttle Co, 1958.

Kidder, Daniel P. and James C. Fletcher. *Brazil and the Brazilians, Portrayed in Historical and Descriptive Sketches.* Philadelphia: Childs & Peterson, 1857.

King, Dean, John B. Hattendorf, and J. Worth Estes. *A Sea of Words: A Lexicon and Companion for Patrick O'Brian's Seafaring Tales.* New York: Henry Holt, 1995.

King, Pauline. *The Diaries of David Lawrence Gregg: An American Diplomat in Hawaii 1853–1858.* Honolulu: Hawaiian Historical Society, 1982.

Lavery, Brian. *The Ship of the Line.* Annapolis, MD: Naval Institute Press, 1983.

Lawrence, James B. *China and Japan, and a voyage thither: an account of a cruise in the waters of the East Indies, China, and Japan.* Hartford, CT: Press of Case, Lockwood and Brainard, 1870.

Lee, Edmund Jennings, ed. *Lee of Virginia, 1642–1892: Biographical and Genealogical Sketches of the Descendants of Colonel Richard Lee.* Philadelphia: Edmund Jennings Lee, 1895.

Leland, Charles Godfrey. *Fusang or the Discovery of America by Chinese Buddhist Priests in the Fifth Century.* New York: J. W. Bouton, 1875.

Lim, Patricia. *Forgotten Souls: A Social History of the Hong Kong Cemetery.* Hong Kong: Hong Kong University Press, 2011.

Lipschutz, Mark R. and R. Kent Rasmussen. *Dictionary of African Historical Biography.* Second Edition. Berkeley and Los Angeles: University of California Press, 1986.

Louis-Frédéric. *Japan Encyclopedia.* Translated by Kathe Roth. Cambridge, MA: Belknap Press of Harvard University Press, 2002.

Maclean, John. *A Compendium of Kafir Laws & Customs, including Genealogical Tables of Kafir Chiefs and Various Tribal Census Returns*. Grahamstown, South Africa: J. Slater, 1906.

The Maine Register and State Reference Book, 1852. Hallowell: Masters, Smith & Company, 1852.

Malte-Brun, Conrad. *Universal Geography or A Description of All the Parts of the World on a New Plan, According to the Great Natural Divisions of the Globe*. Philadelphia: Anthony Finley, 1827.

Manning, Martin J. and Clarence R. Wyatt. *Encyclopedia of Media and Propaganda in Wartime America*. Santa Barbara, CA: ABC-CLIO, LLC, 2011.

Masters, Tom, Jan Dodd, and Jean-Bernard Carillet. *Mauritius, Réunion & Seychelles*. Footscray, Victoria, Australia: Lonely Planet, 2007.

Mayers, William Fred., N. B. Dennys, and Charles King. *The treaty ports of China and Japan: A complete guide to the open ports of those countries, together with Peking, Yedo, Hongkong and Macao*. Edited by N. B. Dennys. London: Trubner and Co., 1867.

Memorials of Protestant Missionaries to the Chinese: Giving a List of their Publications, and Obituary Notices of the Deceased. Shanghai: American Presbyterian Mission Press, 1867.

Meriwether, Colyer, ed. *Publications of the Southern History Association*. Vol. X. Washington, D.C.: The Southern History Association, 1906.

Message from the President of the United States in answer to a resolution of the Senate, calling for information in relation to the mission of Mr. Balestier, late United States consul at Singapore to Eastern Asia. Thirty-second Congress First Session, Senate Executive Document 38 (1851).

Miller, Nathan. *The U.S. Navy: An Illustrated History*. New York: American Heritage/Bonanza Books, 1982.

Millett, Allan Reed and Jack Shulimson. *Commandants of the Marine Corps*. Annapolis, MD: Naval Institute Press, 2004.

Monro, Alexander. *New Brunswick; with a brief outline of Nova Scotia and Prince Edward Island*. Halifax, NS, Canada: Richard Nugent, 1855.

Montgomery, Helen Barrett. *Following the Sunrise: A Century of Baptist Missions, 1813–1913*. Philadelphia: American Baptist Publication Society, 1913.

Morison, Samuel Eliot. *"Old Bruin": Commodore Matthew C. Perry, 1794–1858*. Boston: Little, Brown and Company, 1967.

Morris, Robert, compiler. *Congressional Directory for the Third Session of the Thirty-Fourth Congress of the United States of America*. Washington, D.C.: Gideon and Co., 1856.

Morrow, James. *A Scientist with Perry in Japan: The Journal of Dr. James Morrow.* Edited by Allan B. Cole. Chapel Hill: University of North Carolina Press, 1947.

Needham, Joseph. *Science and Civilization in China: Volume 1—Introductory Orientations.* Cambridge, MA: University Press, 1954.

Nelson, Stewart B. *Oceanographic Ships: Fore and Aft.* Washington, D.C.: Office of the Oceanographer of the Navy, 1971, reprinted 1982.

Noel, John V. Jr. and Edward L. Brach. *Naval Terms Dictionary.* Annapolis, MD: Naval Institute Press, 1988.

Official Army Register for 1907. Washington, D.C.: Government Printing Office, 1907.

Pacific Mail Steamship Company. *Charter of the Pacific Mail Steamship Company, with its amendments; also, the by-laws, as recently adopted.* New York: Slate & Janes, 1863.

Paine, Lincoln P. *Ships of the World.* New York: Houghton Mifflin Company, 1997.

Palmer, Aaron Haight. *Letter to the Hon. John M. Clayton, Secretary of State, Enclosing A Paper, Geographical, Political, and Commercial, on the Independent Oriental Nations; and Submitting a Plan for Opening, Extending, and Protecting American Commerce in the East, &c: Respectfully Submitted to the President and Cabinet, By Aaron Haight Palmer, Counsellor of the Supreme Court of the U.S.—Published by Direction of the Department of State in the National Intelligencer of the 6th September, 1849. Revised, and Now Republished with an Appendix.* Washington, D.C.: Gideon & Co., 1849.

Palmer, Joseph, compiler. *Jane's Dictionary of Naval Terms.* London: MacDonald and Jane's, 1975.

Papinot, Edmond. *Historical and Geographical Dictionary of Japan.* New York: Frederick Ungar Publishing Co., 1910, republished 1964, second printing 1968.

Perry, Matthew Calbraith. *A Paper by Commodore M. C. Perry, U.S.N.: read before the American Geographical and Statistical Society—March 6th, 1856.* New York: D. Appleton, 1856.

Perry, Matthew Calbraith and Francis L. Hawks. *Narrative of the Expedition of an American Squadron to the China Seas and Japan: Performed in the Years 1852, 1853, and 1854, Under the Command of Commodore M. C. Perry, United States Navy, by Order of the Government of the United States.* New York: D. Appleton, 1856.

Pineau, Roger, ed. *The Japan Expedition, 1852-54: The Personal Journal of Commodore Matthew C. Perry.* Washington, D.C.: Smithsonian Institution Press, 1968.

Pinsel, Marc I. *150 Years of Service on the Seas: A Pictorial History of the U.S. Naval Oceanographic Office from 1830 to 1980—Volume I (1830-1946).* Washington, D.C.: Government Printing Office, 1981.

Preble, George Henry. *The Opening of Japan: A Diary of Discovery in the Far East, 1853–1856*. Edited by Boleslaw Szczesniak. Norman: University of Oklahoma Press, 1962.

Proceedings in the North Atlantic Coast Fisheries Arbitration before the Permanent County of Arbitration at the Hague Under the Provisions of the General Treaty of Arbitration of April 4, 1908, and the Special Agreement of January 27, 1909, between the United States of America and Great Britain. Washington, D.C.: Government Printing Office, 1912.

Procter, George H. *The Fishermen's Memorial and Record Book, containing a list of vessels and their crews, lost from the port of Gloucester from the year 1830 to October 1, 1873.* Gloucester, MA: Procter Brothers, 1873.

Proust, Alain and Alan Mountain. *This Is Mauritius*. London: New Holland, 1995.

Pugsley, Alfred. *The Works of Isambard Kingdom Brunel: An Engineering Appreciation*. London: Institution of Civil Engineers, 1976.

Putnam, George Granville. *Salem Vessels and Their Voyages*. Salem, MA: Essex Institute, 1924.

Raimer, John W., ed. *Directory of the Governors of the United States*. Westport, CT: Mechler Publishing, 1978.

Ride, Lindsay and May Ride. *An East India Company Cemetery: Protestant Burials in Macao, Edited by Bernard Mellor*. Hong Kong: Hong Kong University Press, 1996.

Robinson, John and George Francis Dow. *The Sailing Ships of New England 1607–1907*. Salem, MA: Marine Research Society, 1922.

Rodriques, João. *This Island of Japan: João Rodriques' Account of 16th-Century Japan*. Translated and edited by Michael Cooper. Tokyo: Kodansha International, 1973.

Rosenthal, Eric. *Southern African Dictionary of National Biography*. London and New York: Frederick Warne & Co., 1966.

Royal Geographical Society. *A Gazetter of the World, or Dictionary of Geographical Knowledge, compiled from the most recent authorities, and forming a complete body of modern geography, physical, political, statistical, historical, and ethnographical*. London and Dublin: A. Fullarton & Co., 1856.

Scherer, James A. B. *Japan—Whither?: A Discussion of Japanese Problems*. Tokyo: The Hokuseido Press, 1933.

Schroeder, John H. *Matthew Calbraith Perry: Antebellum Sailor and Diplomat*. Annapolis, MD: Naval Institute Press, 2001.

———. *Shaping a Maritime Empire: The Commercial and Diplomatic Role of the American Navy, 1829–1861*. Westport, CT, and London: Greenwood Press, 1985.

Shanghae Almanac for the Bissextile or Leap Year 1856 and Miscellany. Shanghai: The "N.C. Herald" Office, 1856.

Shavit, David. *The United States in Asia: A Historical Dictionary*. New York: Greenwood Press, 1990.

Silverstone, Paul H. *The Sailing Navy, 1775–1854*. Annapolis, MD: Naval Institute Press, 2001.

Society of the Cincinnati of Maryland. *Register of the Society of the Cincinnati of Maryland Brought Down to February 22nd, 1897*. Baltimore: Society of the Cincinnati of Maryland, 1897.

Spalding, J. Willett. *The Japan Expedition. Japan and Around the World; an Account of Three Visits to the Japanese Empire, with Sketches of Madeira, St. Helena, Cape of Good Hope, Mauritius, Ceylon, Singapore, China, and Loo-Choo*. New York: Redfield, 1855.

Sproston, John Glendy. *A Private Journal of John Glendy Sproston, U.S.N.* Edited by Shiho Sakanishi. Tokyo: Sophia University, 1968.

Stanlaw, James. *Japanese English: Language and Culture Contact*. Hong Kong: Hong Kong University Press, 2004.

Statler, Oliver. *The Black Ship Scroll. An account of the Perry expedition at Shimoda in 1854 and the lively beginnings of people-to-people relations between Japan & America, based on contemporary records, with translations by Richard Lane, Ph.D. and scroll paintings in full color by an anonymous Japanese eyewitness*. Rutland, VT: Charles E. Tuttle Company, 1964.

Symonds, Craig L. and William J. Clipson. *The Naval Institute Historical Atlas of the U.S. Navy*. Annapolis, MD: Naval Institute Press, 1995.

Taylor, A. D., compiler. *The West Coast of Hundustan Pilot including the Gulf of Manar, the Maldive and Laccadive Islands*. London: The Hydrographic Office, 1898.

Taylor, Nathaniel W. *Life on a Whaler or Antarctic Adventures in the Isle of Desolation*. Edited by Howard Palmer. New London, CT: New London County Historical Society, 1929.

Thayer, William Roscoe, ed. *The Harvard Graduates Magazine: Volume XV (1906–1907)*. Boston: The Harvard Graduates' Magazine Association, 1907.

Theal, George McCall. *History of South Africa from 1873 to 1884, Twelve Eventful Years*. London: George Allen & Unwin, Ltd., 1919.

———. *History of South Africa Under the Administration of the Dutch East India Company (1652 to 1795)*. London: Swan Sonnenschein & Co., Ltd., 1897.

Trubner, Henry, William Jay Rathbun, and Yin-wah Ashton. *China's Influence on American Culture in the 18th and 19th Centuries: A Special Bicentennial Exhibition Drawn from Private and Museum Collections, China Institute in*

America/China House Gallery . . . April 8 Through June 13, 1976, Seattle Art Museum . . . October 7 Through November 28, 1976: Catalog. New York: China Institute in America, 1976.

Tunis, Edwin. *Oars, Sails and Steam.* Cleveland and New York: World Publishing Company, 1952.

Twain, Mark. *Roughing It.* Edited by Harriet Elinor Smith et al. Berkeley: University of California Press, 1993.

United States. *Sailing Directions (Enroute): Japan. Volume 1.* Annapolis, MD: Lighthouse Press, 2005.

United States. Office of Naval Records and Library United States Navy Department. *Register of Officers of the Confederate States Navy, 1861–1865.* Mattituck, NY: J. M. Carrol & Company, 1983.

United States Navy Hydrographic Office. *Asiatic Pilot: Volume II—The Japan Islands.* Washington, D.C.: Government Printing Office, 1920.

———. *Asiatic Pilot: Volume III—Coast of China, Yalu River to Hong Kong Entrance.* Washington, D.C.: Government Printing Office, 1920.

———. *Asiatic Pilot: Volume IV—The Shores of the China Sea from Singapore Strait to and including Hongkong.* Washington, D.C.: Government Printing Office, 1915.

Van Denburgh, Elizabeth Douglas. *My Voyage in the United States Frigate "Congress."* New York: Desmond FitzGerald, Inc., 1913.

Vande Walle, W. F. and Noel Golvers, eds. *The History of the Relations Between the Low Countries and China in the Qing Era (1644–1911).* Leuven, Belgium: Leuven University Press, 2003.

Vetch, R. H., ed. *Life of Lieut.-General The Hon. Sir Andrew Clarke G.C.M.G., C.B., C.I.E.* New York: E. P. Dutton and Company, 1905.

Walton Advertising and Printing Company, compiler. *Some Ships of the Clipper Ship Era, Their Builders, Owners, and Captains: A Glance at an Interesting Phase of the American Merchant Marine so Far as It Relates to Boston.* Boston: State Street Trust Company, 1913.

Waring, Joseph Ioor. *A History of Medicine in South Carolina 1825–1900.* Columbia: South Carolina Medical Association, 1967.

Watson, James. *The Dog Book: A Popular History of the Dog, with Practical Information as to Care and Management of House, Kennel, and Exhibition Dogs; and Descriptions of All the Important Breeds.* New York: Doubleday, Page & Co., 1906.

Wiley, Peter Booth and Korogi Ichiro. *Yankees in the Land of the Gods: Commodore Perry and the Opening of Japan.* New York: N.Y. Viking, 1990.

Wilkes, Charles. *Autobiography of Rear Admiral Charles Wilkes, U.S. Navy, 1798-1877*. Edited by William James Morgan et al. Washington, D.C.: Naval History Division, Department of the Navy, 1978.

Williams, Frederick Wells. *The Life and Letters of Samuel Wells Williams, LL.D.: Missionary Diplomatist, Sinologue*. New York and London: G. P. Putnam's Sons, 1889.

Young, Charles F. T. *The Fouling and Corrosion of Iron Ships: Their Causes and Means of Prevention with the Mode of Application to the Existing Iron-clads*. London: The London Drawing Association, 1867.

Articles

Bartlett, Merrill L. "Commodore James Biddle and the First Naval Mission to Japan, 1845-1846." *American Neptune* 41 no. 1 (1981): 25-35.

Beasley, W. G. "From Conflict to Co-operation: British Naval Surveying in Japanese Waters, 1845-82," in *The History of Anglo-Japanese Relations, 1600-2000. Vol. 1, The Political-Diplomatic Dimension, 1600-1930*, edited by Ian Nish and Yoichi Kibata. Basingstoke: Macmillan, 2000, 87-106.

Brownback, Samuel (KS). "Senate Resolution 172—Relative to the Democratic Socialist Republic of Sri Lanka." *Congressional Record: Proceedings and Debates of the 105th Congress, Second Session* (February 3, 1998): 503.

Chamberlain, Basil Hall. "The Luchu Islands and Their Inhabitants: I. Introductory Remarks." *The Geographical Journal* 5 no. 4 (April 1895): 289-319.

Craddock, Stephen Culver. "'To the Honor and Credit of the Country': A History of the Warships Mississippi." *Journal of the Mississippi History* 54 (May 1992): 129-48.

Gallagher, Robert S. "Castaways on Forbidden Shores." *American Heritage* 19 no. 4 (1968): 34-37.

Goldsborough, John Rodger. "Commodore Perry's Landing in Japan, 1853." *The American Neptune* VII (1947): 9-20.

Griffis, William Elliot. "American Makers of the New Japan." *The Century Illustrated* LXXXVI no. 1 (May 1913): 597-605.

Hale, William Harlan. "When Perry Unblocked the 'Gate of the Sun.'" *American Neptune* 9 no. 3 (1958): 12-21, 94-101.

Langley, Harold D. "A Naval Dependent in Washington, 1837-1842: Letters of Marian Coote Speiden." *Records of the Columbia Historical Society, Washington, D.C.* 50 (1980): 105-22.

Littlehales, G. W. "The Navy as a Motor in Geographical and Commercial Progress." *Journal of the American Geographical Society of New York* 31 no. 2 (1899): 123-49.

Macleod, Julia H. "Three Letters Relating to the Perry Expedition to Japan." *The Huntington Library Quarterly* 6 no. 2 (February 1943): 228–237.

"Mauritius," *Appletons' Journal of Literature, Science and Art* VII no. 145 (January 6, 1872): 14–15.

Morison, Samuel Eliot. "Commodore Perry's Japan Expedition Press and Shipboard Theatre." *Proceedings of the American Antiquarian Society* 77 no. 1 (1967): 35–43.

Neumann, William L. "Religion, Morality, and Freedom: The Ideological Background of the Perry Expedition." *Pacific Historical Review* 23 no. 3 (1954): 247–258.

"Obituary—Prof. S. Wells Williams," *The Publishers' Weekly* XXV (1884): 243.

"Oriental Literary Intelligence," *Trubner's American Oriental Literary Record* 7 (September 21, 1865): 131–132.

Romer, Grant. "Near the Temple at Yokushen. . . ." *Image: Journal of Photography and Motion Pictures of the International Museum of Photography at George Eastman House* 29 no. 2 (August 1986): 1–11.

Sakamaki, Shunzo. "Western Concepts of Japan and the Japanese, 1800–1854." *The Pacific Historical Review* 6 no. 1 (March 1937): 1–14.

Salisbury, Edward E. "United States Expedition to Japan." *Journal of the American Oriental Society* 3 (1853): 492–494.

Schwartz, William Leonard, ed. "Commodore Perry at Okinawa from the Unpublished Diary of a British Missionary." *American Historical Review* 51 (January 1946): 262–276.

Shaw, Renata V. "Japanese Picture Scrolls of the First Americans in Japan." *Quarterly Journal of the Library of Congress* 25 (April 1968): 134–153.

Speiden, William, Jr. "How the United States Opened Japan to the World." *Japan and America* 2 (December 1902): 15, 22–29.

Stahl, Laurie. "Oregon to Antarctica to Japan: Navy Purser William Speiden." *Heritage Gazette* (Fall 2006): 4.

Towle, Edward L. "Lieutenant Silas Bent's Device to Eliminate Variation Correction in the Magnetic Compass, 1849." *The American Neptune* XXV (1965): 93–98.

Vernon, Manfred C. "The Dutch and the Opening of Japan by the United States." *The Pacific Historical Review* 28 no. 1 (February 1959): 39–48.

Von Doenhoff, Richard A. "Biddle, Perry, and Japan." *Proceedings* 92 no. 11 (1966): 78–87.

Yuzo, Kato. "The Opening of Japan and the Meiji Restoration, 1837–72," in *The History of Anglo-Japanese Relations. Vol. 1, The Political-Diplomatic Dimension, 1600–1930*, edited by Ian Nish and Yoichi Kibata. Basingstoke: Macmillan, 2000, 60–73.

Reference

Adams, Charles Kendall, ed. *The Universal Cyclopedia*. 12 volumes. New York: D. Appleton and Company, 1900.

Broderick, Robert C., ed. *The Catholic Encyclopedia*. Nashville, TN: T. Nelson, 1976.

Cohen, Saul B. *The Columbia Gazetteer of the World*. New York: Columbia University Press, 1998.

Dictionary of Canadian Biography. Toronto: University of Toronto Press, 1966.

Encyclopedia of People of Okinawan History. Naha, Okinawa: Okinawa Bunka-sha, 1996.

Garraty, John A. and Mark C. Carnes, eds. *American National Biography*. New York: Oxford University Press, 1999.

Johnson, Allen and Dumas Malone, eds. *Dictionary of American Biography*. New York: Charles Scribner's Sons, 1958.

Lee, Sidney, Leslie Stephen, and George Smith, eds. *The Dictionary of National Biography*. London: Oxford University Press, 1938.

Logbooks of the U.S.S Mississippi (Record Group 24) Records of the Bureau of Naval Personnel.

Magnusson, Magnus, ed. *Cambridge Biographical Dictionary*. Cambridge, MA: Cambridge University Press, 1990.

Merriam-Webster, Inc. *Webster's New Biographical Dictionary*. Springfield, MA: Merriam-Webster, 1988.

Merriam-Webster's Geographical Dictionary. 3rd ed. Springfield, MA.: Merriam-Webster, 2007.

Mooney, James L. *Dictionary of American Naval Fighting Ships*. Washington, D.C.: Navy Department, Office of the Chief of Naval Operations, Naval History Division, 1959–1981.

National American Biography. New York: James T. White & Co., 1907.

The National Cyclopaedia of American Biography. New York: J. T. White, 1892.

United States, Andrew R. Dodge, and Betty K. Koed, eds. *Biographical Directory of the United States Congress, 1774–2005: The Continental Congress, September 5, 1774, to October 21, 1788, and the Congress of the United States, from the First Through the One Hundred Eighth Congresses, March 4, 1789, to January 3, 2005, Inclusive*. Washington, D.C.: Government Printing Office, 2005.

United States. Naval War Records Office. *Official Records of the Union and Confederate Navies in the War of the Rebellion*. Series I, Volume 2. Washington, D.C.: Government Printing Office, 1895.

Webster's Third New International Dictionary of the English Language Unabridged.
Springfield, MA: Merriam-Webster, 1986.

Wilson, James Grant and John Fiske, eds. *Appleton's Cyclopaedia of American Biography.* New York: D. Appleton and Company, 1887.

Newspapers

Boston Daily Atlas

Brooklyn Daily Eagle

California Farmer and Journal of Useful Sciences

New York Times

New York Tribune

Richmond Times-Dispatch

Straits Times and Singapore Journal of Commerce

Syracuse Post-Standard

Census

California. Sacramento. 1850 U.S. Census, population schedule. Digital images. Ancestry.com. http://www.ancestry.com/ : 2011. (Accessed January 25, 2011).

California. Sacramento. 1860 U.S. Census, population schedule. Digital images. Ancestry.com. http://www.ancestry.com/ : 2011. (Accessed January 25, 2011).

California. Sacramento. 1870 U.S. Census, population schedule. Digital images. Ancestry.com. http://www.ancestry.com/ : 2011. (Accessed January 25, 2011).

District of Columbia. Washington. 1850 U.S. Census, population schedule. Digital images. Ancestry.com. http://www.ancestry.com/ : 2011. (Accessed January 25, 2011).

Maine. Washington. 1860 U.S. Census, population schedule. Digital images. Ancestry.com. http://www.ancestry.com/ : 2011. (Accessed January 25, 2011).

Missouri. Linn. 1870 U.S. Census, population schedule. Digital images. Ancestry. com. http://www.ancestry.com/ : 2011. (Accessed January 25, 2011).

New Hampshire. Rockingham. 1850 U.S. Census, population schedule. Digital images. Ancestry.com. http://www.ancestry.com/ : 2011. (Accessed January 25, 2011).

Online Resources

Allom, Thomas. "The City of Ning Po." 2010. http://www.chinese-outpost.com/history/thomas-allom-china-illustrated/the-city-of-ning-po.asp. (Accessed January 25, 2011).

"Archer-Mitchell-Stump-Williams Family Papers, 18th–20th century (MS. 1948)," January 24, 1973. Finding aid at the Maryland Historical Society Library, Baltimore, MD: Maryland Historical Society. http://www.mdhs.org/library/Mss/ms001948.html. (Assessed January 25, 2011).

Duval, Dominic. "Chief Maqoma." South Africa History Online. 2008. http://www.sahistory.org.za/pages/people/bios/maqoma-chief.htm. (Accessed January 25, 2011).

Hamm, Thomas, Jr. "Speiden Family Tree." December 2008. http://worldconnect.rootsweb.ancestry.com. (Accessed January 25, 2011).

Levy, D. Blethen Adams. "The Maritime Heritage Project." 2009. http://www.maritimeheritage.org/ships/ss.html. (Accessed January 25, 2011).

McLallen, J. I. "Family Members Personal Histories and Links." August 2008. http://www.mclallens.com/Dulany/commodore_dulany.htm. (Accessed January 25, 2011).

Overby, Chuck. "Six Letters from Japan." 2007. http://www.article9society.org/pp-17.pdf. (Accessed January 25, 2011).

Peebles, Shyama. "Old Protestant Cemetery in Macau." Gwulo: Old Hong Kong. October 2010. http://gwulo.com/sites/gwulo.com/files/Gwulo-Macau-Old-Protestant-Cemetery.pdf. (Accessed January 25, 2011).

Roberts, Stephen S. "French Navy Ships, 1816–1859." 2010. http://www.shipscribe.com/marvap/. (Accessed January 25, 2011).

The Ships List. "The Fleets: General Screw Steam Shipping Company 1848–1857." September, 2007. http://www.theshipslist.com/ships/lines/generalscrewssc.htm. (Accessed January 25, 2011).

Truesdell, Paul E., Jr. "Interment.net Cemetery Records Online." International Cemetery—Tomari, Naha City, Okinawa, Japan. May 28 2006. http://www.interment.net/data/japan/international_cemetery.htm. (Accessed January 25, 2011).

About the Editors

———∽∿∽———

John A. Wolter is a former chief of the Library of Congress Geography and Map Division. A merchant marine veteran of World War II and a U.S. Army veteran of the Korean War, he holds BA, MA, and PhD degrees from the University of Minnesota–Twin Cities. He is the author of numerous articles, reviews, and edited works in the fields of geography, cartography, and maritime history.

David A. Ranzan is the University Archivist at Salisbury University. Prior to that, he was a research associate for the Thomas A. Edison Papers at Rutgers University. He earned an MA in history from East Stroudsburg University and an MLIS from Rutgers University. He is the editor of *Surviving Andersonville: One Prisoner's Recollections of the Civil War's Most Notorious Camp* (Jefferson, NC: McFarland and Company, 2013).

The late **John J. McDonough** was a manuscript historian at the Library of Congress from 1961 to 1998. A Navy veteran of World War II, he edited and published journals of political figures of the antebellum period. He was a 1950 history graduate of Boston College and received an MA in history from Georgetown University in 1953.

The Naval Institute Press is the book-publishing arm of the U.S. Naval Institute, a private, nonprofit, membership society for sea service professionals and others who share an interest in naval and maritime affairs. Established in 1873 at the U.S. Naval Academy in Annapolis, Maryland, where its offices remain today, the Naval Institute has members worldwide.

Members of the Naval Institute support the education programs of the society and receive the influential monthly magazine *Proceedings* or the colorful bimonthly magazine *Naval History* and discounts on fine nautical prints and on ship and aircraft photos. They also have access to the transcripts of the Institute's Oral History Program and get discounted admission to any of the Institute-sponsored seminars offered around the country.

The Naval Institute's book-publishing program, begun in 1898 with basic guides to naval practices, has broadened its scope to include books of more general interest. Now the Naval Institute Press publishes about seventy titles each year, ranging from how-to books on boating and navigation to battle histories, biographies, ship and aircraft guides, and novels. Institute members receive significant discounts on the Press's more than eight hundred books in print.

Full-time students are eligible for special half-price membership rates. Life memberships are also available.

For a free catalog describing Naval Institute Press books currently available, and for further information about joining the U.S. Naval Institute, please write to:

Member Services
U.S. Naval Institute
291 Wood Road
Annapolis, MD 21402-5034
Telephone: (800) 233-8764
Fax: (410) 571-1703
Web address: www.usni.org